Ken Marsh is also the author of
Independent Video

KEN MARSH

THE WAY THE NEW TECHNOLOGY WORKS

CLEAR, SIMPLE, ILLUSTRATED DESCRIPTIONS OF THE TECHNOLOGICAL MIRACLES OF OUR TIME

A Fireside Book
Published by Simon and Schuster
New York

Copyright © 1982 by Ken Marsh
All rights reserved
including the right of reproduction
in whole or in part in any form
A Fireside Book
Published by Simon and Schuster
A Division of Gulf & Western Corporation
Simon & Schuster Building
Rockefeller Center
1230 Avenue of the Americas
New York, New York 10020

FIRESIDE and colophon are trademarks of Simon & Schuster
Designed by Irving Perkins Associates
Manufactured in the United States of America
Printed and bound by The Murray Printing Co.

1   2   3   4   5   6   7   8   9   10

Library of Congress Cataloging in Publication Data
Marsh,
Ken.
    The way the new technology works.

    "A Fireside book."
    Bibliography: p.
    Includes index.
    1. Telecommunication—Popular works.
2. Electronic data processing—Popular works.
I. Title.
TK5101.M298   621.38   82-796
                                        AA-CR2

    ISBN 0-671-24675-5

ACKNOWLEDGMENTS

To the many whose brains were picked for information, assistance, and encouragement, I express my deepest gratitude. I wish specifically to note the efforts of Andy Denison, the IBM Kingston Library staff, The Computer Corner of White Plains, Mike Kutcher (IBM), Boeing Computer Services, The Mid-Hudson Library System, Richard Murray (IGC), David Dension (NYSE), and those who gave of their time for interviews—Dr. Milton Zaret, Jim Baker, Ed Zimmerman, and others, some of whom are identified in sections of the book. Thanks also to Gene Finger, Seth Rosenbaum, and Louise Van Dyck Shipway for their readings of the text and suggestions. And finally, I thank my wife, Elaine, for her forbearance and Natasha Milosh for her support.

Now and to come
for Katherine

CONTENTS

ABBREVIATIONS AND ACRONYMS

AC	alternating current
A/D	analog/digital
ADP	automatic data processing
ALGOL	Algorithmic Language
ALU	arithmetic/logic unit
APL	A Programming Language
APT	Automatically Programmed Tools
BASIC	Beginners All-Purpose Symbolic Instruction Code
BCD	Binary Coded Decimal
bit	binary digit
bps	bits per second
b/w	black and white
CAD	computer-aided design
CAI	computer-aided instruction
CAM	computer-assisted manufacturing
CCD	charge-coupled device
CCIS	common channel interoffice signaling
CIM	computer input micrographics
coax	coaxial cable
COBOL	Common Business Oriented Language
COM	computer output micrographics
cps	characters per second
CPU	central processing unit
CRT	cathode ray tube
CU	control unit
CW	continuous wave
D/A	digital/analog
DAA	data access arrangement
DBMS	data base management system
DC	direct current
DDP	distributed data processing
DP	data processing
DSA	data set adaptor
EBCDIC	Extended Binary Coded Decimal Interchange Code
EDP	electronic data processing
EFT	electronic funds transfer
ELF	extremely low frequency
EMS	electronic message (or mail) system
EPROM	erasable programmable read-only memory
ESS	electronic switching system
fax	facsimile
FDM	frequency division multiplexing
FM	frequency modulation
FORTRAN	Formula Translation
fsk	frequency shift keying
GHz	gigahertz
GPSS	General Purpose Simulation System
HF	high frequency
Hz	hertz
IC	integrated circuit
i.f.	intermediate frequency
I/O	input/output
ips	inches per second
kbps	kilobits per second
kHz	kilohertz
kWh	kilowatt-hour
laser	light amplification by stimulated emission of radiation
LED	light-emitting diode

LSI	large-scale integration	RGB	red, green, and blue
LSS	loop switching system	ROM	read-only memory
maser	microwave amplification by stimulated emission of radiation	RPG	Report Program Generation
MEG	magnetoencephalography	rpm	revolutions per minute
MHz	megahertz	SDA	source data acquisitions
MICR	magnetic ink character recognition	SHF	superhigh frequency
		SPC	stored-program control
MIS	management information system	TBC	time-base corrector
modem	modulator-demodulator	TDM	time division multiplexing
mW	milliwatt	TRF	tuned radio frequency
μW	microwatt	tropo	tropospheric scatter communications
OCR	optical character recognition	TSI	time slot interchange
PAM	pulse amplitude modulation	UHF	ultra-high frequency
PCM	pulse code modulation	ULSI	ultralarge-scale integration
pixel	picture element	UPC	Universal Product Code
PL/1	Programming Language/One	UV	ultraviolet light
PM	phase modulation	VCR	video cassette recorder
POS	point of sale	VDT	video display terminal
PROM	programmable read-only memory	VHF	very high frequency
PSN	public switched network	VHS	video home system
quad	quadrophonic (sound recording); quadruplex (video recording)	VIR	vertical interval reference
		VLSI	very large-scale integration
radar	radio detection and ranging	VTR	video tape recorder
RAM	random-access memory	WP	word processing
r.f.	radio frequency	wpm	words per minute

THE WAY THE NEW TECHNOLOGY WORKS

INTRODUCTION

OVER the last 150 years, we have made great strides in the development and application of technologies that extend and complement our intellectual capabilities. Vast and far-reaching lines of communications and instantaneous access to resources of knowledge now comprise a technological environment that is as important to us as the natural biosphere in which we live.

All areas of human activity have been affected by the new technologies: how we learn; practice religion; bank and trade; manage affairs in government, in industry, and at home; shop; get around; keep and get in touch; seek comfort and obtain pleasure; stay healthy and cure disease; maintain peace and safety; understand and interact with the natural environment. With electrically powered telecommunications and information processing machines, we have entered the Information Age, an era in which our welfare is enhanced and our survival dependent on our use of information.

Satellite, cable TV, and upgraded telephone networks are creating an abundance of lines of communications that will likely increase channels to and from home, office, factory, and school by a factor of ten by the year 2000. Television, voice, and computer links comprise a growing web of visible and invisible paths connecting up people and machines around the globe and out into space.

In the home of the near future the computer will play many roles in maintaining a safe and properly

Technology Times

The World Is Changing!

Once upon a time, in the mid-twentieth century, Ms. Chicken Little was reading a computer industry report that her broker had given her " . . . systems feature host channel speed interfaces, off loading, image buffer, local hardcopy output and high-speed interactive displays." Suddenly she realized she couldn't understand a thing she was reading. Fearing that some devious plot was afoot, she jumped up and cried, "The world is changing, the world is changing!" and ran off to warn the others.

In the late 1970s, during a surge of growth of information technologies and services, the industry generated a plethora of terms to describe its new wares and the purposes to which they were to be put. As a result, industry technical and advertising writers, the lexicographers of the Information Age, along with scientists and engineers, *did* help to change the world.

With the first use of electric telegraph in the 1840s, you could transmit one bit of information every second. By the 1970s, transmission capacities of telecommunications systems reached levels of hundreds of million of bits per second (bps). If, for example, it took 10 bits of information to represent a letter of the alphabet and an average five-letter word consumes 50 bits, then with 100 million bits you could transmit 2 million words or 8,000 pages every second—a sizable increase in the quantity-to-time ratio for distributing information. That capability and others have changed the way we know what we know, use it, and talk about it.

The difficulty in comprehending much technical information is unfamiliarity with the language. Every field has its own jargon to denote its special circumstances and paraphernalia. Highly technological environments have more jargon to deal with the more equipment and procedures are inherent in them. Jargon can be confusing to the uninitiated, but its use is not necessarily devious. For instance, TV producers don't intend

functioning environment. Home computer terminals, connecting up the home to the marketplace, schools and libraries, and sources of entertainment, will eventually become as ubiquitous as the telephone.

In the office, many workers are already using keyboard terminals and TV screens to interact with computers, which are replacing file drawers and typewriters. Future workers might stay at home and plug in to their job sites, interacting via two-way, audio-visual hookups. Business conferencing via television has already become an established practice.

Computer-assisted instruction is gaining broader use and may one day revolutionize the classroom. The school of the future was demonstrated, in a fashion, during the winter of 1977, when bad weather forced schools in the Midwest to close: Educators used television to carry on schoolwork with students stranded at home. The home-school link might be enhanced with computers to provide individualized instruction and fingertip access to the resources of learning for the whole family.

A form of electronic banking has been in use since the mid 1970s. In lieu of receiving checks through the mail, Social Security recipients can elect to have their bank accounts directly credited. Automated tellers and banking by telephone might altogether replace the bank as we have known it. In the meantime, bankers say that computerization is bringing back the personal service of yesteryear. With a computer terminal at his or her side, the customer can receive information and services that would otherwise require the assistance of numerous human specialists.

AT&T is no longer "the phone company." In the Information Age, Ma Bell is "the communications company." Bell is marketing devices and services for transmitting voice, picture, and data in a deregulated market. Business and resident subscribers are being offered new services based on newly built, computerized switching systems. Among the services are one-button dialing, call forwarding, signaling of incoming calls when the phone is in use, conferencing, and more.

The stocks and bonds market began using electronic marketing systems in the late 1970s. A comparison of photographs (see pages 176-77) of the floor of the New York Stock Exchange in 1979 and a few years earlier reveals the installation of a multitude of TV screens perched above the trading posts. Further examination reveals a number of floor-based terminals that provide brokers with access to the Intermarket Trading System (ITS), which was developed in 1976 in response to a congressional mandate for a national electronic investors' market.

Doctors and computer programmers are working together to design machines that diagnose disease, endowing them with skills once considered the sole province of humans. Medical consultations via television are becoming standard practice, especially in areas where there are shortages of trained personnel. Doctors are keeping up with developments in medicine in their offices and hospitals through special TV and radio programming transmitted from major medical centers.

The U.S. government under President Carter developed the Domestic Information Display System (DIDS). The system is used to display population data, such as age, income, and educational level, by distribution throughout the country. Color-coded maps are created for instantaneous viewing on a TV screen. The Office of the Executive hopes the system will promote better cooperation between Congress and the White House by providing them with a common ground of information. Congress itself began its own "electronification" in 1979, with initiation of its TV production of House sessions.

The Postal Service is implementing an "electronic mail" system, seeking to ensure the speedy delivery of correspondences via satellite and land line networks. Perhaps the post office motto will one day be changed to: "Neither sunspot activity nor black- or brownout, nor snapped wire, nor busy line, will prevent these postal persons from connecting their appointed daily circuits."

Weather observation and prediction have been remarkably advanced since the early 1960s with the use of satellites, computers, and telecommunications networks. The National Weather Service predicts nearly 100 percent reliability of its short-term (twenty-four-hour) weather predictions by the year 2000. Satellite photography has given us the macroscopic eyesight to see our own planet; in addition to better weather observation, this has improved mapmaking, military reconnaissance, and tracking of biological and geological characteristics on land and in the seas.

A fire alarm response system in Brooklyn, the busiest firefighting city in the world, has cut dispatcher processing time from nearly three minutes to less than 40 seconds. The computer dispatch system has also helped in cutting down on needless response to false alarms.

Few of us avoid daily contact with the machinery to confuse computer programmers when they speak of "programs" and "software," although by those terms they mean shows and video tapes, whereas the programmer understands both terms to refer to sets of instruction used to direct computers to do specific jobs. For the Chicken Littles among us, familiarity with some new vocabulary can go a long way in helping to dispel uncertainty about the changing world and its technology. Glossaries of special terms are appended to parts II (see page 151) and III (see page 224) of this book.

We have always needed to acquire or collect, process, store, retrieve, distribute or communicate, and put to use information in some form or another. These activities have been performed since humankind began socially interacting and using information as the intellect's and the psyche's barter of exchange. Today we are inundated with technologies to enhance "informationizing." We have a broad array of equipment and methods by which we handle information at rates and volumes never before known in recorded history.

The Information Age is marked most by two resources: *Telecommunications* resources provide for the transmission of information through the air and in cables interconnecting nearby and distant locations around the globe and out into space. *Automatic information processing* resources, also referred to as automatic or electronic data processing (ADP or EDP), provide for the manipulation of information—performing arithmetic calculation, correlating and/or reorganizing data, etc.—which can mean controlling air traffic, maintaining indoor conditions of skyscrapers, predicting election returns, editing news copy, drawing architectural plans, and so forth.

Telecommunications and automatic information processing have had and will continue to have the effect of expanding the base of human knowledge. Based on that effect, some thinkers estimate that over 95 percent of all the knowledge we will possess in the year 2020 will have been acquired just since the 1970s.

of the Information Age, which quietly purrs away collecting, organizing, and making available the information that we all produce as naturally as the carbon dioxide we exhale when breathing. Information is a by-product of almost everything we do, and has become the critical ingredient we need to do it all better. In the world today, information is mined, refined, packaged, distributed, and traded in the marketplace. Its source is all of us.

Our technological environment first began to take its present shape in the mid-nineteenth century with the advent of the electric telegraph. At the time, about 50 percent of this country's workers had agricultural jobs. Fewer than 10 percent were involved with information work. In the late 1980s, while fewer than 4 percent will have agricultural jobs, more than 60 percent of the working population will be employed in information fields involving the generation, reproduction, distribution, and marketing of information in both service and product forms. That includes lawyers, doctors, executives, managers, secretaries, writers, artists, inventors, scientists, technicians and machine operators, computer programmers, accountants and bookkeepers, teachers, researchers, librarians, media programmers, journalists, and others. Work is evolving from dominantly muscle-power to brain-power activities.

In the last 150 years, we have developed telegraphy, photography, telephony, the phonograph, cinematography, radio, television, electronic data processing, magnetic and optical recording, electrophotography, holography, and all the linking technologies: transcontinental and transoceanic cable, cable TV, terrestrial microwave, and satellite and optical communications. For all previous recorded history, the flow of information and communications was limited to conversation, oratory, theater, dance, music, drum or smoke signaling, painting, travel, messenger, hieroglyphics, writing, and the printing press, which lead to books, pamphlets, broadsides, newspapers, and journals.

The key that opened the new age to us was electricity. Although this phenomenon was observed first by Homer as early as the twelfth century B.C., it was not named until the 1600s. Around 1750, Benjamin Franklin was flying kites in storms and carrying on other experiments that resulted in his naming the two types of electricity "negative" and "positive." A contemporary of Franklin's in France, Pierre Charles Lemonnier, discovered a "state of electricity" in our atmosphere at all times. This came some 150 years after the work of William Gilbert, who proclaimed that the earth was magnetic. We now know that magnetism and electricity are inseparable partners.

In 1785, Charles de Coulomb worked out the laws of attraction and repulsion between positive and negative electrically charged bodies. The first battery came to use in 1800 from Alessandro Volta. André Ampère, in 1820, showed how to measure the magnetic effect of electrical current. At the same time, Hans Christian Oersted discovered the electromagnetic field—electric and magnetic energy moving through space—from which has developed the technology for all high-speed communications.

As we began to uncover the laws of our cosmos, we developed the means to use what was revealed to us as instinctively as early ancestors must have observed and exploited fire. The "new fire" was the energy of electrons and protons, particles within the atoms that make up our universe, which we can cause to flow along wires and through circuits, putting their energy to work to turn motors, provide light and heat, and store and move information, even through space. We have so refined our ability to generate and detect moving energy in space that we daily crowd our atmosphere with nearly uncountable numbers of information-carrying waves.

This book focuses on the technological aspects of the Information Age, such as how a television system carries sights and sounds from place to far-off place and how a computer processes a volume of information in a fraction of a second—a task that would take a hundred people ten years to do.

Other than those whose jobs require such specialized knowledge, most of us have remained ignorant of the technical side of our world. How things work has been of little or no importance as long as we have been able to get things to work for us. We have been a civilization of expert switch flickers, button pushers, pedal stompers, dialer turners, wheel twisters, and line pluggers. With this lately evolved manual and pedal dexterity, we have been able to instantaneously unleash hundreds of horse power to move ourselves in space and command the invisible powers of subatomic particles to light the dark and share what we see and hear with others around the globe.

Of late, the public has begun to awaken to the need to know more. For instance, the fossil fuel shortages have made us aware of alternatives and led to a greater understanding of energy. Nuclear accidents, scrutinized by the media, have brought nuclear physics into prime-time TV viewing. Inflation, which in the 1970s gobbled up the luxury margin of the average income, has forced many to act more prudently and with more information about consumption of natural and manufactured resources. We are prodded, even from the laboratories of our scientists, toward more participation in the universe. As Gary Zukav puts it in *The Dancing Wu Li Masters:* "Now, after three centuries, . . . 'We are not sure,' they [the scientists] tell us, 'but we have accumulated evidence which indicates that the key to understanding the universe is *you*.' . . . The new physics tells us that an observer cannot observe without altering what he sees."

The adjective *new* is being prefixed to many major scientific disciplines. We have a new biology with its awesome genetic engineering, the new physics as Zukav reports, and the new electronics with its miniaturized circuitry replacing what, in the 1950s, was so big that it filled a room. We are gaining, however slowly among the public, a new literacy of the universe, energy literacy, biological literacy, and, in regard to our technological environment, electronic literacy. More of us are understanding the elements of the technological environment, organizing them, and guiding their development. We need not be engineers and scientists to appreciate technology, use it, benefit from it, be responsible for it, and put it aside when it works to our detriment. In a democratic society, everyone can participate in shaping the impact that technology has and will have on the quality of life. In an Information Age democracy, such participation seems imperative.

This is not a political handbook revealing how to get control of your local technology, or how to lobby government to act to protect you from suspected radiation, or how to protect yourself from electronic invasions of privacy. Those and other issues that will emerge will be resolved most appropriately through continuing dialogue among informed people who give and take information. The growing popular understanding of the technological environment will help.

PART I

SOME BASICS

TECHNOLOGY, in the end, is the result of the knowledge we gain of the laws of the universe. Like us, our machines exist within the limits of those laws. Thus, a discussion of some of those laws is in order. For instance, the universe is composed of matter and energy in many forms, which convert back and forth between one another. In fact, all activity of the universe is involved in the processes of matter/energy *conversion*. Our sun is a burning ball of matter from which energy radiates throughout the solar system and beyond. Plants and animals on earth thrive on that energy and, in turn, generate energy from their own matter.

Akin to conversion is *transduction*, the process by which one form of energy is transformed into another. Plants and animals are natural transducers, as well as matter/energy converters. Our senses are transducers changing the energy, for example, of sound into an energy form that our brains can use. Sound is a form of what is called *mechanical energy*. Bodies, ranging in size from atoms to planets that go bump in the universe, display mechanical energy. The bumping of air molecules, or groups of atoms, that results from pressure in a volume of air can produce a level of mechanical energy that we experience as hearing. The ears detect that range of mechanical energy and change it into signals the brain can process. Specifically, the ear transduces mechanical energy into what is called *electrochemical energy*.

FIG. I-1. All activities of the universe involve matter/energy conversion.

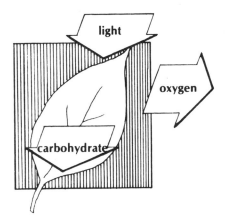

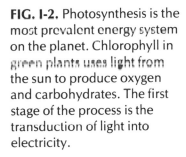

FIG. I-2. Photosynthesis is the most prevalent energy system on the planet. Chlorophyll in green plants uses light from the sun to produce oxygen and carbohydrates. The first stage of the process is the transduction of light into electricity.

FIG. I-3. How sound is heard

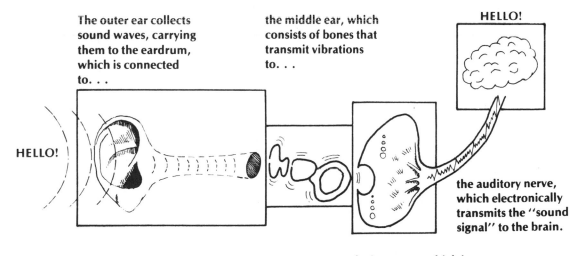

The outer ear collects sound waves, carrying them to the eardrum, which is connected to. . .

the middle ear, which consists of bones that transmit vibrations to. . .

HELLO!

the auditory nerve, which electronically transmits the "sound signal" to the brain.

HELLO!

the inner ear, which is fluid-filled and lined with tiny hairs that are connected to. . .

Alexander Bell's telephone, developed in the 1870s, provided the means to turn sound into electrical signals. (See Fig. I-4.) In Thomas Edison's sound recording machine, invented in the same decade, sound vibrations affected a needle's penetration of a wax cylinder that was turning. When the recording was played back, the needle bounced in the grooves it had previously cut and caused a diaphragm, a thin piece of stretched material, to vibrate the air, making the same sounds again.

In the 1920s, weather bureaus, law enforcers, and news wire services started using machines for transmitting pictures, called *facsimile* (or "fax") machines. In a fax machine, electrical or optical signals are used to represent the black-and-white spots that make up an image. Receiving devices reverse the process, turning signals into spots on paper or film, thereby producing a duplicate.

In effect, our telecommunicating and information processing machines are transduction systems. They change what we see, hear, and write—information— into machine-readable signals and back again into formats we can use. Such signals are easily transmitted over distances. Information represented as machine-readable signals can be processed by machines in far greater volume and at a far greater rate of speed than information in its original form can be processed by us.

Basically, four machine functions are associated with information technologies. First are those machines used to enter information into a system. They change typed language, pictures, sounds, measures such as temperature and air pressure, and other data into signals. Second are the data processing devices that combine, separate, reorder, and store signals. Third are the devices that transmit signals over distances, and fourth are the devices for changing signals back into typed language, pictures, sounds, and so on.

In machines, information in the form of signals is represented as either electrical, magnetic, or electromagnetic energy.

Electrical energy comes from moving electrons. Electrons, protons, and other particles make up atoms. Both protons and electrons have electrical charges. The proton's charge draws the electron's to it. Like charges (two electrons or two protons) repel each other. Opposite charges attract. When an atom has more electrons than protons, the extra electrons are free to move to other atoms with extra protons. A continuous flow of electrical energy can be made to

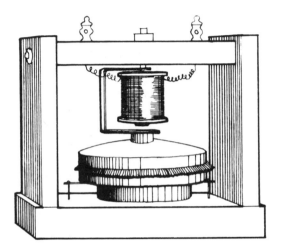

FIG. I-4. Alexander Graham Bell's first phone, 1875

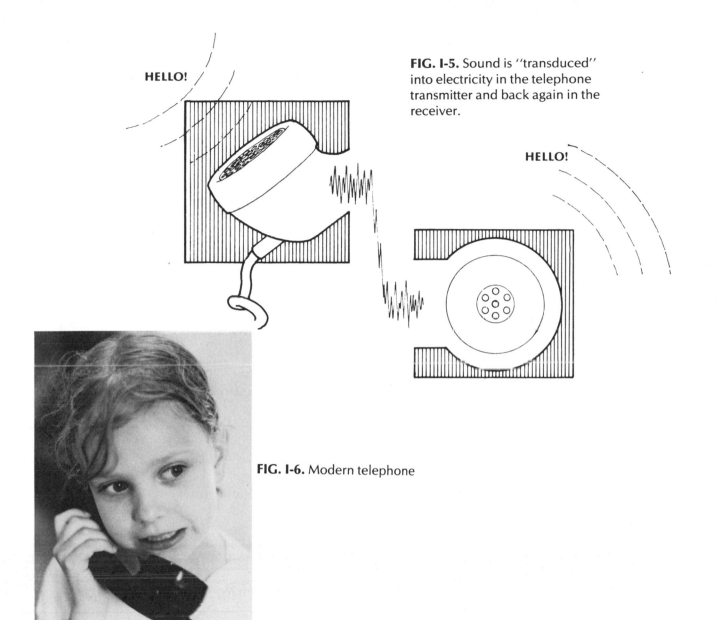

HELLO!

FIG. I-5. Sound is "transduced" into electricity in the telephone transmitter and back again in the receiver.

HELLO!

FIG. I-6. Modern telephone

FIG. I-7. Functions of information technology

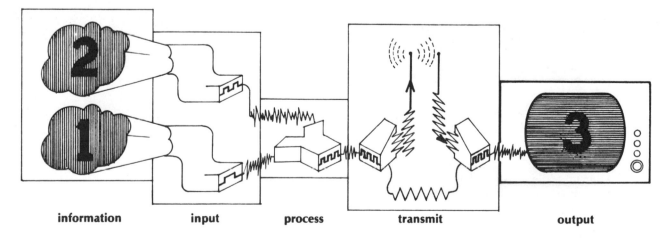

| information | input | process | transmit | output |

FIG. I-8. The telegraph made information "electric" by making a code of starting and stopping the flow of electricity along a wire connecting two points.

occur in a wire by putting a bunch of atoms with extra electrons at one end and a bunch of atoms with extra protons at the other end. (See Fig. I-9.) Electricity does not actually move within wires or circuits, but moves in an energy field around them along the directed path. An electric field occupies a much larger space than that of the wire or circuits along which it travels. Sometimes electric fields can extend thousands of feet out from a conductive path, as is the case with high-voltage transmission lines carrying electricity from generating plants to substations en route to users. Metals are excellent electrical conductors because they have many free electrons among their atoms. The flow of electrical energy or current primarily agitates atoms, which produces heat. In an electric heater, the heat is used for warmth. In an incandescent electric light bulb, the heat produces light. In information machines, heat is minimized and levels of current are used to represent signals.

Magnetic energy comes from the spinning motion

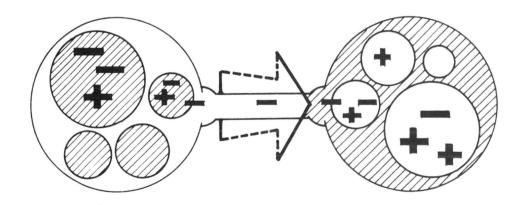

FIG. 1-9. The flow of electrical energy

From more electrons (−) than protons (+). . .

to more protons (+) than electrons (−).

FIG. I-10. High-voltage transmission lines carry electricity from generating plants to distribution transformers.

FIG. I-11. The common utility pole supports local transmission lines for the delivery of electricity to customers.

of electrons. It flows from the north pole of an electron's axis and loops around the electron's mass to its south pole. (See Fig. I-12.) When the flow of magnetic energy is intersected by a wire, electric current flows in that wire. Magnetic energy can therefore be used to generate electricity. The spin direction of an electron can be either to the right or to the left. A material is said to be magnetized when most of its atoms' electrons spin in the same direction. The direction of electron spin can be influenced by electricity. These phenomena are fundamental to the operations of electric motors and magnetic recording systems.

Electromagnetic energy is energy traveling through space at or along a guided path at nearly the speed of light (about 186,000 miles per second). It is made up of both electric and magnetic fields which alternate back and forth. A transition of one energy state to another is called a *cycle*. The physical distance traversed during a cycle is called a *wavelength*. The number of cycles per second is called the *frequency* of an electromagnetic wave. For transmitting information in the air, electromagnetic propagation is the only game in the cosmos. For communications we use electromagnetic frequencies from thousands to trillions of *hertz* (Hz), or cycles per second—and more when it comes to light waves. Light or optical energy is electromagnetism at frequencies that our

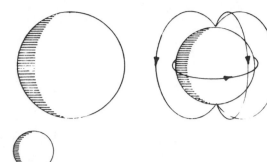
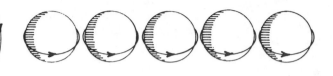

The atom has a positive-charged nucleus and negative-charged electrons.

The electron spins on its axis and generates a magnetic field.

Top: **A material is magnetized when all of its electrons spin in the same direction.** *Bottom:* **A material is not magnetized when some electrons spin in one direction and others in the opposite direction.**

FIG. I-12. Electron and magnetism

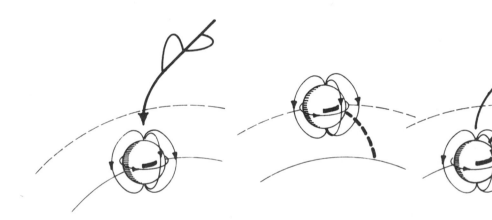

1. An electron is hit by a photon.

2. The electron gains energy and moves to an outer orbit of its atom.

3. The electron falls back to its original orbit, giving off a photon.

FIG. I-13. The photoelectric effect

eyes can detect, ranging into the quadrillions of cycles per second having wavelength of twenty-millionths of a centimeter. Light energy and electrons interact in what we call photosensitive materials. Electricity is produced when such materials are hit by light. This phenomenon is called the *photoelectric effect.* On the other hand, when electrons are extremely agitated, they give off light energy packets called *photons.* (See Fig. I-13.) Such phenomena are fundamental for television.

In general terms, energy is defined as the ability to perform work. In electrical things, stored energy—the potential for doing work electrically—is referred to as *charge*. For example, a battery has a charge when it contains a store of electrical energy. Work is performed at a rate, such as supplying heat to a pot of water for five minutes to bring the water to a boil. The rate at which work is performed is referred to as *power*. The faster the work is done, the higher the power rating.

One of the first terms used to denote power was horsepower. One horsepower represents working as fast as a horse or, more precisely, lifting 55 pounds to a height of 10 feet in one second. The watt is the measure of electrical power. The equation between watts and horsepower is about 750 watts to one horsepower.

To measure the consumption of electrical energy, power is integrated with time: watts × time. For instance, a 1,200-watt burner left on for one hour consumes 1,200 watt-hours or 1.2 kilowatt-hours (kWh) of energy. If left on for 2.5 hours, consumption would be 3 kWh. Electric companies price electricity in kWh units, such as ten cents per kWh. At that price, the 1,200-watt burner left on for 2.5 hours would cost thirty cents.

Electrical energy is characterized by amperage, resistance, voltage, and wattage.

Amperage is the rate of flow of electricity—that is, the amount of electrical charge passing a given point in a second. One ampere (or amp) is equal to 6 quintillion (6 followed by eighteen zeros) electrons passing a given point per second. Amperage levels in household appliances range from fractions of amps to about 10 amps for hair dryers and electric space heaters. Radios, tape recorders, and stereo systems have relatively low amperages. In such devices, power consumption is minimal and electricity is used primarily as signal to represent information.

Resistance is the opposite of conductivity. It is measured in ohms. A good conductor, such as gold or

1
Electricity

FIG. 1-1. Household appliances such as these vary in amperage levels.

copper, is made up of atoms with many free electrons to release for the flow of electrical energy. An ordinary lamp cord made of copper wire has a low resistance measuring about 0.03 ohm. A good insulator, or highly resistive material, has atoms with few or no free electrons. Resistance levels are measured in hundreds of millions of ohms in good insulators like rubber, plastic, and ceramics. Levels of resistance also depend on the volume of material. For example, a thick wire has less resistance than a thin wire, and a longer wire has more resistance than a shorter wire. Temperature also affects resistance levels. In copper, a temperature increase causes a resistance increase. In some materials, increased temperature can decrease resistance.

Voltage is the pulling force acting on electrons flowing between the two poles of electrical charge. The amount of force affects the amperage. Voltage levels are established when setting up an electrical supply source. In the United States, the electrical system has been developed to supply 120 volts of alternating current (AC). Thus, appliances designed to be powered electrically from the system are matched to it. They are built to receive 120 volts AC of electricity. Inside an appliance, voltages within individual circuits can be at different levels. For instance, a computer circuit can require a voltage as low as 3 volts; a cathode ray tube (CRT) or TV screen requires an extremely high voltage of thousands of volts. Voltage changes can be done with transformers (see page 37) or through changing the relationship between voltage, amperage, and resistance in a circuit. A varying voltage can be used to carry information, such as a television picture signal.

Wattage, as the measure of electrical power, results from electrical flow. Wattage can be determined by multiplying voltage times amperage. For example, a hair dryer is rated at 10 amps and the house supply is 120 volts; thus, 10 times 120 produces 1,200 watts of heat-generating power with which to dry one's hair.

Ohm's law is the equation representing the relationship of voltage, amperage, and resistance. Ohm's law is, in effect, the electrical law of nature. It states, first, that the voltage is always equal to the amperage multiplied by the resistance. In other words, a flow of electricity at, say, 0.5 amps passing through a resistance of 240 ohms will have resulted from a pulling force of 120 volts:

$$0.5 \text{ amps} \times 240 \text{ ohms} = 120 \text{ volts}$$

A second variation of the equation is for determining the amperage, which is always equal to the voltage divided by the resistance. For example, 120 volts of electricity impressed across a resistance of 240 ohms will have a flow rate of 0.5 amps:

$$120 \text{ volts} \div 240 \text{ ohms} = 0.5 \text{ amps}.$$

A third variation of the equation is for determining the resistance, which is always equal to the voltage divided by the amperage. In other words, 120 volts of electricity moving at a rate of 0.5 amps flows through a resistance of 240 ohms:

$$120 \text{ volts} \div 0.5 \text{ amps} = 240 \text{ ohms}.$$

All electrical devices are designed in accordance with Ohm's law—for example, the electric hair dryer. The design of electrical appliances often starts from the desired result, in this case, 1,200 watts of heat. Given the standard 120 volts, the designer can figure out the amperage level by dividing the voltage into the wattage:

$$1,200 \text{ watts} \div 120 \text{ volts} = 10 \text{ amps}.$$

Then, knowing the amperage and voltage, the designer can use the equation of Ohm's law for finding the resistance:

$$120 \text{ volts} \div 10 \text{ amps} = 12 \text{ ohms}.$$

A circuit is then constructed to those specifications.

Circuits are composed of (1) a source of electrical power; (2) conductors for carrying the current; and (3) resistors, which use the power, such as light bulb filaments, transistors, and heating coils. Resistors control the flow of power and put it to work. They are placed in the path of electricity to route and consume it. For instance, electricity routed through a tungsten filament in a vacuum encased in a glass bulb produces heat, which causes incandescence, which results in light. In effect, the electrical energy boils the tungsten's electrons, causing them to give off "particles" of light, or photons. (See Fig. 1-2.)

Short circuits are electrical states in which electricity is out of control. Shorts occur when all resistance to current is absent and the energy is released to burn up the materials through which it flows. For instance, electrical wiring is made up of three conductors: a ground wire (more about this presently), a line along which electricity flows into a device, and a line along which it flows from the device after passing through it. In AC, of course, the lines alternate. Shorting commonly occurs when those two lines touch and effectively make a direct connection between the poles of charges. The full energy of the source of power is unleashed, generating immense heat that burns anything it can reach. On the other hand, in an open circuit, no current flows.

Fuses are used to minimize the effects of shorts. A fuse is made of a wire with a low melting temperature. Placed in the path of electrical flow, it conducts electricity under normal conditions. When a short occurs, however, its low tolerance to heat causes it to break and cut devices off from the source of electricity. Fuses can be placed at several points along circuit paths to keep components safe from shorts that can occur inside devices, just as they can in wiring.

The earth is a drainage field for dumping electrical buildups. It naturally draws electrical energy to it. Since everything is made up of atoms, electrical energy is everywhere. These so-called "static" electrical charges can build up in electrical devices and become safety hazards. To drain them off, a wire is connected to circuits and fed to the earth. It is commonly called the *ground wire*.

Direct current (DC) and *alternating current* (AC) are the two ways electricity flows. DC refers to current flowing in one direction, consistently from one charge pole to the other. Batteries supply DC power by converting chemical, solar, nuclear, or thermal energy to electricity. Household and car bat-

FIG. 1-2. The light bulb circuit

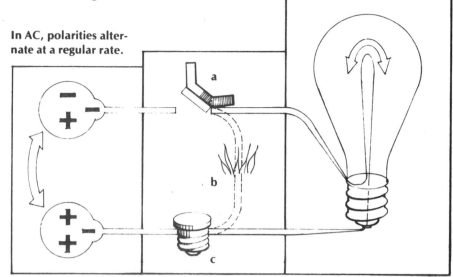

In AC, polarities alternate at a regular rate.

The electrical energy flows through the light bulb's filament en route to the "more protons" pole.

(a) With the switch "off," the circuit is open—no current flows.

(b) A short unleashes excessive current— potential fire.

(c) The fuse is a "weak link" that will break in case of a short.

teries are *electrolytic*—made of substances that in chemical dissolution produce electron flow The electrons' energy flows from one pole or terminal of the battery through the device it is powering (e.g., a flashlight or portable radio) and is drawn to the other terminal. AC is the type of flow produced when the poles of charge are rapidly changed back and forth. In other words, the energy flows from pole A to pole B, then from pole B to pole A, alternating its direction back and forth. Electricity in the U.S. system is AC changing at a rate of sixty times per second—60 Hz. In Europe, 50 Hz is standard. When devices are designed, the AC rate must be matched to the electical system to be used for power, just as voltage level is matched.

Electric generators rely on the interplay of electrical and magnetic energies. A simple generator is made up of a wire loop fixed to the end of a shaft that is mechanically rotated in a magnetic field. The magnetism causes electricity to flow in the wire loop. (See Fig. 1-3, in which a C-shaped magnetic is used, the

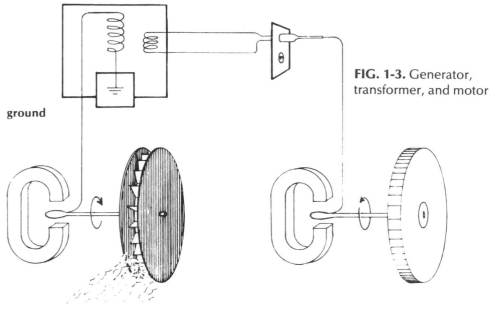

FIG. 1-3. Generator, transformer, and motor

ground

a simple water-powered generator supplying current to. . .

a simple motor turning a grinding wheel

wire loop placed between its poles.) Attaching a second wire to the shaft serves as a tap for the electricity. Rotation of the shaft can be done by controlling falling waters from a dam (hydroelectric power plant) or by burning fossil, wood, or nuclear fuels to make steam. Using the falling waters, a water wheel-type structure (turbine) is fitted to the shaft, and as the water hits it, the shaft is rotated. Steam is used to drive a turbine or piston-type engine equipped with a series of rods and flywheel for rotating the shaft. In

FIG. 1-4. Transformer

power plant generators, large electromagnets are used which provide great magnetic fields and thus greater voltages.

Electric motors are a variation of electric generators. A shaft with a wire loop placed between the poles of a magnet will rotate when electricity is fed to the loop. (See Fig. 1-3.) The magnet's field and the magnetic field resulting from the flow of electricity in the loop interact, causing the loop to rotate, which, in turn, rotates the shaft.

Transformers also rely on the interplay of magnetism and electricity. When a wire is coiled like a spring or wrapped around a metal rod, AC flowing through it produces a magnetic field, which causes electricity to flow in another closely located coil of wire. (See Fig. 1-4.) If the number of loops in the secondary coil is greater than in the primary coil, the voltage of the electricity in the second coil is increased. Fewer coil loops in the secondary produce a decrease in voltage. Transformers play an important role in numerous electrical appliances to step up or step down voltage levels. For instance, in a stereo amplifier, 120 volts can be stepped down to 12 volts for the individual signal amplifier circuits.

2

Electronics

Electronics is the field of science and engineering concerned with the behavior and use of the energy of electrons in devices. In contrast to electric or electrical devices, which primarily use the flow of large currents of electricity in metal conductors to produce heat and its effects or to run motors, electronic devices involve small currents for their signal-carrying capacity.

Signals can be represented in either analog or digital form. *Analog* signals are represented by a continuous flow of energy that often functions as an electrical "copy" of the information being signified. For example, the telephone is an analog device in which sound waves are changed into electric waves. The amperage of the electric waves changes in correspondence to the variations of the sound waves. The louder the sound, the greater the amperage.

In a *digital* device, a signal is a string of *bits*—short for "binary digits." The term *binary* refers to a number system that uses only the two digits 1 and 0. Digital computers, for example, process numbers and letters, which are translated into binary code—strings of 1s and 0s. In contrast to a varying, continuous electric current or analog signal, the digital signal is made up of discrete, discontinuous electrical states positioned one after the other in time. (See Fig. 2-1.) Analog and digital signals can coexist in electronic systems, and conversion between the two is not uncommon. (More on this in chapter 4.)

Among the first electronic devices were *vacuum tubes*, the use of which has dwindled since the advent of transistors. Radio and TV could not have developed without the vacuum tube devices known as the *diode* (two-element circuit) and the *triode* (three-element circuit). The disadvantages of tubes are their high power consumption, their bulkiness, and their cost. In tubes, excessive power is used to "boil off" electrons from metal plates to generate electricity in a vacuum. (See Fig. 2-2.) In radio transmission, where high power is required for radiating electromagnetic waves, tubes still play a dominant role over their semiconductor counterparts.

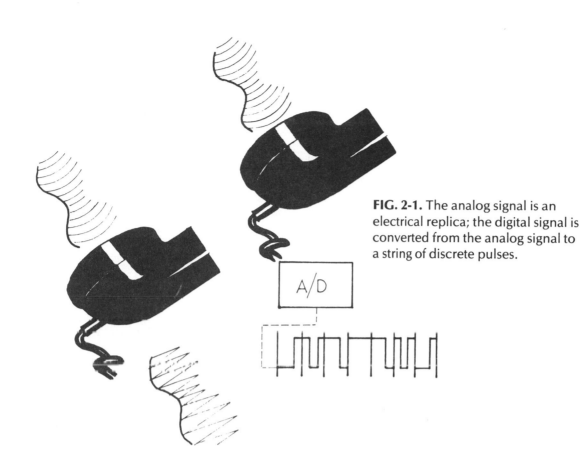

FIG. 2-1. The analog signal is an electrical replica; the digital signal is converted from the analog signal to a string of discrete pulses.

The functions served by vacuum tubes and transistors are primarily amplification and AC frequency oscillation.

Amplifiers change low-level signals to higher levels. For example, a microphone acts to change a sound wave into an electric wave, but does nothing about signal level. When the microphone is plugged into a public address system consisting of an amplifier and speakers, an enlarged and exact copy of the sound picked up by the microphone is emitted from the speakers. An amplifier has a reservoir of electrical charge, a control valve, and an output line. (See Fig. 2-3.) For both tube-type and transistor amplifiers, the operating principle is the same: to apply a small input signal to the control valve which shapes the flow of a larger electrical current flowing from the reservoir to the output line. The output becomes an enlargement of the input.

Oscillators are circuits that generate and detect selected AC frequencies. One type of oscillator is made by using an amplifier-type circuit and feeding the output back to the control valve. (See Fig. 2-3.) The same signal is thus produced repeatedly. Crystal oscillators employ the piezoelectric effect: A small sliver of crystal is mechanically energized or vibrated when placed between two metal plates to which a voltage is

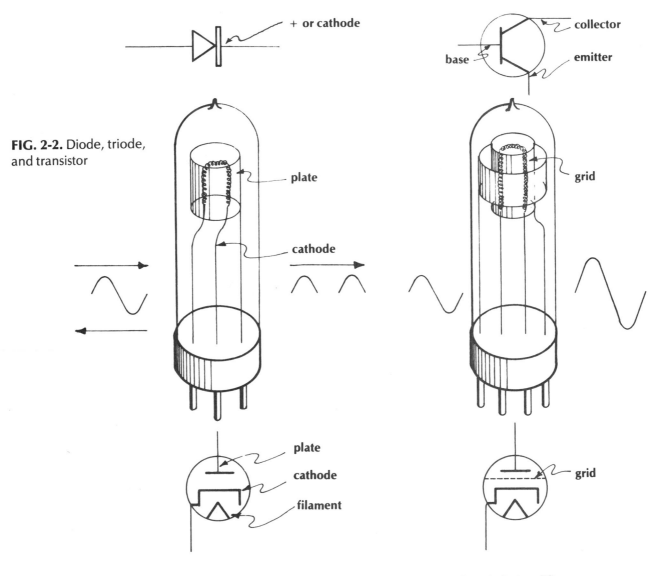

Semiconductor Diode

+ or cathode

NPN-type Transistor Amplifier

collector

base

emitter

FIG. 2-2. Diode, triode, and transistor

plate

cathode

grid

plate

cathode

filament

grid

Tube Diode Rectifier

Tube Triode Amplifier

fed. Conversely, when a crystal in such an arrangement is mechanically vibrated, a voltage is generated across the metal plates. AC frequencies, for example, are used for broadcast signals; the oscillator is used for transmitting and receiving signals. A frequency generated by a transmitter's oscillator radiates as electromagnetic energy in the air. A receiver's tuning circuitry includes an oscillator of that same frequency. When the frequency of the tuner and the signal in the air match, the signal is received.

Integrated circuits (ICs) are fingernail-size and smaller multicircuits that are made up of the basic components of electronics, which engineers call

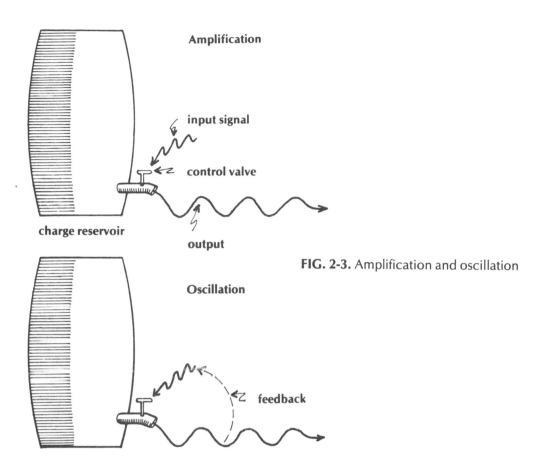

Amplification

input signal

control valve

charge reservoir

output

Oscillation

feedback

FIG. 2-3. Amplification and oscillation

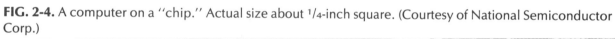

FIG. 2-4. A computer on a "chip." Actual size about ¼-inch square. (Courtesy of National Semiconductor Corp.)

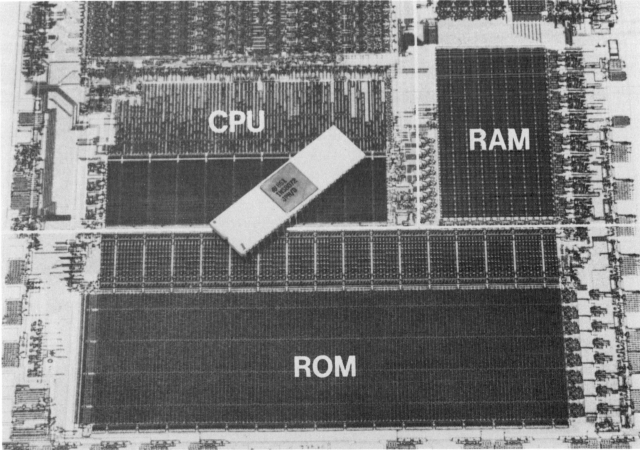

CPU

RAM

ROM

"gates"; these gates can be opened and closed in various ways to modify the flow of electricity. (See Fig. 2-4.) ICs themselves are highly complex gates that have become the basic building blocks of solid-state electronics, the class of devices that has replaced the use of vacuum tubes.

The basic components of electronics are resistors, capacitors, rectifiers, inductors, and semiconductors or transistors.

Resistors are components that have fixed levels of resistance or a specific variable range of resistance levels. A radio volume dial, for example, is a variable resistor. Placed in the path of electricity, resistors increase or decrease the voltage or amperage. They are the most versatile and essential of electronic components. Some ICs are made up of resistors and little else.

Capacitors are components that store electricity. A battery is a type of capacitor in which electricity is stored chemically. However, in most capacitors, electricity is stored in an electronic field. A simple capacitor is made up of two metal plates separated by an insulator (also called a dielectric), such as air, paper, or glass. In a DC condition, the first plate collects all the electrical charge fed to the capacitor, draining also the electrons of the second plate. This sets up a voltage or pulling force between the plates across the insulator, and electricity ceases to flow in the capacitor. The energy is held as if in a tank, and can only be emptied by bridging the two plates. In an AC condition, the tanking capacity changes from plate to plate with every change of flow direction. During the fill/empty process a small amount of electricity slips

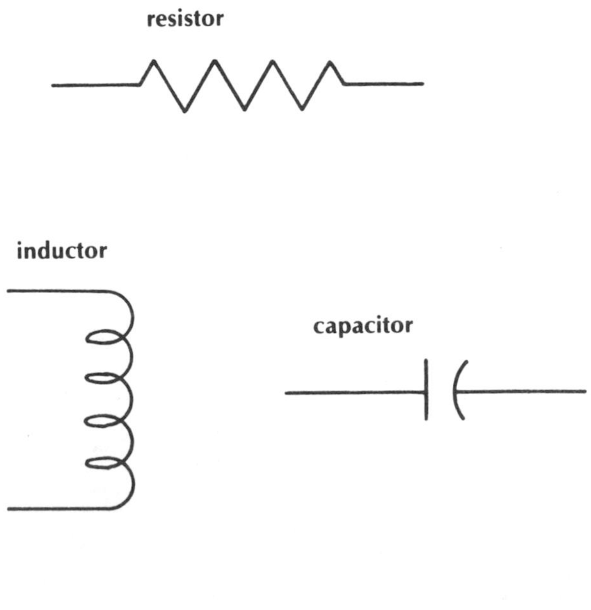

resistor

FIG. 2-5. Component symbols

inductor

capacitor

FIG. 2-6. Capacitor

through the insulator. Thus, energy flows through the capacitor. A higher rate of AC causes more electricity to flow through; a lower rate causes less to flow through. Overall, capacitors store electricity, inhibit DC, and control the flow of AC.

Rectifiers are components used to change AC to DC. A rectifier allows electrical current to pass in only one direction. One of many jobs of the rectifier is to power tube plates and transistor terminals, for which DC is required. (See Fig. 2-7.)

Inductors are coils as described on page 37, in the paragraph on transformers. (See Fig. 1-3.) Whereas electrical energy in a capacitor is stored in an electric field, inductors act to store energy in a magnetic field, which is a natural result of electricity flowing in wires. An electrical current in a wire produces a second current in that wire, flowing in the opposite direction. The two currents interact, and the result is a draining and holding of energy in a magnetic field around the wire. In a DC condition, the inductance phenomenon occurs only as the electricity begins to flow, and then ceases when a stable flow rate is reached. In an AC condition, the constant changes of flow direction cause a continuing interaction of the opposing currents. The greater the frequency of the AC, the greater the voltage of the second current. In a coiled wire (i.e., an inductor), inductance is greater, and AC fed through it is delayed. Inductors and capacitors are combined to make what are called resonant frequency circuits to act as filters that can be set to allow selected AC signals to pass while blocking all others. This type of circuit is required for radio and TV reception.

Semiconductors or transistors are made of substances that are between conductors and insulators. A conductor has many free electrons that can be stimulated by a voltage, resulting in the flow of electricity.

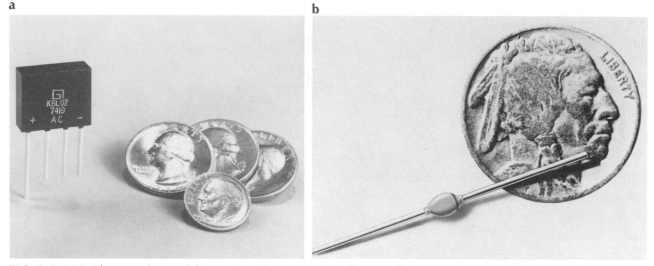

FIG. 2-7. (a) Bridge rectifier and (b) minirectifier (Courtesy of General Instrument Corp.)

FIG. 2-8. (a) Power transistors (Courtesy of General Electric Co., Semiconductor Products Dept., Auburn, N.Y.) and (b) transistor on a circuit board

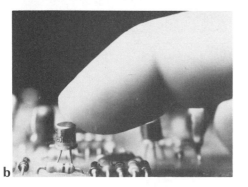

An insulator of very high resistance has few or no free electrons, and electricity does not flow. A semiconductor has some free electrons, which can be stimulated by a small voltage to produce a small electrical current. Materials that are intrinsic semiconductors are silicon, germanium, and gallium arsenide. In the process of making semiconductive components, other materials are added to intrinsic semiconductors to alter electrical conduction. In semiconductive devices, conduction can occur in two ways: (1) by electron movement and (2) by the movement of "holes," the vacancies in atoms left by electrons that have moved on. An *N-type* semiconductor has moving electrons, while the *P-type* has moving holes. In the making of a *transistor*, N-type and P-type functions are combined. Transistor components are used for rectification, amplifying signals, and switching. (See Fig. 2-9.)

Solid-state and microelectronic circuitry has grown out of the development of transistors, which began in the 1940s. The devices of the 1950s were the prototypes for digital electronic circuitry. Evolving from the vacuum tube and its extravagant use of power, microelectronics has been moving toward the eventual, miserly conduction of just a few electrons. For signal processing, a measurable electrical effect achieved by the least amount of electrons is most suitable. Although electricity travels at about one foot per nanosecond (billionth of a second), the less distance it has to travel, the faster it works and the more it can be used to do within a given space. In electronics, the smallest circuitry is the smartest.

In 1961, the first integrated circuits became available commercially. They consisted of about ten transistors crowded together on a tiny quarter-inch square of silicon called a *chip*. Later in the 1960s, the next major step was taken and is referred to as *large-scale integration* or LSI. An LSI chip contained about 400 components made up of many separately functioning circuits. At first, LSI chips were suited only to single purposes, so for every application a different chip was needed. Then, in 1971, the "miracle" chip was developed around the idea of putting the entire circuitry for an electronic calculator on a single chip. Also known as a *microprocessor*, the device contained more than 2,000 transistors and other components all packed onto a piece of silicon less than one quarter inch square. The same device could be used in many situations by simply using an additional "memory" chip containing an appropriate set of instructions. By the late 1970s, VLSI, or very large-scale integration, with 40,000 components and ULSI, or ultra-LSI, with 100,000 components came on the scene.

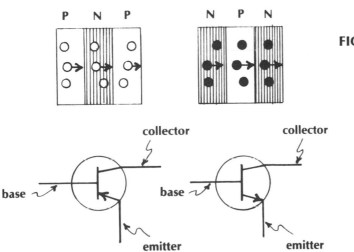

Holes Moving   **Electrons Moving**

FIG. 2-9. Transistors

The speed of operation or switching time of microelectronic devices reached nanosecond rates in the 1970s. They require only 5 volts. If the trend should continue, by 1990, chips will have 100 million components and switching times in the thousandths of a nanosecond, requiring only 0.5 volts to operate.

Techniques for manufacturing integrated circuits have been at the root of the continuing improvement of chips. The process starts with laboratory-grown, two-, three-, or four-inch-diameter cylinders of N- or P-type silicon crystals sliced into thin wafers. The wafers are baked in an oxygenated gas to coat them with an insulating layer of glass or silicon dioxide, then coated again with a photosensitive emulsion (called a photoresist), which can be exposed in ultraviolet light (UV). Tiny masks scaled down from large circuit drawings are placed on the wafer and exposed to UV. Those areas struck by the light harden, forming another layer of insulation. The areas not exposed to the light are washed away in an acid bath. The acid etches through to the silicon. A semiconductive material opposite to that of the wafer is diffused into the exposed channels. For example, if the wafer was P-type, the first level of diffusion would be N-type. The second level, after a further coating of insulation, photoresist, another mask, UV, and the acid bath, would be again P-type. And so it goes, in some cases for ten levels of diffusion. An aluminum coating that is also engraved with a circuit design is the final layer before the wafer is inspected for deficient sections and the individual chips are cut apart. Each chip is then externally wired and sealed in plastic or metal, ready for use. The yield of good chips is about 10 to 50 percent, depending on circuit complexity. Laser beams, which are about 300 millionths of a meter wide, are used in the photographic processes, providing the precision necessary for the scale of work. A variety of IC chips are manufactured: for example, memory circuits that can hold instructions or store binary-coded data, microprocessors for computers and for use as control circuits in larger devices, and special-purpose signal generators, such as for TV synchronization signals.

Josephson-junction technology is another important area of circuitry development. Named for the scientist B. D. Josephson, who discovered it, the Josephson effect is the ability of electrons to cross a hairline gap separating two superconductors. A *superconductor* is a metal, such as tin or lead, that loses all resistance when its temperature is reduced to near absolute zero, the point at which all molecular ac-

FIG. 2-10. Segment of a photomask used in the making of a random access memory chip (Courtesy of National Semiconductor Corp.)

tivity ceases ($-273°C$). When a voltage is placed across the gap, the electrical current ceases to flow and produces a high-frequency signal. Of rather recent development, experimental Josephson-junction circuits or superconductors have been used in place of transistors requiring only minute amounts of power and having operation rates hundreds of times faster than transistors.

3
Digital Electronics

The development of digital electronics and the subsequent displacement of analog devices are spurred on by the need for greater precision in signal processing. An analog signal, as a continuous flow of electricity, is vulnerable to outside interference and distortions. An analog signal can be what is called "noisy." Affected by nearby, spurious signals, an analog signal can fail to clearly and cleanly represent the information it is carrying. On the other hand, a digital signal is almost nondistortable. Each signal bit in a string of bits is either one of only two voltage levels. A digital signal can contain a pure representation of the information it carries. Newly available digital audio recording systems in use in recording studios are providing a purity of sound reproduction to which analog audio systems just can't compare.

Analog/digital (A/D) conversion and the reverse, D/A conversion, are common practice. To convert an analog signal to digital, distinct levels of energy within the analog signal must be identified. Each distinct level, as it is detected, is given a specific value from among a range of specified values, broad enough to encompass the highest and lowest extremes of the analog signal. The frequency rate at which detection and value notation are made must be at a rate great enough to render a "digitized" copy of the analog signal. (See Fig. 3-1.) Once the signal is digitized, it is coded into binary. For example, a given digitized value of a sampled segment of the analog signal is a 7 in a range of 0 to 7. With the binary number system, a three-digit number made up of 1s and 0s can represent all the values from 0 to 7: 000 represents 0; 001 = 1; 010 = 2; 011 = 4; 101 = 5; 110 = 6; and 111 = 7. Thus, the digitized value 7 is converted to 111. Keep in mind that 1s and 0s represent electrical states; for instance, 1 = a specific high voltage, and 0 = a specific low voltage. Thus, a string of binary-equivalent values becomes a series of discrete high and low "pulses" that carry the information of the original analog signal. In the conversion of digital signals to analog, the process is reversed. An example

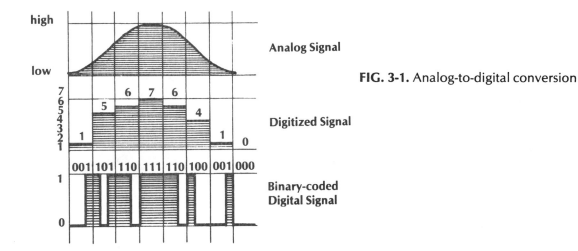

FIG. 3-1. Analog-to-digital conversion

of the use of A/D and D/A conversion can be seen in studio audio recording. Microphones pick up sound, which is itself an analog signal. They transduce the sound into analog electrical signals, which are then converted to digital. For playback, the digital signals must be converted back to analog to drive the speakers.

Although A/D and D/A conversions are feasible in many situations, they are not always economical. Another consideration, one that is under regular revision because of ever-upgrading circuitry, is the capacity of the medium through which the signal is sent. Digital signals require greater bandwidth, or signal-carrying capacity, than do analog signals. For instance, a television picture is transmitted in analog form. Some 7.5 million distinguishable voltage levels every second make up that signal. In the process of converting such a signal to digital form, there is an increase to 105 million distinguishable pulses per second. That signal rate happens, at present, to be beyond the capability of the conventional metal conductors used in television transmission systems.

Digital signal processing was first applied to computers. In the first written description of an electronic computer, in 1946, John von Neumann, Herman H. Goldstine, and Arthur W. Burks laid down the basics of digital operations still valid today. Their "Preliminary Discussion of the Logical Design of an Electronic Computing Instrument," written for the U.S. Army, at the Institute for Advanced Studies at Princeton, states that such a device is made up of a collection of many two-state elements organized to represent binary numbers and coded instructions.

Boolean logic, or switching algebra, governs the way computers carry out logical operations. It stems from the work of George Boole, a nineteenth-century

Technology Times

Noise—the Opposite of Signal

Inherent to electrical systems is *noise*— unwanted and ever-present signal that can alter the data carried through a system. The design and engineering of electronic devices must take noise into account and build into systems the circuits and parameters of operation that minimize noise and rise above it. Signal-to-noise ratios must be calculated so that above the ever-present din of electrical activity—colliding electrons—the signal can be clearly detected.

Attenuation, the decrease of a signal's amplitude as it moves through circuits and along transmission lines, is another natural occurrence to be overcome. Rates of attenuation can be calculated and must be counteraffected by the use of circuits, such as amplifiers spaced along coaxial cable to revitalize attenuating signals transmitted along them.

Closely located or coupled circuits are sometimes plagued by a *crosstalk*—a form of interference in which a signal, either electromagnetic or electrical, from one circuit strays into another. Crosstalk sometimes occurs during a telephone conversation, when the two speakers hear another conversation under their own.

Peculiar to digital signals is *quantizing noise* or *quantization distortion,* which is the result of converting an analog signal to digital form. It results from breaking a smooth, continuous wave into a series of squared-off bits. The process of digitizing involves a limited set of values to which sampled levels of the analog signal are converted. If a specific sampled level of the analog signal falls between the digital values available for conversion, an inexact rendition of the signal is the result. That distortion of the original data is referred to as the quantizing error, which is one of the few forms of distortion in digital signaling.

Interference and distortion resulting from noise and circuit functions can be overcome through the use of the appropriate devices designed to counteract them. Quantizing errors can be smoothed over, signals can be amplified to levels that are big enough relative to noise to be clear and strong, and crosstalk can be limited. Transmission errors

mathematician. To solve problems in logic, Boole created a mathematical system using symbols to represent language statements. In his system, reasoning is, in effect, turned into calculation. When statements are properly represented as prescribed by Boole, they obey certain laws of combination and thus can be added, subtracted, etc.

All statements are treated as either true or false and nothing else. True is represented by the binary digit 1; false by binary 0. For the handling of information in such a two-state format, instructions are expressed with the use of three logical operations: AND, OR, and NOT.

- AND operation: If a statement is true AND another statement (or all others) is true, then both (or all) statements together are true. If a statement in the group is false or all are false, then all statements together are false.
- OR operation: If a statement OR another (or all others) is true, then either one or both (or all) are true. If all are false, then together all are false.
- NOT operation: One statement is NOT another statement.

Fig. 3-2. TRUTH TABLES

Statements		Conclusions	
A	B	AND (A and B)	OR (A or B)
0	0	0	0
0	1	0	1
1	0	0	1
1	1	1	1

Statement	Conclusion
A	Not A
0	1
1	0

Truth tables are used to show the possible combinations of elements in a logic problem related to an operation. Figure 3-2 shows sample truth tables for AND, OR, and NOT operations using 1s and 0s. Note that in the AND operation, all inputs have to be 1s to produce a 1 output. In the OR operation, only one or more inputs need be 1 to produce a 1 output. In the NOT operation, whatever the input, the output is opposite.

In the late 1930s, Claude Shannon, a graduate student at M.I.T., showed that Boolean algebra could be applied to two-state electronic devices, which opened the way for development of electronic computation as we know it today. With a simple circuit containing a switch and light bulb, 1 and 0 are represented electrically. (See Fig. 3-3.) The 1 equates to the switch being closed and current flowing to the light bulb. The 0 equates to the switch being opened and current being prevented from reaching the light bulb. Adding a second switch in series creates an AND circuit. Both switches have to be closed if current is to reach the light bulb. If either one or both are open, no current reaches the bulb. If the second switch is added in parallel, we have an OR circuit. Only one of the two or both switches need be closed for current to reach the light bulb. Only if both (or all) are not closed is current prevented from reaching the light bulb. The NOT circuit is constructed using a switch that is normally closed. When current flows to the switch, it opens, cutting off current to the light bulb. When current ceases to flow to the switch, it closes. OR and AND circuits can be combined with NOT to make NOR and NAND circuits.

in digital codes which result from unpredictable *glitches,* or temporary noise impulses, can be guarded against by using parity checking techniques.

Parity checking is a process in which a bit is added to a group of information-carrying bits for error-detection purposes. The bit is inserted to indicate whether the group has an odd or even number of 1s. Parity checking may be either odd or even. In odd parity, the parity bit is 1 when there is an even number of 1s in the group to make the total number of 1s odd. If, at reception, an even number of 1s is detected, retransmission of that group is performed. Because of parity checking, error rates in digital transmission are very low.

Since noise, in general, is thermal—created by energized atoms—devices that operate at cooler temperatures are less noisy. Josephson junctions and other low-temperature devices, beginning to be used in the 1980s, help to overcome some of the problems of noise in electronic and electrical systems. However, noise, attenuation, crosstalk, quantization distortion, and other lesser forms of interference will not be completely conquered. They are to these systems what gravity and friction are to global flight.

FIG. 3-3. AND/OR circuits

Digital circuits are made up of two-state devices.

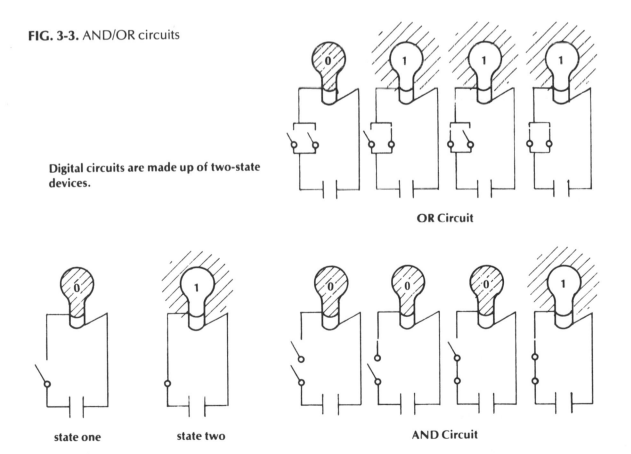

OR Circuit

state one   state two   AND Circuit

A practical application of an AND circuit is in a car. For example, seat belts are fastened AND the key is turned in the ignition to start the car. An applied OR circuit is an automatic garage door which is opened by a signal from the car OR by pressing the button in the garage. The NOT circuit practically applied serves as a safety switch. For example, the seat belt/ignition AND circuit includes a NOT circuit which opens when the car door is opened.

Networks of logic circuits are either combinational or sequential. In *combinational logic*, all circuits in a network respond simultaneously. With *sequential logic* networks, signals are stored, acted upon, and passed on serially. Among the useful combinational

FIG. 3-4

Digital Circuit Symbols

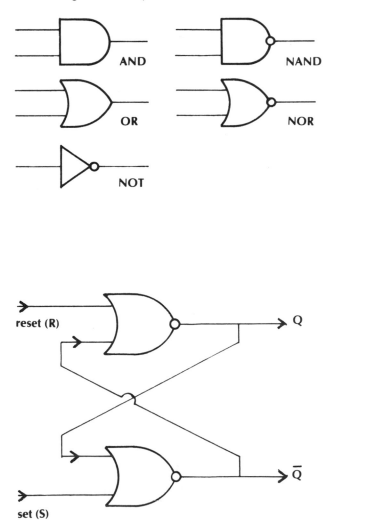

A reset-set flip-flop is made up of two NOR circuits.

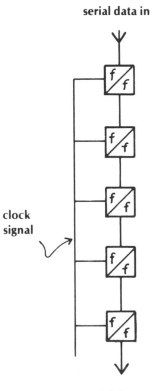

serial data in

clock signal

serial data out

A shift register is made up of a group of flip-flops that transmit data in a single wire one bit at a time.

logic circuits are pulse detectors used, for example, to monitor errors that can occur during the transmission of long sequences of signal pulses; half adders used to add two digits; full adders for adding three digits; encoders and decoders for translating signals in and out of various symbolic states; and multiplexers and de-multiplexers, which, respectively, make signal input selections and signal output selections, like railroad track switchmen, routing signals along their proper paths. Combinational circuits have no signal-storage capability. They produce an output only when an appropriate input is fed them.

In sequential logic circuits, signals can be stored. A basic sequential logic circuit is a *flip-flop* made up of

Fig. 3-5. TRUTH TABLE: FLIP-FLOP

S_0	R_0	Q_1
0	0	0_0
0	1	0
1	0	1
1	1	?

FIG. 3-5. Truth table: flip-flop. Subscript $_0$ means before clock pulse; subscript $_1$ means after clock pulse; ? means unknown.

FIG. 3-6. The half adder is for adding two binary digits.

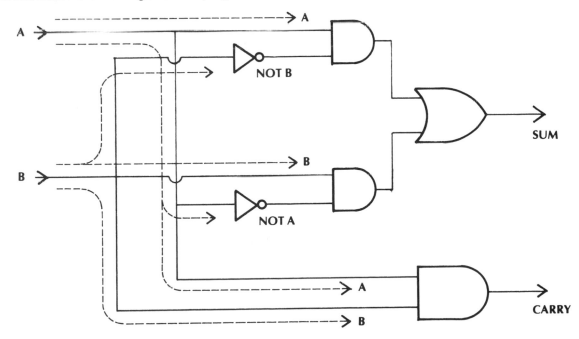

Fig. 3-7. TRUTH TABLE: HALF-ADDER

If A =	If B =	Carry	Sum
0	0	0	0
0	1	0	1
1	0	0	1
1	1	1	0

two crisscrossed NAND circuits. It can store a single signal pulse. Grouped together, flip-flops are used for generating time signals that control the operations of the systems in which they are used. For example, a *clock* is an important part of a computer that sets the timing of the various operations being carried out (see page 219). The clock—an oscillator—generates a sequence of pulses that are counted by flip-flop circuits, which in turn set specific computer functions into action. Sequential logic circuits are also used as short-term signal-storage devices called *registers*, which hold groups of signals. For instance, during an addition execution in an electronic calculator, the accumulating total is held in a register. Shift registers act to shift groups of signals from one flip-flop chain to another.

Memory circuits constitute a large part of digital electronics. They include magnetic cores, magnetic bubbles, charge-coupled devices (CCDs), and semiconductor memories.

Magnetic core memory is the senior citizen of the electronic memory community. Core memory arrays are made of tiny, doughnut-shaped ferrite (a ceramic iron-oxide material) units strung on a grid of wire. Three wires pass through each core. As current passes through the vertical wire, called the *write* wire, the core is magnetized. When current in the wire travels downward, the core is magnetized in one direction, and when it travels upward, the core is magnetized in the other direction, thus providing the two conditions required for encoding 1s and 0s. The horizontal wire is called the *sense* wire and is used to read a stored signal. The third wire is called the *inhibit* wire, and it prevents the write and sense currents from affecting cores adjacent to those addressed. Core systems are *random access*, meaning that any location of storage can be directly accessed as opposed to having to sequence through a series of storage locations to get to a selected one. Cores are *nonvolatile*, meaning that they retain signals even if power to them is cut off, whereas *volatile* devices lose their memories when power is cut. Core memory capacities can be quite large, and though they have been replaced by many newer, less costly devices, they will remain a viable storage option for some time to come.

Magnetic bubble devices store 1s as tiny cylinder-shaped magnetic regions measuring but a fraction of the diameter of a human hair. The bubbles are created in a thin film of magnetized garnet. The absence of bubbles represents 0s. A magnetic field created by a set of tiny coils controls the movement of the bubbles within the film. Bubbles are read by detector circuits as they move along defined paths designed into the device. Bubble memory is *serial access*, meaning that a stored signal is only locatable among a series of stored signals sequencing through the device. Bubbles are nonvolatile. Bubble memories can store up in the hundreds of thousands of signals, and improvements are in the making. Signal movement rates through bubble memories are currently in microseconds and are expected to be ten times greater in the newer devices.

Charge-coupled devices (CCDs) are made on silicon chips and, like semiconductor memories, have their memory points set in grid arrays. CCDs circulate signals for storage serially, signal by signal through the devices. They are volatile, requiring a small amount of power to preserve their stored signals. CCDs are being developed for use in television cameras to replace present-day light-sensing circuits. Because of the way they are made and what they are made of, they change light into electricity and produce a digital signal output.

Semiconductor memories are fabricated as described above and are composed of logical digital circuits made up of transistors. They include the types of registers discussed on page 54. However, the main body of devices used for memory applications—in computers, for instance—are two-dimensional arrays of from dozens to thousands of individual storage elements, each capable of storing binary 1s and 0s. (See Fig. 3-8.) Of the two types of semiconductor memories, one is designed for storing and retrieving signals over and over again. These memories are called *random-access memories* (RAMs) or *read/write memories*. In computers, RAMs are used for what is called main memory, the reusable "file drawer" that holds the data and instructions that are ready for processing. The other type of semiconductor memory is called *read-only memory* (ROM). It comes from the manufacturer already packed with a set of stored sig-

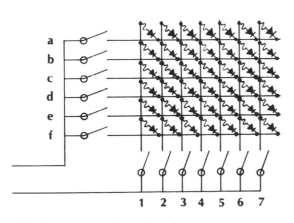

FIG. 3-8. A two-dimensional memory array that provides random access

nals to be used for a particular application, such as a set of signals required to instruct a computer to perform a particular task. RAMs are volatile and ROMs are nonvolatile. They are both random-access devices. Access times are in nanosecond ranges—that is, the time it takes to retrieve a signal from a location and deliver it to where it is needed; for instance, in a computer, to the *central processing unit* (CPU). The signal-storing capacity of semiconductor memories ranges into the hundreds of thousands. Two parameters are used to classify memory capacity: the number of storage points, called *addresses*, and the number of binary digits stored at each address. For instance, 256K bytes means 256×2^{10} equals 60,144 storage points times 8 bits at each storage point. (A byte is a signal group consisting of 8 bits.) RAMs can be either dynamic or static. In a dynamic RAM, only one bit can be stored at an address and held for only a fraction of a second. In static RAMs, up to a full byte can be stored at an address for as long as power is supplied to the device. ROMs are static only.

For further discussion of memory and external storage, see Chapter 23.

4

Optoelectronics

Optoelectronics refers to systems that use electrical energy to generate optical energy or light and vice versa. The major optoelectronic devices are light-emitting diodes (LEDs), photoconductive cells, lasers, and optical fibers. LEDs are used for numerical displays in digital watches, electronic test equipment, etc. Photoconductive cells (or photocells) are used to convert light to electricity; they have been used in space to supply power to satellites by converting the energy of the sun. Lasers are used in holography for making 3-D images and for industrial cutting processes and medical surgery. Optical fibers conduct light signals used to carry information. All these devices play a role in optical communication systems, in which light, in lieu of electricity, is used to carry information over distances (see chapter 8).

Electromagnetic radiation, or light, is emitted by all objects as long as they have temperatures above absolute zero. The human body emits infrared radiation with a wavelength of about 10 microns (millionths of a meter). Optical energy, or "visible" electromagnetic radiation, has wavelengths from 700 nanometers (billionths of a meter) down to 350 nanometers. Optoelectronic devices can be designed for operation on any wavelength between 1 millimeter, the low end of infrared, to 10 nanometers, the far edge of ultraviolet radiation. (See Fig. 4-1.)

Light sources are few in number. The sun pretty much corners the market when it comes to natural light sources. Distant stars do supply a twinkle here and there, but such light illuminates the soul more than the body. Fire by way of consumption of matter gives light. Since 1807, with the invention of the carbon arc lamps like those at movie premieres, electric light has been available. And in 1879, the familiar Edison incandescent light bulb was perfected.

Light bulbs are heat-to-light devices as discussed on page 34. In a fluorescent light tube, light is a result of atomic processes. The tube is lined with a phosphor coating and filled with gas. Electricity traveling through the gas causes it to radiate ultraviolet light,

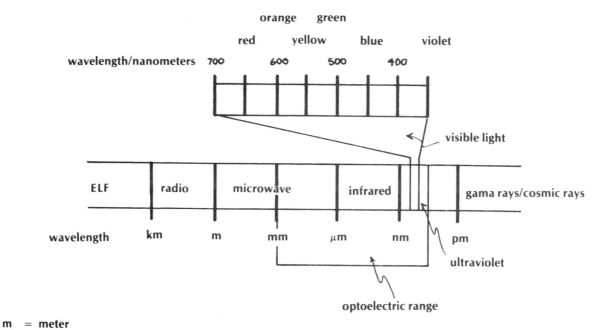

FIG. 4-1. The electromagnetic spectrum

m = meter
km = kilometer = 1,000 m
mm = millimeter = one-thousandth m
μm = micrometer = one-millionth m
nm = nanometer = one-billionth m
pm = picometer = one-trillionth m

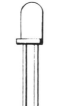

FIG. 4-2. Light-emitting diode (LED)

which in turn causes the phosphor to radiate energy in the visible spectrum. Light is given off by electrons when they gain and lose energy from an external source. In an incandescent light bulb, the external energy is electricity causing heat. In the fluorescent tube, the ultraviolet radiation does the trick for the electrons of the phosphor's atoms. Neon and xenon lamps also work atomically. All these artificial light sources give off what is called *incoherent light*, consisting of a wide range of wavelengths and colors. To produce a single color of light, a filter must be used.

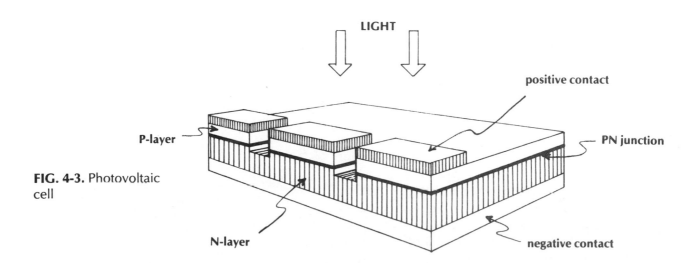

FIG. 4-3. Photovoltaic cell

LEDs

Light-emitting diodes are like tiny solid-state light bulbs. Their light is a result of electrons moving in a tiny semiconductor. A voltage is fed to a LED device, forcing its electrons to cross a junction separating two poles of charge. As their energy levels are raised and then return to their original states, light of a very narrow range of wavelengths is emitted. LEDs can be made to emit different colors and infrared radiation. They consume very little power and have exceedingly long lives, better than fifty years. They can be turned off and on within billionths of a second.

PHOTOCELLS

Photocells are transducers of light to electricity. Among the types of photocells are photoresistors and photovoltaic cells.

Photoresistors are made of materials, such as cadmium sulfide, which have inherent high resistance in darkness. When they are exposed to light, the resistance level in these materials is lowered. Photoresistors are fabricated semiconductors that, when exposed to light, give off a small electrical current. The current is a result of electrons gaining energy from the light and moving across a junction. A photoresistor can be designed for a particular wavelength of light, such as an infrared photoresistor for detecting infrared light exclusively.

Photovoltaic cells produce a voltage when hit by light. This type of photocell is the one commonly known as the solar cell used in devices, such as radios and watches, that are powered by solar energy. Photovoltaic devices are made with materials, such as selenium, that give off electrical energy when hit by light. In 1880, using a selenium cell, Alexander Graham Bell constructed an optical communications system for transmitting voice signals. The cell was used to detect voice signals that were carried on a beam of light reflected off a mirror.

LASERS

Laser is an acronym for "light amplification by stimulated emission of radiation." Normal light is made up of many wavelengths or colors of light; it is incoherent. A coherent light, if it existed naturally, would have a single wavelength or pure color. In the cosmos, a natural source of coherent light has not been found.

Technology Times
Energies of the Future

The search for useful particles and effects occurring in the subatomic world has only just begun. The atom's electron and the electromagnetic wave's photon are the first of what will likely prove to be many related energy resources that our science and engineering will exploit. The proton, for example, is the focus of research in nuclear fusion, the sought-after process to produce clean nuclear power. The proton, which carries the opposite charge to the electron, is located in the atom's nucleus. Nuclear fusion involves the merging of nuclei or proton charges. When protons are forced together from different nuclei, a great deal of energy is produced in the form of extreme heat. Though yet to be perfected on an economical level, fusion (or we might call it "protonics") will likely have technological applications unimagined today.

Some of the phenomena that scientists have observed and begun to experiment with are phonons, spin waves, and neutrinos.

Phonons are sound waves at extremely high frequencies, 10 billion cycles per second and up. We hear sound waves with frequencies of about 50 to 20,000 cycles per second. In the phonon range, sound waves in solids demonstrate what is called the acoustoelectric effect, in which tiny electrical imbalances are caused in atoms vibrated by phonon energy. Phonons have been used to make magnets several hundred thousand times more powerful than the earth's magnetic field. Phonons may someday play a role in the fabrication of a material that will act like a small public address system; when you speak at it, the sound will be amplified.

Spin waves are magnetic energy "waves" that travel through solids exposed to certain frequencies of radio or electromagnetic waves. The phenomenon could provide the means for magnetically affecting electromagnetic signals, such as their amplification.

Neutrinos have been a subject of experimentation since 1978 that might result in a new medium of communications. A neutrino is a particle with almost no electrical charge and mass. It tends not to collide with other particles as it travels through space. In a beam, however, some neutrinos do collide with the atoms of a body of water and produce tiny flashes. These flashes can be detected and counted, and their number is proportional to the number of neutrinos in the beam. Pulsed beams with varying numbers of neutrinos could be used to carry information through the densest of matter over any distance. A practical application of this is communications with submerged submarines, which cannot receive ordinary radio signals.

Instantaneous transportation is a capability predicted by some futurists as the ultimate synthesis of all energy-transforming technologies. In part, the human need to communicate is rooted in the desire to overcome distance. As information is refined and the means for its transport enhanced, are we not working to find a way to take the total information of something, transmit it, and have it manifest in its totality at the place to which it was transmitted—instantaneous transportation?

Future discoveries about the cosmos will likely reveal new energy resources for the development of as yet unimaginable technologies. In view of the quantum-leaping advances of the last 150 years, and the growing pace of curiosity, continued investment, and development, our technology can only improve to serve our further and successful survival if we, in fact, put it to that purpose.

The laser, for all practical purposes, is a human-made generator of coherent light. With a laser, energy traveling at 186,000 miles per second can be focused into a single beam that can strike a single cell of human tissue or blow a fist-size hole in the side of a tank. A laser being developed for atomic fusion applications can supply 40 trillion watts of power right on target to an atom. Laser temperatures in the range of the sun's surface, 100 million degrees, have been achieved.

The principles of lasing go back to the work of Albert Einstein and the Danish physicist Niels Bohr. In the period 1913–1917, they discovered that electrons exposed to external sources of energy are raised to higher energy levels momentarily, and that when the energized electrons fall back to their original energy states, they give off energy in the form of light or electromagnetism. Further, electrons of the same material give off light of the same wavelength. A laser, in effect, is a "pump" that takes advantage of Einstein's and Bohr's discovery. Some materials (such as ruby crystals) are more easily pumped or lased than others.

As a side note, laser technology was invented in 1960 at the Hughes Aircraft Company by Theodore Maiman following a 1958 publication by Charles Townes and Arthur Schawlow which described the basic design for a laser. A fourth party to the invention is Gordon Gould, who in 1957 came up with the idea, wrote it down, had it notarized, and approached the Pentagon for funding. The military, having death-ray on its mind, impounded Gould's notebooks, declaring them top secret. Gould won a patent challenge in the late 1970s and is on his way to winning more.

Among the types of lasers are pulse ruby lasers and continuous wave lasers (See Fig. 4-4), solid-state lasers, and carbon dioxide lasers.

Pulse ruby lasers contain a power supply that activates an optical pumping element that surrounds a ruby crystal rod. Optical pumping is the process by which the electrons of the ruby are exposed to their own light to stimulate their further emission of radiation. Two mirrors are placed at the ends of the rod between which the emitted radiation bounces back and forth. As the light travels through the ruby, it stimulates more electrons to emit more light. One of the mirrors is partially transparent and allows light to pass through it and out of the laser cavity. That escaping beam of light is coherent; it is a single wavelength of light. The beam can have an output of several thousand watts of power and can last from

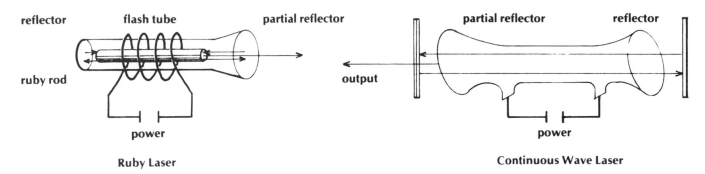

FIG. 4-4. Lasers

three to five milliseconds. When rapid changes of power are made to the laser cavity, shorter pulses of about twenty nanoseconds with a billion watts of power can be obtained. The range of the beam is relatively short, about one mile. These pulse-type lasers are used where high power concentration over a small area is required, such as for retinal coagulation in eye surgery and in the manufacture of microelectronic components.

Continuous wave lasers are mostly made with helium and neon gases and are electrically stimulated, rather than optically pumped. A continuous wave gas laser contains a power supply that delivers high voltage to a tube filled with the gas(es). Mirrors, one partially transparent, are located at opposite ends of the tube. As long as there is power, a coherent light beam is produced by the electrons of the gas(es). Circulating liquids, in lieu of gases, are suitable for lasing in a continuous wave laser. Chemical lasers are being developed and require no external source of power. A combination of hydrogen and fluorine gases lase without electricity and will be well suited for use in spacecraft where power supplies are limited. The continuous wave laser has been used in communications, in holography, and in industrial instrumentation alignment.

Solid-state lasers, the size of a sliver of glass, can be continuous wave or pulsed at microsecond durations with a peak of about 10 watts of power.

Carbon dioxide lasers are continuous wave devices and among the most efficient and powerful. Their beams radiate at a wavelength of 10.6 microns, which makes them invisible to the human eye. This type of laser provides high wattage and, thus, heat. Fifteen thousand watts of coherent light can melt almost anything. That's well within the range of carbon dioxide lasers.

OPTICAL FIBERS

Optical fibers are light-conducting strands of glass or plastic. Each strand is about the thickness of a human hair. A light travels or propagates through the fiber by bouncing or reflecting from side to side off the fiber's highly polished and transparent inner surfaces. Fibers are most often bundled together to provide enough signal-carrying capacity to suit a selected purpose. A bundle of fibers has the ability to transmit light around curves and into otherwise inaccessible places with very little loss of intensity or clarity. Optical fibers are to optical energy systems what copper wire has been to electrical systems. Fiber bundle lenses are fitted to TV cameras used for exploration of the human body for medical purposes, such as examinations of the internal conditions of organs and arteries.

PART II

TELECOMMUNICATIONS

N the mid-1500s it was believed that two needles magnetized from the same loadstone had a "sympathetic" connection without regard to how far apart they might be from one another. The "rumor" had it that if you moved one needle, the other needle would move the same amount. It was proposed that such a set of needles could comprise a system for communications across great distances, for if the needles were placed on a wheel of letters, a sender could merely turn his needle to each successive letter spelling out a message, which the receiver could write down, observing the movement of his needle on its wheel.

But, alas, no such phenomenon exists. Though the principle of telecommunications was clearly embodied in that figment of sixteenth-century imagination, it was not until almost three hundred years later that a genuine telecommunications system came into wide use, and that was the telegraph. During those three hundred years much groundwork was accomplished. Ben Franklin performed some experiments transmitting electrical pulses along some two miles of wire strung on poles, but did not attempt to use it for communications. Also in the late 1700s, several attempts were made at telegraphy, most based on constructing a separate circuit for each character to be transmitted. And, finally, the idea of coding information was attempted, using electricity for signals. Sometime in the first decade of the nineteenth century, with the use of the then newly developed battery, intelligence was transmitted with a device that used electrically charged poles immersed in water from which bubbles emerged when current passed through them. Numbers of bubbles represented specific characters.

Finally, in 1844, Samuel F. B. Morse introduced to the world his electric telegraph and code on a government-funded line built between Baltimore and Washington, D.C., with his famous prophetic inquiry, "What hath God wrought?" From that time on, the world and humankind began to shrink under the time- and distance-negating effects of telecommunications. Soon after the telegraph came the telephone, in the 1870s. By the turn of the century came radio, and within fifty years of that had come facsimile, radar, mobile radio, and television.

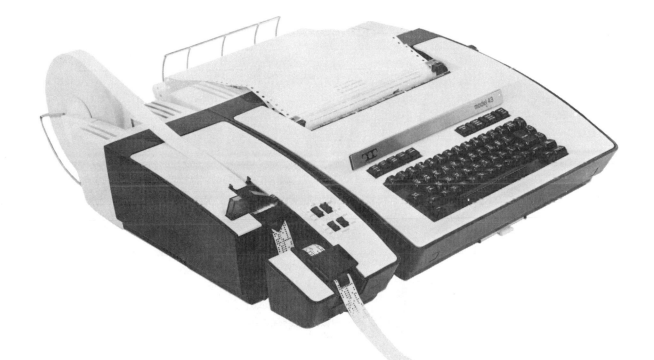

5

Transmission

Telecommunications is accomplished either by use of electromagnetism in the air, electrical energy in metal wires, or light energy (a form of electromagnetism) in optical fiber lines. Electromagnetic waves in the air and along wires can be generated by giving added electrical charges to electrons. An electron's own charge is like a still pool of water in its usual state within an atom. When it is disturbed, given an excess of energy, it ripples. The rippling of an electric charge is the outward movement of electric and magnetic fields alternating back and forth, or what is called the "propagation of an electromagnetic wave." All matter radiates some electromagnetic energy, and electromagnetic waves are all over the place themselves, energetically interacting with the materials they hit. In the process of *transmission*, electromagnetic waves are generated in patterns that represent information.

WAVES

The characteristics of a wave are its speed of travel, frequency, wavelength, and amplitude or energy level.

A wave's *speed of travel* (the speed of light) is a constant 186,000 miles per second or 300,000,000 meters per second in free space and only slightly less in materials and the air. In terms of distances on the planet, such a speed can be considered instantaneous. Going into space, such as to the moon, a wave requires a few seconds to make the trip. All information handled by machines moves at the speed of waves.

The number of alternations of fields (first an electric, then a magnetic) occurring in a second is a wave's *frequency*. The range of frequencies is from 1 per second to 10^{23} (1 with 23 zeros after it) per second. For information transmission, frequencies of between under 100 Hz (cycles per second) and 10^{15} Hz are used. The high end of this range takes in the frequencies that we detect with our eyes—visible light. The low

FIG. 5-1. A stone dropped in a pool demonstrates how an electromagnetic wave propagates.

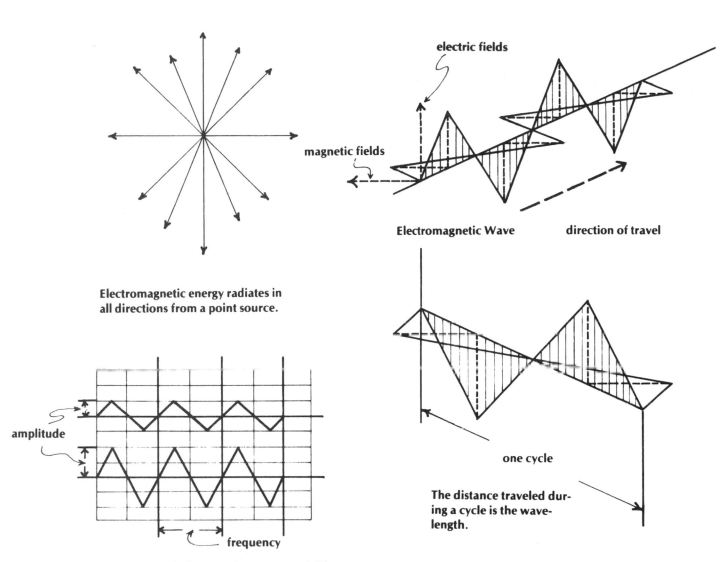

Electromagnetic energy radiates in all directions from a point source.

electric fields

magnetic fields

Electromagnetic Wave   direction of travel

amplitude

frequency

two waves with the same frequency and different amplitudes

one cycle

The distance traveled during a cycle is the wavelength.

FIG. 5-2. Electromagnetic energy

end might be an electronic signal generated in a circuit.

The physical distance spanned during an alternation or cycle is called a *wavelength*. Wavelengths range from over 2,000 miles long for waves of extremely low frequency (ELF) to 3×10^{-15} meters for waves of the highest frequencies.

In a wave, each field is rising and collapsing regularly. Each has a maximum and minimum field strength. The highest energy level of a field is its *amplitude*. Both electric and magnetic fields have measurable amplitudes. To determine the energy level of a wave in watts of power, the amplitude of the electric field is multiplied by that of the magnetic field and the product is divided by 2.

Our ability to transmit information is dependent on causing electric charges to emit waves and detecting those waves by measuring their effect on electric charges within materials that they hit. Generally, any radiation can be detected by its heating effect. A wave is an injection of energy to the materials it hits, hence the expression "a dose of radiation." It acts to energize electrons, causing their atoms to vibrate, and that is heat. Radiation is also measurable as an electrical effect.

Atomic-level effects of radiation are different depending on the type of wave. Basically, three types of effects have been broadly identified: *heat*, as mentioned above, is the vibrating of atoms; the *photoelectric effect* is when electrons within atoms are energized enough to jump to higher orbits temporarily, giving off energy in a form of light when they drop back down; and the *ionizing effect*, which is the ejection of electrons from atoms, leaving the atoms electrically unbalanced with an unequal number of protons and electrons. (See Fig. 5-3.)

The light frequencies, including infrared, visible, and ultraviolet, have photo and heating effects (see Table 5-1). All the microwave and radio frequencies below light are said to have only heating and electrical effects. X-rays, gamma rays, and cosmic rays are the ionizing waves; x-rays also have the heating and photo effects. Each type of effect is detectable by an appropriate sensor. For example, crystal detectors and transistors are used to detect microwave and radio wave propagation, photosensitive detectors for light waves, and geiger counters for ionizing radiation.

Electromagnetic waves radiate outward from their point source in all directions. Though they easily pass

FIG. 5-3. The three effects of electromagnetic energy radiation

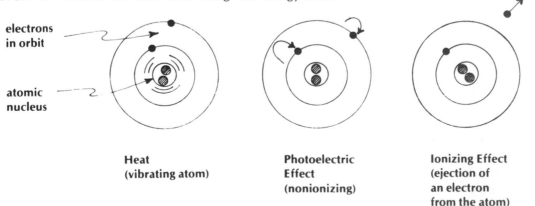

electrons
in orbit

atomic
nucleus

Heat
(vibrating atom)

Photoelectric
Effect
(nonionizing)

Ionizing Effect
(ejection of
an electron
from the atom)

Table 5.1. THE ELECTROMAGNETIC SPECTRUM

Wave band	Frequency (Hz)	Wavelength (meters)	Source	Atomic effect
Cosmic photon	10^{23}	3×10^{-15}	astronomical	ionizing
Gamma rays	10^{22}	3×10^{-14}	radioactive nuclei	ionizing
X-rays	10^{20}	3×10^{-12}	atomic inner shell	ionizing, photon-releasing, heat
Ultraviolet	10^{16}	3×10^{-8}	atoms in arcs and sparks	photon-releasing, heat
Visible	10^{15}	3×10^{-7}	atoms, hot bodies, molecules, lasers	photon-releasing, heat
Infrared	10^{13}	3×10^{-5}		
Extremely high frequency (EHF): microwaves	10^{11}	3×10^{-3}		
Super high frequency (SHF)	10^{10}	3×10^{-2}		
Ultrahigh frequency (UHF): radar	10^{9}	3×10^{-1}		
Very high frequency (VHF): TV, FM radio	10^{8}	3	electronic devices	heat
High frequency (HF): shortwave radio	10^{7}	30		
Medium frequency (MF): AM radio	10^{6}	300		
Low frequency (LF): longwave radio	10^{5}	3,000		
Very low frequency (VLF): induction heating	10^{4}	3×10^{4}		
Extremely low frequency (ELF): power	10	3×10^{7}	rotating machinery	electron flow
Direct current (DC)	0	infinity	batteries	electron flow

through many materials, their impact is lessened as they spread apart in their outward movement. Propagating waves are subject to reflection, refraction, and absorption.

In *reflection*, waves are reflected by or bounced off mountain sides, the moon and earth, tall buildings, etc., and the ionosphere—the electrically unbalanced upper layers of the earth's atmosphere.

A wave passing through a material can result in a change in that wave's velocity. This causes *refraction*, a slight change in the direction of travel.

The dissipation of a wave's energy as a result of interaction with matter is *absorption*.

ANTENNAS

Antennas are used for both transmission and reception of waves. For transmission, an antenna couples transmitter-generated waves with the air. For reception, the antenna couples airborne waves with receiver circuits. Transmission requires considerable electrical power to stimulate radiation. On the other hand, for reception, a fractional measure of a wave's power is easily detectable. Power from a transmitter energizes the electrical charges of the transmitting antenna to produce waves. The waves hitting a reception antenna energize its electrical charges, which the receiver detects.

FIG. 5-4. Transmitter-receiver system

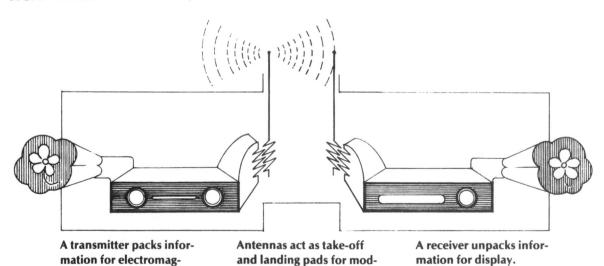

A transmitter packs information for electromagnetic transmission.

Antennas act as take-off and landing pads for modulated waves.

A receiver unpacks information for display.

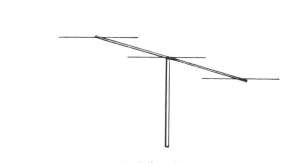

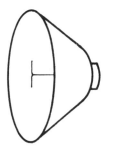

FIG. 5-5. The basic antennas

Dipole   **Multiband Beam**   **Parabolic Reflector**

Antennas for extremely low frequency must be very long to detect the long wavelengths. The sizes of antennas are proportional to the wavelengths they are made to receive. Because of the extreme size of low-frequency antennas, such transmission is not suitable for many communications needs. High-frequency antennas, like those for TV and radio, need only be a few feet or less in size. (See Fig. 5-5.)

Waves propagated from an antenna form an enlarging sphere surrounding the antenna as they move outward in all directions. Some travel in paths along the surface of the earth. Referred to as *ground waves*, they follow the curvature of the earth, their use being limited to a few hundred miles. Other waves, called *airwaves*, move skyward and into the atmosphere to the ionosphere. Depending on their angle of approach, these waves are either reflected or refracted back to earth, or pass through the ionosphere out into space. In some cases, a wave can be bounced back and forth between the earth and the ionosphere. In this way it can be relayed around the globe.

The sun's energy causes atoms of the ionosphere to ionize. Therefore, the ionosphere is farthest from the earth during the day and closest at night, making the time of day also a factor of transmission. For example, anyone tuning a car radio at night notices the increase in the number and distant reach of stations that can be picked up. The ionosphere is a natural reflector without which our use of electromagnetic waves would be much less effective. (See Fig. 5-6.)

Broadcast waves are those radiated in all directions for the largest possible area of reception. Waves can also be transmitted in a focused beam. Radar and microwave transmission, both on land and via satellite, rely on narrow-beam, line-of-sight transmission. An antenna must be visible to another from which it receives or to which it sends a transmitted signal. Mi-

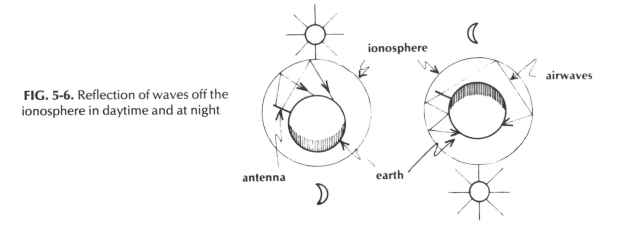

FIG. 5-6. Reflection of waves off the ionosphere in daytime and at night

crowave networks are constructed of strings of antenna towers spaced tens of miles apart depending on the terrain. Satellites orbiting the earth receive and retransmit microwaves, acting as space relay stations. Though narrowcast, a satellite's transmitted beam can cover a wide area, such as the contiguous United States.

CABLES

In the travel of waves along metal wires, propagation is parallel to the conductor. Penetration of a wave's energy into the conductor is minimal, and its radiation away from the conductor is not very far. The flow of electrons in an alternating current invariably produces electromagnetism. Waves in wires deteriorate unless periodic amplification is performed. Waves can be transmitted in rectangular pipes called *waveguides*, and along several types of conductors: wire pairs for waves up to 1 million Hz, coaxial cable for high-frequency waves, and, in optical communications, optical fibers for light waves. Wire pairs or open transmission lines are subject to radiation losses, especially over longer runs, whereas coaxial cable (coax) is designed to limit such losses, as well as interference from external sources, to a relative minimum.

FIG. 5-7. Transmission cables

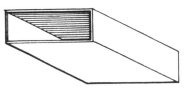

waveguide

wire pairs

coaxial cable

TRANSMITTERS

Transmitters can be made to generate almost any frequency of wave and provide varying power to it. In a transmitter, an oscillator is used to generate a selected carrier frequency with which information signals are mixed. In a receiver, the carrier frequency is separated from the information signals, which are then decoded for output.

Carrier communications goes back to the beginnings of radio and is based on the need to use high-frequency—that is, radio frequency (r.f)—waves with wavelengths of about three meters and less, which can be received with small antennas. Voice and music, for example, have sound frequencies within the human hearing range of under 100 to 20,000 Hz. In a simple telephone circuit or public address system, sound frequencies are changed into analog electrical signals and back again. For air transmission, the electrical signals are shifted up to r.f. by use of a carrier wave and shifted back down at the receiver. It is interesting to note, also, that if sounds were transmitted at their own frequencies, signals from multiple radio stations would interfere with each other, making clear reception impossible.

Bandwidth is the set of frequencies occupied for transmission. Voice, for example, uses a set of sound frequencies somewhere between 200 and 4,000 Hz. Voice transmission, therefore, requires a bandwidth of 4,000 Hz, a set of frequencies spanning some 4,000 discrete levels. A carrier frequency must be great enough to accommodate the bandwidth of a transmitted signal. All the components of voice could not be transmitted with a carrier wave set at 2,500 Hz.

The mixing of information signals with a carrier wave is called *modulation*. The unmixing of information signals and carrier wave is *demodulation*. The carrier wave is modulated or shaped by the information signal, itself a wave, either continuous, and thus analog, or made up of discrete bits in sequence, and thus digital. The informational wave and the carrier wave are transmitted side by side. For ex-

FIG. 5-8. Modulation/demodulation

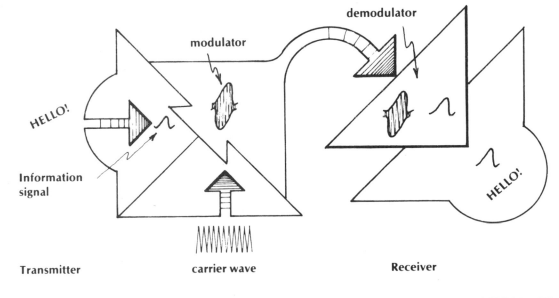

Information signal

Transmitter

modulator

carrier wave

demodulator

Receiver

ample, an FM radio station with a carrier frequency of 90 megahertz (MHz) transmits music requiring a bandwidth of 20,000 Hz. Three frequencies leave the transmitter: the 90-MHz carrier wave; it plus the 20,000-Hz signal wave; and it minus the signal wave—90,000,000 Hz; 90,020,000 Hz; and 89,980,000 Hz. The 20,000-Hz bandwidths below and above the carrier frequency are called *sidebands*, and in them the information is carried. Since both sidebands carry the exact same information, one of them can be filtered out to create what is called single sideband transmission, which uses less frequency space.

The primary methods of modulation are *amplitude modulation* (AM), in which the amplitude of the sideband(s) is varied in accordance with the information signals' frequency variations; *frequency modulation* (FM), in which the frequency of the sideband(s) is varied in accordance with the information signals' amplitude; and *phase modulation* (PM), in which the information is carried in the degree and rate of shifting of a second wave compared with the carrier.

Multiplexing is the process of mixing together a number of different information signals and transmitting them as a single signal, which at reception can be separated back into its components. When a group of signals are stacked one above the other, each occupying its own separate portion of a wider bandwidth, they are being *frequency division multiplexed* (FDM).

Time division multiplexing (TDM) makes available the total bandwidth of the sideband to all information signals, but limits time. Each signal has its turn in sequence. At reception, signals are sampled at a rate of time synchronized with the transmitter for reconstruction of each complete signal.

For converting analog signals to digital, *pulse code modulation* (PCM) is used. PCM eliminates analog transmission by using *pulse amplitude modulation* (PAM). In the PAM process, signals are digitized or quantized, made to fit a set of predetermined values. Then the digitized signals are sampled at regular rates of time to give a pulse signal to their amplitudes. These pulse signals are further converted to binary format; each is represented by one of two values according to its presence or absence rather than size. A network employing PCM, capable of operating rates of 270 megabits per second is commonly called a *T-carrier* system.

The transmission of data character by character is

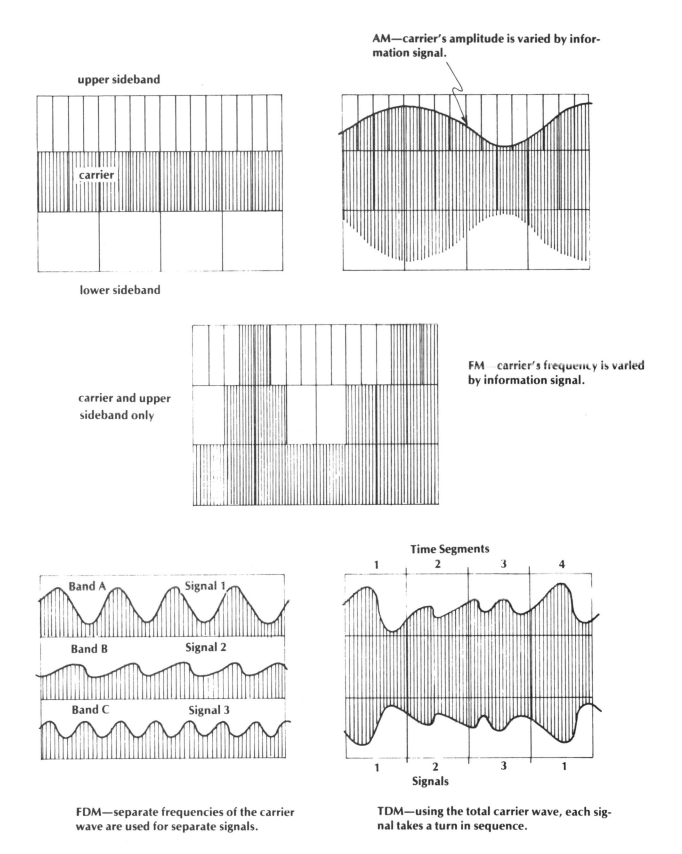

upper sideband

carrier

lower sideband

AM—carrier's amplitude is varied by information signal.

carrier and upper sideband only

FM—carrier's frequency is varied by information signal.

Band A   Signal 1

Band B   Signal 2

Band C   Signal 3

Time Segments
1   2   3   4

1   2   3   1
Signals

FDM—separate frequencies of the carrier wave are used for separate signals.

TDM—using the total carrier wave, each signal takes a turn in sequence.

FIG. 5-9. Methods of modulation: AM, FM, FDM, TDM

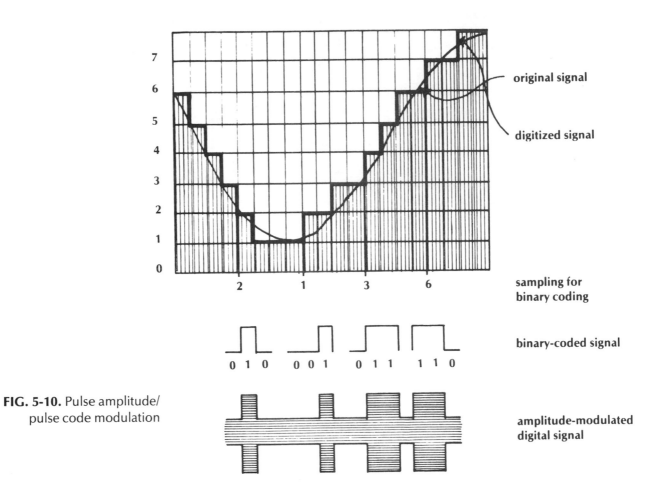

FIG. 5-10. Pulse amplitude/ pulse code modulation

original signal

digitized signal

sampling for binary coding

binary-coded signal

0 1 0   0 0 1   0 1 1   1 1 0

amplitude-modulated digital signal

PAM/PCM—the original signal is digitized, then sampled to create PAM signals that are then binary-coded; these PCM signals can then be AM- or FM-transmitted.

called *asynchronous transmission*. A set of independent information bits precedes and follows each and every character transmitted. Asynchronous data are transmitted from low-speed (up to about 2,000 bps—bits per second) keyboard teleprinters and data terminals.

Synchronous data transmission is the transmission of groups of characters, group by group, each preceded and followed by a set of independent information bits. A group can contain from 25 6-bit characters to 1,000 8-bit characters. Synchronous data are transmitted from computers and their high-speed terminals at rates up to 9,600 bps over analog voice channels.

Modems, or modulator-demodulators, also called data sets, are used to convert digital signals to analog for transmission over analog voice channels—phone lines—and vice versa at the receiving end. A typical transfer rate of data over an analog channel is one bit of information for every hertz of usable bandwidth. *Usable* or *effective bandwidth* refers to the portion of the bandwidth that is not degraded by distortion. In a voice channel of 4,000-Hz bandwidth, about a maximum of 2,400 Hz are usable for bit-to-hertz conversion; thus, 2,400 bps could be accommodated on a voice channel: That's 300 characters (8 bits per character inclusive of separation bits). Modems of more sophisticated design can increase the bit-to-hertz ratio from 1-to-1 to 4-to-1. Low-speed modems transmit at rates of up to 2,400 bps; medium-speed devices handle up to 10,000 bps; and with bandwidth greater than 4,000 Hz, high-speed modems can exceed 10,000 bps.

NETWORKS

A transmission network, such as the telephone system, is composed of (1) local loops, which connect users to central offices; (2) intracity trunks, which connect up central offices and toll offices within a city; and (3) intercity trunks, which interconnect toll offices of different cities. In addition to the telephone network, two other major networks are the Telex and TWX networks. Telex is the automatic teleprinter exchange service of Western Union for worldwide message transmission. TWX is its teletypewriter exchange service in the United States and Canada, which it acquired in 1971 from AT&T. Such networks provide *switched services*, the term referring to their capability of permitting contact between subscribers anywhere within the network. Subscribers to Telex and TWX can also use computer-controlled store-and-forward switching. In the store-and-forward process, groups of bits are transmitted as packets along the most available (not the most direct) route at every instant. A message, broken into packets traveling different routes to the point of reception, can be routed along the least congested paths. When all packets have arrived at the reception point, the message is reconstructed. This process is referred to as *packet switching*.

Also available for information transmission between two or more points are the private wire services. They provide dedicated hookups. A *dedicated* service provides a singular, custom-tailored use, in contrast to a *dial-up* network, which permits numerous uses and interconnections. Some of the types of private wire services are (1) the 2,000 Series for voice transmission only; (2) the 3,000 Series, using a voice channel for data for machine control and monitoring purposes; (3) the 4,000 Series, like the 3,000 Series, with additional facsimile transmission capability; (4) the 5,000 Series, or TELPAK, for voice, teletypewriter, data, and more, over 60 to 240 channels; and (5) the 8,000 Series of twelve voice channels for voice or wideband, high-speed data, and facsimile.

Transmission networks can also include terrestrial microwave and space satellite relay links. Frequencies above one billion hertz, or 1 gigahertz (GHz), and up to 3,000 GHz are classified as *microwaves*. Radiations at GHz energy levels are above the naturally occurring and human-made noise. Therefore, microwave signals need not be transmitted at as high powers as are signals transmitted in the radio band and lower bands where the signal-to-noise ratio must be kept high to prevent noise interference.

Microwaves are concentrated into a narrow beam for point-to-point transmissions rather than broadcast, which would disperse and weaken them. Metallic, parabolic reflector antennas are most commonly used; the larger the reflector, the narrower and higher power is the beam. Reflectors run to two feet and up in size, most being about eight feet. For microwave communications, line-of-sight transmission is a must, whereby antennas are placed on towers or higher locations, such as mountaintops and tall buildings.

A microwave carrier wave is most often frequency-modulated (FM), though other modulation methods can be used. At relay points, a signal is shifted down to an intermediate frequency (i.f.) of usually 70 MHz in the high-frequency radio band, amplified, shifted back to the microwave frequency, and transmitted on to the next relay link about twenty-five miles away. This process is carried out to minimize the effects of transmission equipment noise inherent to microwave system components.

The troposphere, in which clouds form, is the lower layer of the earth's atmosphere extending up to about 60,000 feet above the equator and 30,000 feet above the poles. *Tropospheric scatter communications*, or tropo, is a method of microwave transmission for connecting points from 70 to 600 miles apart. Tropospheric scatter is the propagation of waves by their collision with matter in the troposphere, causing them to change direction. Similar to

Technology Times

Weather-Watching from Space

On April 1, 1960, the first satellite for weather observation was put into orbit. TIROS 1—Television Infrared Observation Satellite—was for daytime use only, and the pictures it provided were of low resolution. TIRO's camera was fitted to it in such a way that half the time it was pointing out into space. It was crude, but, "for the first time," as weather forecaster Ross LaPorte put it in a 1977 interview, "we were able to look down upon that from which we had always been looking up."

We have learned much about other planets through our ability to observe them from a distance, from space. Satellites have given us the advantage of that perspective on our own planet. In LaPorte's words: "The bottom line is that the weather was always bigger than we were. With satellites, we are bigger than it."

In the Navy during the Korean conflict, LaPorte cited being on a ship with radio silence, having to make a weather forecast with only a single ship's report, that being his own. Today, he sits at a TV monitor and can see the weather actually moving over the hemi-

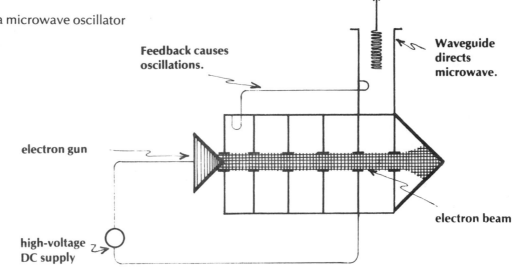

FIG. 6-1. Klystron—a microwave oscillator

Feedback causes oscillations.

Waveguide directs microwave.

electron gun

high-voltage DC supply

electron beam

sphere almost as it's happening. He has gone from the licked finger held to the wind of the Pacific Ocean to a complex of electronic technology occupying the World Weather Building outside Washington, D.C., and outer space.

Ross LaPorte is the site manager of the National Environmental Satellite Services (NESS) station, which is part of the National Oceanic and Atmospheric Administration (NOAA) of the Department of Commerce. He began his working career as a piano player in nightclubs before his Navy stint in Korea. His musicianship landed him with the Navy band, and additional training prepared him for weather forecasting. After the service, with G.I. Bill benefits, he went on to obtain his bachelor's and master's degrees in meteorology. Satellites and computers have become a major part of his continuing education.

After TIROS 1, newer generations of satellites offered better picture quality and sensors for nighttime use. NASA put up the first geostationary or synchronous satellites. They are put into orbit 22,300 miles above the equator so that the satellite orbits the earth at the same speed the earth is turning on its axis. Thus, the satellite is continuously over the same spot on earth.

Geostationary satellites permit observation of storm systems, dust storms, cloud patterns, and other transitioning features of the weather. The GOES—Geostationary Observational Environmental Satellite—the latest series, provides high picture resolution and

the use of the ionosphere for long-range transmission, tropospheric communications is for shorter-range, over-the-horizon transmission.

The detection of microwaves is accomplished with, for example, silicon crystals, which indicate the presence of microwaves by converting their field intensity into electricity, either DC or AC. Another detector is the bolometer, which displays a change of resistance in response to temperature which is the result of microwave absorption in materials. Microwave generators are primarily electronic devices that produce continuous wave (CW) oscillation of a single frequency. Klystrons and magnetrons, for high-power propagation, and traveling wave oscillators for lower-power propagation, are the primary microwave generators in use. Depending on the frequency and type, their power outputs are from microwatts to thousands of kilowatts.

In addition to the use of coax for conducting microwaves are rectangular waveguides made of hollow metal tubes. They can be straight, bent, twisted and joined into T-connections, etc. Microwaves traveling in waveguides are confined within them.

Pulsed wave transmission of microwaves, in which microsecond bursts of signal are transmitted, is used in *radar* (an acronym for "radio detection and ranging"). With radar, objects are identified by detecting reflected waves that bounce off them as they pass through an area in the path of sequences of pulsed waves.

Communication satellites are microwave relay links in space. Generally, there are three types of satellites: weather and observational satellites; communication satellites; and space probes. Sputnik, in

1957, was the first observational satellite; Telstar, in 1962, the first communications satellite. They can be passive reflectors or active repeaters, called *transponders*, comprised of receivers and transmitters.

Satellites are solar battery powered and have equipment for monitoring the conditions in and around themselves and transmitting the data back to earth for control purposes. They also carry reception equipment for control signals from earth for correction of orbital travel, etc. The earth satellites, in contrast to space probes, travel in set orbits from hundreds to thousands of miles above the earth, or in geostationary orbits of 22,300 miles above the equator. Geostationary or synchronous satellites are, in effect, fixed over a particular spot on earth. A geostationary satellite's "footprint," the area it transmits to on earth, is about one-third the circumference of the earth.

Such a wide span of reach gives geostationary satellites, in effect, great "broadcastability." This is not a contradiction to narrow-beam transmission. The signal is no less narrowly focused by a satellite's reflector antenna, but the effects of propagation take over during transmission. At a distance of 22,300 miles, a signal is dispersed over a wide area. It is also subject to much attenuation or decrease in amplitude because of interference and noise. A signal from a satellite is transmitted with 10 watts of power. It is received on earth at a level of about 2×10^{-19} watts and then amplified by use of a *maser* (microwave amplification by stimulated emission of radiation), a device for producing microwaves by energizing atoms to a level where they give off energy of the desired microwave frequency. An earth station's antenna and amplifier act to increase a weak signal a million times.

A signal transmitted from an earth station to a satellite might start out at a power of 2 million kilowatts, but end up for reception by the satellite at a level of about 2 trillionths of a watt.

Most communication satellites have multiple access—they receive from a number of earth stations simultaneously—and transmit simultaneously. The INTELSAT IV-A communications satellite, for example, has an overall height of about twenty-two feet. The diameter of its solar drum is about eight feet. It weighs about a ton. Launched on February 1, 1976, over the Atlantic, it is the primary satellite of the International Telecommunications Satellite Organization (INTELSAT). Its capacity is 6,000 circuits plus two television channels. It has twenty transponders for twenty 36-MHz wide channels

special sensors for heat-sensitive photography. Anything on earth a half-mile in size or larger can be clearly pictured with these satellites. Their heat sensors are used to detect water temperatures for denoting current boundaries. With time-lapse sequences of images of, say, the Gulf Stream, we are able to see the physics of that ocean.

Since the late 1970s, four geostationary satellites have been in orbit for U.S. weather observation. Their viewing areas take in the North and South poles. One satellite covers the area from the Mississippi to New Zealand; the other, from about 500 miles off the California coast to the western coast of Africa. The other two are parked in reserve orbit. They are shut down and on stand-by. Within a few days they can be made operational and can take over should one of the others fail.

The computer has also changed weather study. There are about forty billion cubic miles of air in the atmosphere; forty billion cubic miles with temperature, moisture, different density factors, pollutants, and all of this changing constantly; the effects of solar radiation, gravitational forces, and all of this melding into a conglomeration of systems," LaPorte said.

"It's unbelievable," he continued, "that we do as well as we do at predicting the weather." An associate of LaPorte's who deals with prognoses, mathematical projections of weather events, estimated that it would take a hundred mathematicians working around the clock for forty years to do what one of their computers can do in ten minutes. The computer is the weather forecaster's principal tool for long-range predictions, for which all the factors of the atmosphere must be considered.

On the other hand, the satellite is best used for short-range (zero- to six-hour) weather forecasting: thunderstorms, tornadoes, developing squall lines, dust storms, etc. Satellites and radar keep weather watchers abreast of the small-scale events that can come along and blow us off the maps.

The daily task of the satellite services stations is the collection and distribution of images. Images coming from a satellite are in digital form, which needs to be translated into pictures. The satellite spins on its axis, and every time the camera comes around facing the earth, it takes one scan line. It takes

a

FIG. 6-2. (a) Earth station; (b) satellite in space; (c) microwave antenna; (d) satellite in space and earth stations (Courtesy of RCA Communications)

b

in information from one side of its view to the other; thus, a line of information is scanned (recorded). A reflector mirror slightly shifts position downward, and another scan line is taken as the camera comes around again to face the earth. This occurs a hundred times a minute for nine minutes to obtain the total information to produce a full disc photo of the hemisphere in view. An image is produced every half-hour, twenty-four hours a day, every day.

The image is transmitted as viewed from the satellite via microwave. At a data distribution facility, it is recorded by magnetic tape machines, some of which record only sectors of the total hemisphere. Sectorized images are produced for regional use by local forecasters. From the recorded data, photographic negatives are produced, from which black-and-white prints are made.

c

d

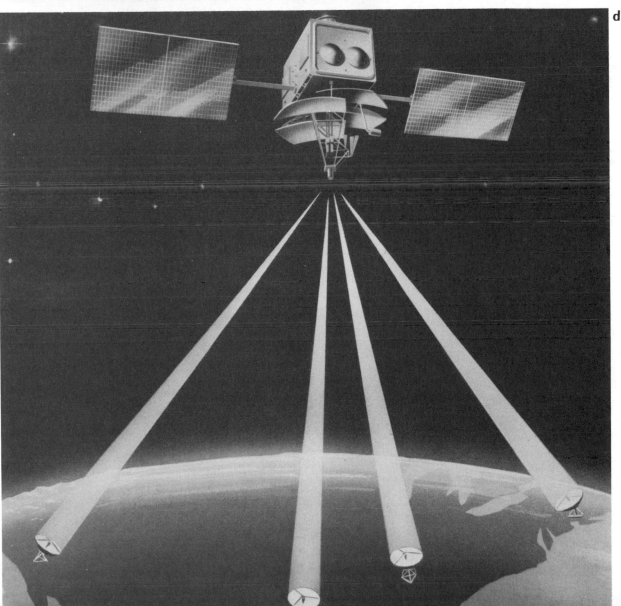

a

The station at the World Weather Building is one of several throughout the country. Others are in Miami, Kansas City, San Francisco, and Honolulu. Users are tied in from around the regions of each station. Land line transmission is used to connect up what might be considered a weather wire service network. Because it is government operated, the service is free of charge to any who pay the costs of hooking into the system and for their own in-house equipment for the display of the information.

Looking to the future, displacement of photographic prints by video imaging is already under way. Video disk storage of satellite-transmitted data was being tested in 1977. A prototype system was producing video images direct from satellite transmissions within the nine minutes it takes to obtain the total information of the full disc image. Though bulky and expensive at about $80,000, with miniaturization an improved model could cost only about $15,000, a price low enough to make large numbers of the systems affordable.

to operate through the satellite. It has twin four-and-a-half foot transmitter dish antennas. Its receiving antenna has sets of feed horns used with a third dish antenna. It has multiple access and simultaneous transmitting capabilities. It was designed to last seven years.

b

FIG. 6-3. Satellite weather photos. (a) Full western hemisphere; (b) central and (c) northern American continent; Pacific Ocean. (Courtesy of National Oceanic and Atmospheric Administration)

c

Direct-from-satellite video images will be complemented by completely automated systems for data analysis to project weather patterns to get an idea of what can develop, and to instantaneously process the vast and diversified data on the oceans and the atmosphere as they are being collected. More and faster computing power is required.

What can we expect of forecasting in the future? Ross LaPorte predicted that within the next twenty-five years he will be almost 100 percent reliable in telling us what the weather will be for a twenty-four-hour period in any area fifty miles by fifty miles. What about the future of long-range weather prediction? "That's an area for meteorologists; think-tank people," said LaPorte. "I'm a forecaster."

Data Transmission

Within a digital computer, direct current signals are binary coded. For transmission to and from a computer, a modem is required for converting DC into frequency and vice versa. Any of the modulation methods can be used for modem operations. With an AM modem, two amplitude levels are used to represent the two states of the binary code; for example, the high amplitude is the 1 state and the low amplitude is the 0 state. AM modems are primarily for low-speed transmissions of up to 300 bps. They are subject to noise and signal distortions. Single sideband AM, however, can be used for high-speed transmissions of 2,000 bps and up.

FM modems use two frequencies for binary encoding. They are used for medium-speed transmission of up to 1,800 bps and for cleaner low-speed transmission. FM modems have better noise immunity than AM. PM modems use phasing changes to encode the binary signals and have excellent noise immunity. They are used for high-speed data transmission up to 9,600 bps.

Asynchronous transmission is used for lower, non-specific bps rates up to 1,800 bps, while synchronous transmission is used for specific high bps rates over 1,800 bps.

Multilevel modulation is the compression of digital data, the combining of several bits into one, to reduce the number of transmitted bits in order to exceed bandwidth capacity. In this way, the usual capacity of a voice channel, with 3,000-Hz effective bandwidth, can be increased from 2,400 to 9,600 bps.

There are generally three classes of transmission capacities: (1) *narrowband* with bandwidth of up to 300 Hz for transmission rates of 150–300 bps; (2) *voiceband* with 4,000 Hz bandwidth and 2,000–2,400 bps transmission rates and higher with special techniques as discussed; and (3) *wideband* with 48,000-Hz bandwidth and transmission rates of 40.8 kilobits per second and up.

At transmission rates above 1,800 bps, different sideband frequencies may travel at slightly different rates, so they are not received at the same instant in time. To ensure the proper reception of signals carried by a group of frequencies, *circuit conditioning* is performed, a process whereby the faster frequencies are delayed to match the slower. Conditioning is usually not performed on dial-up lines because of their lower transmission rates and multiple uses. Private lines are commonly conditioned.

Voice circuits, through which most data is transmitted, are either *half-duplex* or *full-duplex* lines. Half-duplex lines have two wires for two-way, non-simultaneous data transmission. Full-duplex lines have four wires and permit two-way, simultaneous transmission. Most local loops are half duplex, while trunk lines are full duplex. Private line services are full duplex. The private service company adds two wires to a customer's local loop.

Computer communications controllers are central computer peripherals that interface modems to computers by use of *data set adaptors* (DSAs), also called line termination units. While most transmission is serial by bit, a digital computer deals with the data in 8-bit clusters called *bytes*. DSAs break down bytes from the computer into bits for transmission and form bytes for the computer from transmitted bits from terminals.

Light frequencies fall within the range of 3 trillion to 3,000 trillion Hz, encompassing infrared light at the lower end, ultraviolet at the upper, and visible light in between. Using these optical frequencies of the electromagnetic spectrum for information transmission was experimentally attempted with some success by Alexander Bell in 1880. His device, called the photophone, was intended for the transmission of speech by using reflected beams of sunlight as the carrier.

In a sense, light transmissions have been with us since our earliest efforts to communicate across distances. Smoke signals, waved flags, flashing beacons, and the like use existing light as an information carrier; however, the range and bandwidth are very limited. Such systems lack the capability of generating their own light waves, whereas radio transmitters do generate their own electromagnetic waves. With the development of the laser in the late 1950s has come the means for generating waves in the optical frequency range. In 1968, lasers began to be used in *integrated optics*, a discipline that emerged as part of the pursuit to develop optical communications systems, particularly light carrying, miniaturized, integrated circuits. Among optoelectric integrated-optic devices, in addition to solid-state lasers and LEDs are modulators, magnet-optic switches, and electro-optic scanners which serve to vary the phase, intensity, polarization, or physical position of a light beam as a means of superimposing information on it. Other devices of concern to the optics engineer for controlling light waves are waveguides, lenses and prisms, beam splitters, and polarizers.

Optical communications systems are of two types: (1) guided optical transmission, in which light is guided along a confined path; and (2) free-space optical transmission, which can be likened to radio wave transmission at light frequencies. The advantages of optical communications are that (1) the bandwidth capacity of light waves is potentially much greater than that of waves within the radio band, and

8
Optical Communications

sirable biological effects as irregular heartbeat, blood flow, and electricity in the brain, central nervous system disorders, changes to the blood's composition, headaches, stress, behavioral difficulties, and more.

Radiation, in general, naturally occurs throughout the universe. Radiant energy is, in fact, energy moving at about 186,000 miles per second while changing back and forth between electric and magnetic fields at a wide range of cycles per second, or frequency. Electromagnetism is classified by its frequency, which is its energy level. The spectrum includes extremely low frequency (ELF) at under 100 Hz; the radio frequencies, which include longwave, AM, shortwave, TV, and FM with frequencies from 100,000 to 100 million Hz; microwaves (100 billion Hz); light, including infrared, visible, and ultraviolet, with frequencies from 10 trillion to 10,000 trillion Hz; and x-rays, gamma rays, and cosmic rays with frequencies greater than ultraviolet light. Radiant energy also has power that is independent of frequency and is measured in watts.

In our universe, radiation is emitted and absorbed by all objects with temperatures above absolute zero, −273°C. We ourselves emit infrared radiation at extremely low power, giving off heat, and we are constantly absorbing the radiant energy of the atmosphere. Our atmosphere contains "background" radiation from the earth's own magnetic field and crust, the sun, and other distant cosmic bodies and events. Background radiation comes in a wide spectrum, including microwaves, but most is visible light occurring during daytime hours. When the sun is at its highest activity, during sunspots, the total power of the radiated energy hitting the earth is about a tenth of a microwatt per square centimeter of surface (0.135 μW/cm²).

Control of exposure time is one of three things we can do to protect ourselves from radiation; the others are shielding and distance. Shielding materials, like lead, reflect or absorb most radiant energy. As for distance, the farther from a source we are, the less the overall exposure. The power of a particular radiant energy does not change as it travels through space. However, the farther away from the source, the greater the dispersion of the power. Watts per square centimeter of irradiated surface is the common measure

(2) light can be concentrated into narrower beams and confined in smaller waveguides because of its extremely short wavelengths.

Free-space transmission, or radio-optical communications, is used for short transmissions on the ground and for earth-to-satellite and satellite-to-satellite connections. Generally, transmission reliability has not been satisfactory enough for the wide use of earth-based, free-space light-wave communications, except for relatively short connections of about two miles. Within the earth's atmosphere, light waves are distorted and attenuated by climatic factors and especially by inclement weather. Light transmissions are ideal within the vacuum of outer space, but the less precision-engineered microwave links are more commonly used for satellite-to-satellite relays. Closely spaced repeaters can enhance the extendability of a free-space optical transmission line, but the major efforts in optical communications have been in the development of guided-wave systems.

Infrared wave transmission in small, free-space environments, such as large office rooms, factory floors, and even between closely located buildings, was commercially introduced in late 1979. Infrared wave frequencies are not susceptible to electronic interference and are easily confined to a limited area. For transmission, the "near infrared" frequencies, close to the range of visible light, are used.

The infrared transmission systems employ LEDs for sending signals and photodiodes for receiving. Carrier modulation techniques are used to encode and decode transmitted data. Such systems have been introduced for use in lieu of wire connections between terminals and computers, providing greater terminal mobility and easy installation of new terminals where no wiring need be done.

Most optical communications has been accomplished with near-infrared frequencies of about 300 trillion Hz. The application of optical systems, also referred to as *fiber optics*, at such frequencies is expected eventually to displace electronics in the field of data processing. In such optical information processing machines, light conducted in optical fibers will carry information and connect integrated optic circuits just as electrons, conducted along metal wire, carry information and connect integrated electronic circuits in electronic data processsing machines.

The development of optical fibers for guided-wave light transmission was launched in the 1960s when Corning Glass was asked by several members of the communications industry to perfect "glass wires." As of 1979, factory-built optical fiber cables can deliver 50 percent of a light signal over a distance of a kilometer. That degree of clarity in the waters of the oceans would mean we could see their bottoms. Within the optical communications system, repeaters are used to regenerate weak signals. Receiver/transmitter devices serve to regenerate light signals about every fifteen kilometers, better spacing than in electric wire networks.

A fiber consists of three layers: an outer protective layer of plastic; a layer called *cladding* that reflects waves within the fiber; and the core. Both the core and cladding are made of glass of different indexes of refraction. A light wave travels through the fiber by bouncing back and forth off the cladding. Some waves with extremely sharp angles pass through the cladding. Some are not detected because they bounce right by the detector. Some waves reach the detector before others, depending on how much they bounce within the fiber. This causes *modal dispersion*, which distorts transmitted signals. To alleviate modal dispersion, graded index fibers can be used. These fibers are made with different refraction indexes within the core area, which results in equalizing travel rates of the waves. *Spectral dispersion*, another distortion of signals, occurs as a result of the transmission of several different frequencies that travel at different speeds within the core. To minimize spectral dispersion, a purer light source of as few frequencies as possible must be used, or the rate of transmission must be slowed to a level where the dispersion has no effect.

Lasers, LEDs, and photodiodes for converting light into electrical energy and vice versa are the components used for transmitting and receiving of light

FIG. 8-1. Digital transmission of pulsed light-wave signals for a one-way cable system

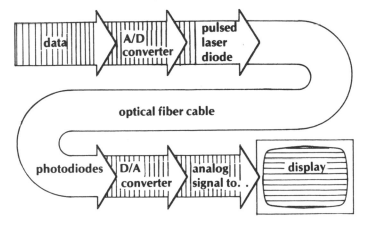

used to express the effective power of radiation.

We add, to the background, radiation of our own making from military and air traffic radar systems, all our uses of radio, TV, microwave, our telephone network, and about a half-million miles of high-voltage lines carrying 60-Hz electricity from power plants to users. "Since World War II," pointed out Dr. Milton M. Zaret during an interview in the fall of 1979, "the amount of power being emitted into the atmosphere has increased by a factor of ten every decade. There has been exponential growth in the number of emitters every decade. In some parts of the spectrum, we are making more activity than the sun." The numbers, by the late 1970s, reached 9 million broadcast transmitters and 30 million CB radios in this country.

Zaret was among the first group of scientists to do research on the biological effects of laser radiation at the onset of the 1960s. As a practicing ophthalmologist, he has not been away from the study and treatment of radiation effects since. He is an authority on the formation of radiant energy cataracts. He describes himself as a neutral in what has become, since the 1950s, a grossly underpublicized controversy that has been impeding government action to set and enforce broadly accepted radiation safety standards. In Zaret's words, "We need not fight. There's no such thing as adversarial medicine. We don't have to get rid of technology. But we can't make it safe by decree. Only solid information can make it safe. It requires that we just face up to the question: Is it possible that there are hazards?"

In the early twentieth century, physicists divided the electromagnetic spectrum into two classes of radiation. From the atomic perspective, when an electron gains energy, as it does when irradiated, either it can be ejected from its atom or it can ascend to a higher energy level within its atom. The radiation that causes ejection is called ionizing radiation. That which does not is nonionizing radiation. An atom is ionized when it either gains or loses an electron and is electrically unbalanced; the important point is that it is drastically altered in structure. The alteration can be temporary or long-lasting, depending on the material irradiated and the energy level and quantity of radiation. X-rays, gamma rays, and cosmic rays are ionizing radiation. Ultraviolet light and all the longer-wavelength frequencies are considered nonionizing radiation.

Talking about the mutating effects of ionizing radiation, Zaret explained, "What we are interested in, in biological materials, is DNA, the macromolecules of our genes. Radiation changes their configuration, maybe in only one, two, or three out of a half-million connections, but changes do take place. We are talking about delayed biochemical effects. Eventually they are expressed." Zaret likened the effect to a computer memory in which a minute number of bits are inadvertently altered. "Look at it as a switching circuit; until it's time for that switch to go off, there's no apparent change to the memory."

He continued, "We've learned that nonionizing radiation also affects DNA." The effect of nonionizing radiation on the electron is instantaneous. The electron absorbs a dose of energy, ascends to a higher energy state (orbit) within the atom, emits energy itself, and descends to the lower energy state again. In a laser, for example, such a sequence is made to happen repeatedly and rapidly to build up the concentrated power that makes laser radiation, which is nonionizing, as devastating to matter as any ionizing radiation. Zaret suspects that the pumping of electrons, as is done in lasers, can occur under other conditions with nonionizing radiation, spectrum-wide. "There's no difference between ionizing and nonionizing radiation except for where they are in the spectrum and the ways they reach the state to cause radical atomic changes."

Efforts to go beyond the ionizing/nonionizing distinction in understanding radiation's biological effects have been a priority in the Soviet Union. Viewing Soviet data, some American researchers, in the late 1970s, began to suggest that certain biological materials might be sensitive to certain frequencies and not to others, and that's what triggers a biological effect. Leo Birenbaum, professor of electrical engineering at New York Polytechnic Institute, in a fall 1979 interview, talked about a Soviet experiment that he and a group of other scientists were attempting to duplicate. "Two Soviet scientists, using high-frequency microwaves, irradiated *E. coli,* a type of bacteria that makes colecin, and found that colecin

signals. Since individual fibers bundled together to make up cables are as thin as a strand of human hair, connecting and splicing them requires precision to minimize light loss and misalignment. Fibers are as strong as metal wires and lighter. They can be hung on poles or distributed through underground ducts, taking up less space for more transmission capacity than metal conductors.

FIG. 8-2. Optoelectronic devices. *Left to right:* photo cell, silicon photo transmitter, infrared emitter and detector pair.

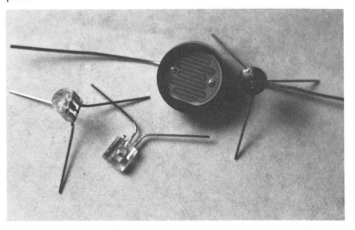

In a late-1970s demonstration of optical communications, AT&T installed optical fiber lines in Chicago between two central offices. Each half-inch cable they used is made up of twenty-four fibers, each cable carrying 8,000 simultaneous phone conversations. The success of the demonstration has led AT&T toward development of total optical communications systems, which are to be, in part, installed in major cities in the 1980s. As the energy crisis and metals scarcity grow, entrenched electrical communications will undoubtedly give way to greater use of optical systems, which use less power, are virtually unaffected by electrical interference, have immense bandwidth for carrying more signal, and are more difficult to breach for invasions of privacy.

production was enhanced by a factor of three. The enhancement was frequency sensitive; at one frequency it happened, at a nearby frequency it didn't. They lowered the power of the microwaves and there was no change in the enhancement. The effect seems to have nothing to do with power, but is based on frequency. Tickling molecules." Still in a data-gathering stage, the theory is vague, but it points to the possibility that both beneficial and detrimental effects are possible at any frequency. Both Birenbaum and Zaret agree that there's a lot to be done that hasn't been and isn't being done to learn more about spectrum-wide radiation effects.

The basis for understanding radiation injury has been primarily the study of radioactivity, which is the decay of atomic nuclei by the emission of particles and radiant energy. Materials like radium, uranium, and carbon 14 are naturally radioactive. The radiation of radioactivity is ionizing and is broken into three types according to velocity, ability to penetrate matter, and effect of magnetic field. Alpha radiation is the least active, beta next, and gamma the most active. Nuclear power plant accidents are a concern because of the possible release of radioactivity into the air in high enough doses to cause tissue damage to the brain, anemia, hemorrhaging, infection, and dehydration, all of which can be fatal. Zaret referred to such as the "cooking" immediate effects of radiation in contrast to the "simmering" long-range effects as mentioned earlier.

"Cooking" or thermal effects, those quickly observable, had served as the basis for establishing a nonionizing radiation safety standard initiated by the military in the 1950s upon discovery of radiation injury to men working with radar. An early study, funded by the military, found that when animals were irradiated with microwaves at power levels of 100 milliwatts (mW) per square centimeter of skin surface, the animals were burned or developed heat stress and died. At the time, no one had achieved the same result at a lower-power level. Seeking to establish a safe exposure standard for humans, the scientists suggested that a safe level was ten times below the 100 mW figure, or 10 mW/cm². Until the GOA study in the late 1970s, that standard was used by the government, the military, and industry without official question. Personnel working with mi-

crowaves were permitted exposures of up to 10 mW for six minutes every hour, or for continuous exposure of 1 mW. The standard was established for healthy individuals working in controlled environments with low humidity (since radiation enters the body easily in the presence of moisture). The standard was not based on any long-term studies, and in using the square centimeter as the dimensional criterion, the scientists assumed a scale of view too large in which to note molecular aberrations or "simmering" effects.

Bone marrow, the spleen, and the lymph nodes are the most sensitive of human body tissues to the simmering effects of radiation. These effects are both cumulative and additive. Zaret has seen both mutative and additive effects in the formulation of cataracts associated with radiant energy exposure. "*Additive* refers to those exposures that add to a current inflammatory process which is ongoing. *Cumulative* refers to a buildup of exposure effects even after healing," he explained. Zaret and others deem the 10-mW standard for microwaves unsafe. Animals have been killed since the 1950s with lesser power than used then. The simmering effects take years to manifest and, as many in the scientific community point out, only the proper studies can provide the information we need to establish appropriate standards for all types of radiation. For example, ultraviolet radiation has been shown to cause cataracts with time-averaged exposure of only 0.1 μW/cm²; the *American Industrial Hygiene Association Journal* reported in April 1979 that normally operated video data terminals emit ultraviolet radiation at about the level of 0.1 μW/cm².

"There's no question," said Zaret, "that the manmade contribution to the electromagnetic atmosphere is detrimental. There's no controversy about its being dangerous. There's a lack of specific knowledge about the points and conditions of when it's harmful, and we have differences of opinion on that at this time. Diathermy in medicine is abused tremendously. With CB radios, everybody can radiate for his own pleasure. Microwave ovens are permitted to leak more than radio communications systems. TV viewing through cathode ray tubes is potentially dangerous. CRTs emit ultraviolet radiation, which is the most mutagenic radiation you can find. Do we need fifty different channels of open air communications in the New York metropolitan area? Even electric blankets make some people dream terrible dreams. There's an effect on the calcium metabolism in brain cells. So even our sixty-hertz home electricity is not innocuous. And all this electronic smog has an impact on the molecules of our atmosphere. It changes them and adds to the solar constant, a higher-level manmade constant. I see it as a scandal that so little study is being done that bears directly on the human hazard."

In 1842, Alexander Bain of Scotland proposed the first facsimile system—the electrical transmission of images. However, it was not until the 1920s that "fax" began to be widely used for transmission of news photos, weather maps, and, in the following decades, military maps. The business community began using fax in the 1960s, and by a decade later, it has gained the total acceptance of business, government, and professionals as it proved to be more economical and efficient than the mails in handling the high-speed, large-volume circulation of graphic and printed data among offices, plants, and so forth.

A facsimile system, like a television imaging system, incorporates *raster scanning*—a method by which an image (page) is systematically inspected by photosensors, converting the black and white components into electrical signals, either as voltage or current. The image plane can be considered a grid of vertical and horizontal lines forming an array of boxes. A photosensor makes a notation of each "box of image information," referred to as the resolution elements, or *pixels* (picture elements), which make up the video baseband signal of the system.

The raster or imaging area for scanning can be created in many ways, but most commonly are drums or *flatbeds*. A drum, around which the transmitted page is wrapped, rotates at a constant rate as the photosensor and required optics (lenses) are focused on it. Either the sensor/optics slide from side to side as the drum rotates, or the rotating drum itself slides under a fixed sensor/optics. Another alternative is to have the drum fixed and the sensor/optics spin within it. In this case, the drum cylinder is transparent and the page is placed facing inward. With flatbed rasters, either the sensor/optics or the flatbed moves from side to side and up and down to cover the total area.

The scanned image can be illuminated either by floodlighting or flying-spot scanning (using a small beam). If the page is floodlighted, the sensor/optics are sharply focused on the pixel. If a small beam of light is used, the sensor/optics are defocused and only one pixel at a time is illuminated.

9
Facsimile Transmission

FIG. 9-1. Raster scanned image. This 13 × 19 grid consists of 247 pixels. In facsimile systems, 576,000 pixels are the norm, a grid almost 600 × 1,000.

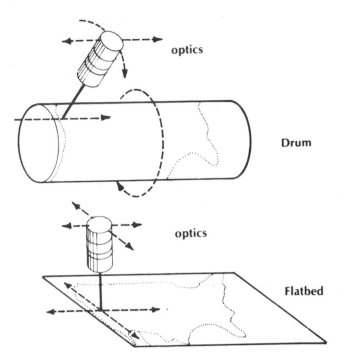

FIG. 9-2. Facsimile systems

optics

Drum

optics

Flatbed

In addition to the various forms of flatbed scanning involving a flying-spot or floodlight—which include CRTs, spinning mirrors, and line-to-circle converters—are scan arrays. These devices are made up of strips of solid state photosensors combined to comprise a raster. Each photosensor detects a pixel. With a lens, the image is focused onto the array.

For transmission, encoding of the video baseband signal can be done, if required, to suit the channel as to bandwidth limitations, or to minimize errors due to interference and noise, or for cryptography. Data compression techniques are used to limit the signal bandwidth. For example, instead of transmitting black, black, black, white, white, etc., the signal is transmitted as 3 black, 2 white, etc., thereby conserving bandwidth. Another technique is to indicate just the first type; the following are understood. For example: 3 black; 2, 4, 1—in other words, 3 black, 2 (white), 4 (black), 1 (white).

Modems are used for fax transmission on telephone lines and are mostly FM, where one frequency represents white and another black. With some machines, black and white and shades of gray are transmitted and, in this case, the transmitted tones cover a range of frequencies. These devices, referred to as binary

FM modems, transmit a maximum of 2,400 pixels per second. Duobinary FM modems double the capacity of the channel by using three frequencies to transmit blacks and whites. This doubled capacity is considered intermediate-speed transmission and can consume from two to three minutes per page. In other terms, the transmission of 576,000 pixels comprising a page takes two minutes via an intermediate speed channel transmitting at 4,800 bps.

High-speed transmissions of less than a minute require extensive encoding (use of data compression algorithms) and higher-capacity channels or highly efficient modems that don't use FM, but use a library of waveforms, each representing a number of successive bits. A single signal can represent three or four successive signals. On a 4,800-bps channel, some 9,600 pixels per second can be transmitted. These transmission rates are being bettered at the time of this writing (late 1081). As better equipment, processing techniques, and lines are developed and put into use, transmission capacity and speed will increase.

FIG. 9-3. Portable facsimile transmitter (Courtesy of Muirhead, Inc.)

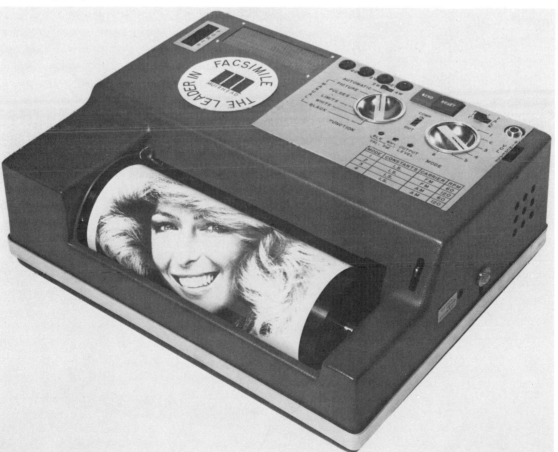

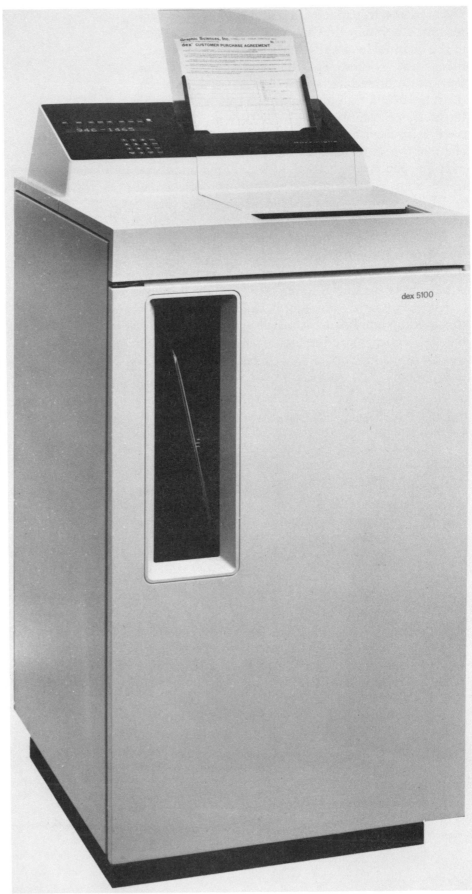

FIG. 9-4. A high-speed digital facsimile transceiver that communicates a full page of text or graphics in as little as 20 seconds (Courtesy of Graphic Sciences, Inc., Burroughs Corp.)

Acoustic coupling of fax machines to telephone lines is achieved by placing the phone handset into a cradle on the machine. The number of the receiver is dialed and the connection made. It's that simple for transmission rates of below 3,000 bps. For higher rates, electrical coupling must be done to protect the fax equipment and the telephone plant from each other. Malfunctions in one can affect the other unless an isolation circuit called a data access arrangement (DAA) is used. Coupling to digital lines, as opposed to analog (telephone) lines, does not require a modem. Digital lines are available through common carrier companies dealing exclusively with data transmission and provide for transmission speeds of greater rates than thus far indicated. An IBM television commercial in early 1980 advertised a fax system with a transmission speed of fifteen seconds per page. However, the instantaneous transmission of hard-copy is still some way off.

At reception, the video baseband signal, as it was photosensed before encoding, if any, and before transmission, is fed to the printing apparatus. Two types of operations can go on between transmitter and receiver machines: open loop or closed loop. In an *open-loop system*, transmitter and receiver do not communicate about reception. The transmitter doesn't know whether its sent data is received, except if voice contact is made between operators. In the *closed-loop system*, automatic communications between the components acts to verify and correct (re-transmit) data where necessary.

Fax printing is of several types: CRT electrostatic, dielectric, electrolytic, xerographic, ink-mist, electrosensitive, and impact.

- *CRT electrostatic* printing is similar to printing a photograph. The fax image written on the CRT is used like a photo transparency, and photoconductive paper is used for the print. Though contrast qualities can be low, speed is fast in this process.
- *Dielectric* processes employ charge-retentive paper on which an array of pens writes the image. The paper is developed by use of a liquid toner and fixed by evaporation of a toner solvent. The process gives good contrast and high speed.
- *Electrolytic* processes use electrolytic solution–wetted paper which is subject to color changes when current is passed through it. Electrolytic printing has lower contrast qualities.
- *Xerographic* processes use a photoconductive medium upon which a light beam writes the image. The image, in turn, deposits a dry toner powder on a

sheet of paper and is fused to it by heat. Xerography offers high contrast and speed.

- *Ink-mist* recording is the process whereby particles of ink are electromechanically deposited directly onto a sheet of paper. Contrast and speed can be very high.
- *Electrosensitive* processes pass electric current through a paper with three layers: a base paper, a carbon layer, and an opaque white layer. As current is increased, more of the white opaqueness is burned off, exposing more of the black carbon layer. Continuous tone images can be produced with good contrast.
- *Impact* printing involves the use of a hammer that strikes specially treated paper, which then turns dark; the harder the strike, the darker the spot. Impact printing is slow.

The copy quality of a fax machine is determined by its resolution and contrast. Facsimile printing resolution is measured in lines per inch. When a printer has a resolution of, say, 100 lines per inch, it means that a transmitted page with parallel black lines, each 0.01 inch wide and separated by a space of the same width, will be clearly reproduced at reception. In other words, the printer can print an image element as small as 0.01 inch.

A facsimile transmission system can be equipped with a document feeder for automatic document input. The document feeder, combined with associated memory, can be programmed to handle fax traffic when the human operator is not present. Programming can include instructions for storing and later forwarding several different multipage fax transmissions to several receivers sequentially. Compatibility among machines of different speeds and manufacture is limited. Devices are available for limited compatibility among similar types of fax machines. The fax machine can be interfaced with a computer and serve as a printer. However, for this purpose either part of the computer program or part of the fax writing control logic has to be capable of generating characters.

Facsimile encompasses wirephoto (wired- or line-transmitted photograph) and telephoto (telecommunicated photograph, which can involve radio transmission of the image from point to point on land or from air to ground).

The first electrical system for communications, developed almost 150 years ago, telegraphy is still widely used by the news wire services, the stock exchange ticker-tape service, public message services, an internal government wire service, certain police and fire alarm systems, fixed and mobile military message services, and private-line companies for data transmission. In contrast to voice communications, telegraphy generally involves the use of electrical signals to carry coded alphanumerics over wires, over land and submarine cables, and by radio using a narrow frequency band—so narrow that, with time-division multiplexing, forty-four telegraph channels transmitting sixty-six words per minute (wpm) can be sent over a single voice channel. Included in a broad definition of telegraphy is facsimile, phototelegraphy, and teletypewriting or teleprinting.

Binary encoding is the essence of telegraphy. Morse's original dots and dashes representing letters and numbers are still in use for manual key operations, as among amateur radio operators. Morse code employs from one to four bits to encode the letters of the alphabet, five bits for each number (0-9), and six bits for punctuation marks. Each bit is either a dot or a dash, which in electrical terms is signified by two contrasting states, such as positive and negative polarities. During transmission, each bit is separated by spaces of equal length. A dash is three times longer than a dot.

Transmission is either single or double current. Single-current operations, in which current flows in one direction, can be of two types: open circuit or closed circuit. In closed-circuit transmission, a closed key causes current to flow, activating responders at a receiving station. For *marking*—that is, transmitting code elements—the key is opened and no current flows. For spacing, the key is closed; again current flows. The opposite process is open-circuit transmission: Current flows for marking (the key is closed) and no current flows for spacing (the key is opened). Double-current transmission employs two separate

Table 10-1. INTERNATIONAL MORSE CODE

A	.-	1	.----	
B	-...	2	..---	
C	-.-.	3	...--	
D	-..	4	....-	
E	.	5	.....	
F	..-.	6	-....	
G	--.	7	--...	
H	....	8	---..	
I	..	9	----.	
J	.---	10	-----	
K	-.-	'	.----.	(apostrophe)
L	.-..	:	---...	
M	--	,	--..--	
N	-.	-	-....-	(hyphen)
O	---	.	.-.-.-	
P	.--.	( )	-.--.-	(parentheses)
Q	--.-	?	..--..	
R	.-.	" "	.-..-.	
S	...	SOS	...---...	
T	-			
U	..-			
V	...-			
W	.--			
X	-..-			
Y	-.--			
Z	--..			

currents in a line, one positive and one negative, one for marking and one for spacing.

For the most part, telegraphy has developed from the hand-operated key station, associated with western frontier railroad depots, to automated teletypewriting networks interconnecting offices throughout the world. Concurrently, Morse code has been modified to suit the newer operations. Primarily, a standard number of code elements per character has been established. Two such codes in wide use are a five-unit code and a seven-unit code. For the stock exchange ticker tape a six-unit code is used. For data transmission the seven- or even an eight-unit code is required.

The Baudot code is made up of five equal-length bits. Each bit is either marked or spaced. Thirty-one usable combinations (excluding all blanks) are thus available to represent twenty-six characters on a typewriter keyboard plus five control signals: (1) figures shift for shifting to digits and punctuation; (2) letters shift for shifting to letters; (3) carriage return; (4) line feed for advancing paper; and (5) space for word spacing. In this arrangement, the upper case is digits and punctuation and an audible bell. The lower case is for letters. As each key is pressed, five code bars are positioned for bit-by-bit character transmission. To maintain clear character separation, a start and stop bit is placed at the beginning and end of each five-unit group. The start bit is a space, and the stop bit is a mark. Baudot operating speed is 66 wpm, or 50 baud. (A *baud* is a unit of code per second.)

The most prevalent seven-unit code is ASCII (American Standard Code of Information Interchange), developed by the American National Standards Institute in 1963. With seven bits, 128 combinations are available for character representation of both capital and lower-case letters, ten digits, punctuation, special symbols, and many control signals oriented, especially, to computer operations for which ASCII keyboards are commonly used. ASCII also employs bit-group separation elements and an error-checking signal called a parity bit. The ASCII stop signal uses two bits; thus, the total number of bits per transmitted character is eleven. ASCII operating speed is 100 wpm (75 baud), or 150 wpm for dual-face keyboards.

In one form of transmission, a keyboard operator types a message to produce a perforated paper tape encoded with the message. The tape can then be fed through an electromechanical or photocell reader, which translates the message to electrical code and

Table 10-2. BAUDOT FIVE-BIT TELEGRAPHY CODE

Start	1	2	3	4	5	Stop	Lower Case	Upper Case International Telegraph Alphabet #2	Upper Case U.S. Teletype Commercial Keyboard
	•	•				•	A	-	-
	•			•	•	•	B	?	?
		•	•	•		•	C	:	:
	•			•		•	D	Who are you?	$
	•					•	E	3	3
	•		•	•		•	F	(*)	!
		•		•	•	•	G	(*)	&
			•		•	•	H	(*)	#
		•	•			•	I	8	8
	•	•		•		•	J	Bell	Bell
	•	•	•	•		•	K	(	(
		•			•	•	L	)	)
			•	•	•	•	M	.	.
			•	•		•	N	,	,
				•	•	•	O	9	9
		•	•		•	•	P	0	0
	•	•	•		•	•	Q	1	1
		•		•		•	R	4	4
	•		•			•	S	,	,
					•	•	T	5	5
	•	•	•			•	U	7	7
		•	•	•	•	•	V	=	;
	•	•			•	•	W	2	2
	•		•	•	•	•	X	/	/
	•		•		•	•	Y	6	6
	•				•	•	Z	+	"
						•	blank		
	•	•	•	•	•	•	letters shift		
	•	•		•	•	•	figures shift		
			•			•	space		
				•		•	carriage return		
		•				•	line feed		

(*) = not allocated; for each country's internal use.

• = positive current mark.

Table 10-3.   USASCII SEVEN-BIT CODE

	000	001	010	011	100	101	110	111
0000	NUL	DLE	SP	0		p	@	p
0001	SOH	DC1	1	1	A	Q	a	q
0010	STX	DC2	"	2	B	R	b	r
0011	ETX	DC3	#	3	C	S	c	s
0100	EOT	DC4	$	4	D	T	d	t
0101	ENQ	NAK	%	5	E	U	e	u
0110	ACK	SYN	&	6	F	V	f	v
0111	BEL	ETB	'	7	G	W	g	w
1000	BS	CAN	(	8	H	X	h	x
1001	HT	EM	)	9	I	Y	i	y
1010	LF	SUB	*	:	J	Z	j	z
1011	VT	ESC	+	;	K	[	k	{
1100	FF	SS	,	<	L	\	l	:
1101	CR	GS	-	=	M	]	m	}
1110	SO	RS	●	>	N	↑	n	~
1111	SI	US	/	?	O	↓	o	DEL

NUL = null/idle
SOH = start of heading
STX = start of text
ETX = end of text
EOT = end of transmission
ENQ = enquiry
ACK = acknowledge
BEL = audible signal
BS = back space
HT = horizontal tab
LF = line feed
VT = vertical tab
FF = form feed
CR = carriage return
SO = shift-out
SI = shift-in
DLE = data link escape
DC1 =
DC2 } = device controls
DC3 =
DC4 = device control stop
NAK = negative acknowledge
SYN = synchronous idle
ETB = end of transmission block
CAN = canceled
EM = end of medium
SUB = substitute character
ESC = escape
SS = start of special sequence
GS = group separator
RS = record separator
US = unit separator
DEL = delete

FIG. 10-1. Two of the latest teletype systems: (a) a punched paper tape/printer system and (b) a magnetic storage/CRT console (Courtesy of Teletype Corp.)

transmits it. At a reception point, the received message may automatically activate (1) a reperforator to produce a duplicate tape for later retransmission; (2) a teletypewriter that types the message for delivery; or (3) other types of terminal equipment, such as accounting machines and computers. More recently developed operations exclude paper tape and directly interconnect teletypewriters through computerized message switching centers. The functions of paper tape are being met by the use of other storage media, such as magnetic tape.

TWX and Telex, the teletypewriter networks, provide point-to-point interconnections through the use of computerized message switching centers which handle storage capabilities for store-and-forward services, routing, accounting, and delivery and retrieval functions, as is the case with Western Union's Info-Master computerized message switching centers. Western Union also maintains three central telephone bureaus that provide toll-free access to many of its services from anywhere in the contiguous United States.

Western Union was organized in 1851 to provide telegraph services. In 1970, Western Union Telegraph Company became the Western Union Corporation, encompassing the Westar satellite system for domestic satellite communications; a 10,000-mile land microwave network displacing the once prized railroad right-of-way, galvanized wire, land line network; a teletypewriter network; Mailgram, a telegram service in conjunction with the Postal Service; and data communications leased systems divisions serving government and private subscribers.

In effect, the telegram of yesteryear has evolved into a teletypewriter communications system. With the use of computers, teletypewriter services from Western Union include the following.

- Extended access via a Telex/TWX keyboard terminal means dialing up a switching center computer to send telegrams, cablegrams (international telegrams), Mailgrams, and money orders.
- Stored address list services are available for sending the same message to a stored list of correspondents in any message format, either immediately or during night hours only for output at a recipient's terminal the following morning.
- Datagram is a service for field workers to report via teletypewriter to headquarters by calling the toll-free telephone bureau.
- FYI news service supplies, either automatically or on dial-up demand, news summaries on a variety of

subjects, somewhat like a subscription electronic newspaper.

With the use of Western Union satellites, transmission services for private system uses include:

- Voice/data channels of 4 kHz or 48 kHz
- Data channels from 75 bps (teleprinter services) to 4,800 bps for point-to-point or multipoint data transmission
- Conditioned channels for data at 9.6 kilobits per second, 50 kbps, 230 kbps, and 1.544 megabits per second
- Wideband channels of 48 kHz, 240 kHz, and 1.2 MHz
- Transponder service with 36-MHz bandwidth for voice, voice/data video transmission, or any combination
- One-direction-only video channel service for black-and-white, color, and accompanying audio

The Westar satellite system (as of 1982) includes three satellites, seven earth stations, twenty-six satellite access cities, and seven TV operating centers, all linked to the Western Union 10,000-mile transcontinental microwave network. By the end of 1982, the Westar system will include two additional satellites.

Some other offerings of Western Union include:

- DataCom, a data communications service between any two of some sixty cities, handling Baudot, Binary Coded Decimal (BCD), and ASCII codes at rates between 150 and 1,200 bps
- Multipoint services requiring that subscribers use their own communications central processing equipment
- InfoCom, a computer-controlled, store-and-forward message switching system that provides subscribers with their own private networks
- Hot Line telephone service, a no-dial, point-to-point voice hookup available in some twenty-five cities
- SpaceTel, a point-to-point private voice/data service using satellite and microwave systems

Radiotelegraphy, the high-frequency (3 to 30 MHz) transmission of coded messages, uses transmitters that are either single-sideband type or frequency-shift-keying (fsk) type. *Frequency-shift transmission* is a process in which the carrier frequency is shifted about 800 Hz. This sets up two predetermined values that are used to represent the mark and space elements. Most radio circuits operate at the standard rate of 66 wpm. For multichannel transmissions, both time-division multiplexing and frequency-division multiplexing can be employed.

11

Telephone

In 1876, with the invention of the telephone, the unique human attribute of speech overcame distance. In Alexander Graham Bell's terms, the telephone was a device for "transmitting speech telegraphically." By 1900, well over a million phones were in use in the United States; eighty years later, over 150 million. Telephony is the use of acoustoelectric transducers (telephone handsets) for changing sound energy into electrical energy, and vice versa, and switching networks for interconnecting users worldwide.

In the handset are the transmitter (mouthpiece) and receiver (earpiece). The transmitter is made up of a diaphragm and a chamber of carbon, through which a steady current of electricity flows when you pick up the phone. The diaphragm is a thin circular piece of aluminum securely fitted at its edges to the mouthpiece housing. The inner part of the diaphragm can vibrate back and forth from the pressure of air waves. Its center is dome-shaped and projects into the carbon chamber, which contains granules of carbon. The granules are compressed when the diaphragm intrudes into the chamber and loosely packed when the diaphragm is in its normal position. Electricity flowing through the chamber increases when the granules are compressed and decreases when they are loose.

Thus, sound vibrations are converted to levels of current flow. The pitch (frequency) of the sound spoken into the mouthpiece determines the number of vibrations per second of the diaphragm. The loudness (amplitude) of the sound determines the degree of granular compression within the chamber. The result is an electrical wave with frequency and amplitude traveling at the speed of light along wires.

The receiver is made up of a circular diaphragm with a permanent magnet around its circumference, and an electromagnet. The receiver's diaphragm, also thin aluminum, is fixed at its edges to the earpiece housing and can vibrate back and forth at its center. The electromagnet is a ring of metal with a coil of wire around it, through which the signal-carrying

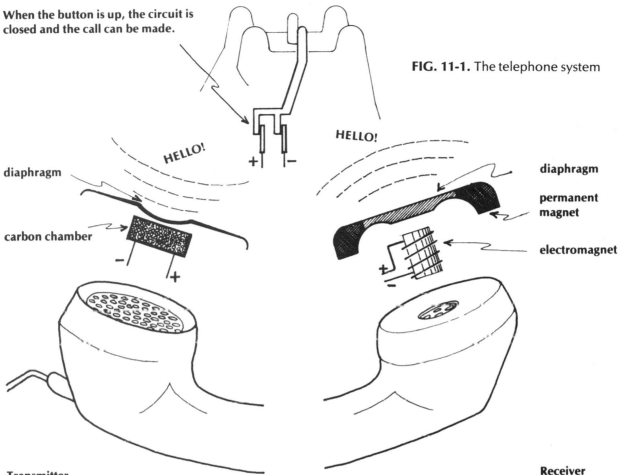

When the button is up, the circuit is closed and the call can be made.

FIG. 11-1. The telephone system

HELLO!

HELLO!

diaphragm

carbon chamber

diaphragm

permanent magnet

electromagnet

Transmitter

Receiver

current flows. Current flowing through the electromagnet causes its magnetism to change in accordance with the changes of the current. Thus, the electrical wave with frequency and amplitude becomes a "magnetic wave" with changing numbers and intensities of magnetic states. The magnetism of the electromagnet and that of the diaphragm's permanent magnet interact, causing the diaphragm to vibrate. This duplicates the vibrations of the transmitter's diaphragm and thereby creates sound waves in the air around the earpiece, which are a copy of those spoken into the mouthpiece.

Switching networks provide "interconnectability" among phones. Given the number of phones in the United States alone, each capable of being connected to any other, centralized switching centers are a must. Initially, operators at exchange switchboards manually hooked up two wires from two phones to make a connection. Then came mechanization, which incorporated devices that automated that part of the operator's work. As electrical engineering developed, electromechanical devices were replaced by

Technology Times

Restructuring the House
That Ma Built

Tom Beshaw is an AT&T marketing manager specializing in business analysis. An ex-IBMer and one time computer systems marketing man for UNIVAC, Beshaw is of a breed of AT&T executives that in the early 1970s had been recruited from outside the Bell System's own talent pool—an unconventional practice for Ma Bell prior to the 1970s. Also unconventional at AT&T over the decades has been the operation of a marketing department; that is, until 1973, when the challenge from competitive equipment manufacturers had to be met. AT&T's pre-

electronic systems with greater speed and versatility.

The problem of switching is best illustrated in the formula used to determine the number of connections required to interconnect a given number of phones so that each is accessible to every other: the number of phones times that number again, minus 1, and then that total divided by 2. For 100 phones, 4,999.50 connections are required; for 10,000 phones, 49,999,999.50 connections. Without switching, the telephone would have become, at best, a long-distance intercom between two fixed points.

Telephone switching networks are composed of (1) subscriber loops, which connect phones to central offices; (2) central offices with switching facilities for interconnecting local phones, and connections to other central offices, nearby and distant; (3) tandem offices, which provide intermediate connections to distant central offices for a group of local central offices in areas where traffic is light; (4) interoffice trunk lines, which directly interconnect central offices be-

FIG. 11-2. Telephone network

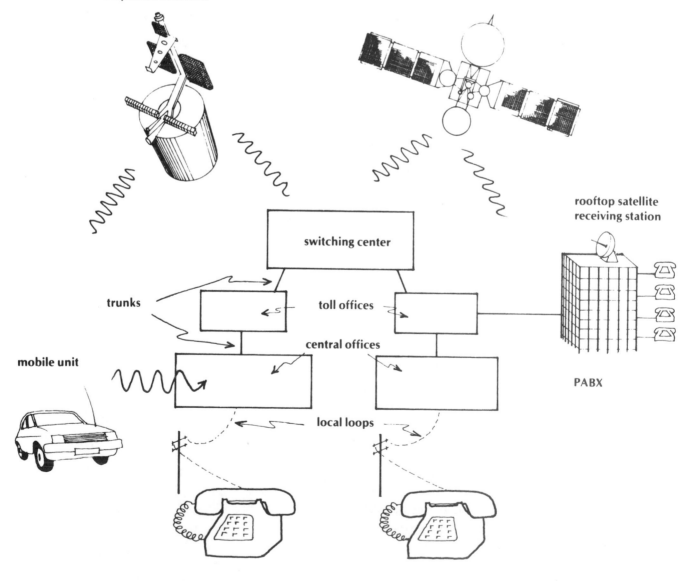

switching center

rooftop satellite
receiving station

trunks

toll offices

central offices

mobile unit

PABX

local loops

tween which traffic is heavy; and (5) city-based long-distance toll offices, which are interconnected by intercity trunk lines. Other higher-order switching centers serve to interconnect regions, zones, etc. AT&T, for example, operates its computer-based Network Operations Center in Bedminster, New Jersey, for monitoring the flow of long-distance traffic throughout North America.

The development of switching mechanisms began with Almon Stowger, who constructed the first "step-by-step" switch in 1890. Spurred on by his irritation with busybody switchboard operators, Stowger, a Kansas City undertaker, devised a set of phone keys that were connected through the central offices for direct signaling to another phone, thereby bypassing the operator. By 1907, his keys were replaced by the circular dial still in use.

Switching a signal through a maze of possible connections to hook up two phones is like twirling the dial of a combination lock in a sequence of numbers to open it. Elements must be positioned in sequence to form an open path through which passes either lock bolt to open the lock or electrical signal to reach its termination point—another phone. In step-by-step switching, each dialed digit acts to locate a relay point, which in combination with others makes the final connection. For example, in a simple telephone selector at the central office, 100 relays are arranged in rows and columns of 10 relays each. A relay is an electromechanical switch that is triggered by electrical conditions. Dialing a local number of four digits works like this: When the first number is dialed, an armature or wiper of the selector moves vertically to the row indicated by the digit and then moves horizontally until it finds an unused relay, which is then closed. The second dialed number directs the wiper to the next relay, which is at the row and column indicated by the number (e.g., 8 means eighth row and eighth column). That relay is closed. The third digit locates the next row for the wiper to find, and the fourth digit directs the wiper to a column of that row, which closes another relay and completes the connection. All the necessary relays have been closed in their proper sequence and the call goes through. The relays remain closed until the connection is broken—the phone is hung up.

Dialing is of two types: circular dialing and push-button tone (Touch-Tone of AT&T). In circular dialing, when, for example, the number 4 is dialed, the steady current or dial tone signal is interrupted four times as the dial spins back to its normal position

viously enjoyed government-regulated monopoly was severely deteriorated by new rulings allowing telephone subscribers freedom to supply their own instruments. Free enterprise penetrated the fortress that Ma built as breakthroughs in electronics and communications technology encouraged new, old, large, and small companies into the marketplace.

Responding to the impact of a growing information age and economy, by the fall of 1978, AT&T implemented a carefully developed plan to reorganize its total corporate structure. The Bell System is now composed of three major divisions: the residence market division; the business market division; and a network that was created out of the Bell Long Lines group to handle all transmission needs for both residence and business divisions.

Beshaw described the new structure in an interview a few days before its adoption as the development of something like two distinct companies with a common support aimed at two distinct markets with different needs and potentials. In time, all Bell System companies throughout the country are to reorganize to fit the new structure, offering new services and products developed by AT&T in an open marketplace with competitors.

Once the blue jeans of communications technologies, the dressed-up telephone of today provides voice, picture, and data communications around the world. "A home telecommunications system is under definition and development," Beshaw promised, though greater efforts were aimed at the business market to meet its needs for word processing, video teleconferencing, electronic mail, data communications, energy control, and alarm and security systems.

Bell Labs, the company's science and technology research subsidiary, remains structurally untouched by the reorganization. Western Electric, the System's own manufacturer, also remains untouched; however, its ownership by AT&T is being jeopardized by possible government regulations that might order its divestiture. At one time the exclusive manufacturing source for AT&T, Western Electric is now the major but not the only supplier of equipment. As Beshaw put it: "Why invent the wheel again? If it's out there with somebody else, we'll buy it."

Under the new structure, the business

market division is aggressively going out to companies to help them determine their needs as well as find the solutions. Beshaw elaborated: "Computers, telephones, all these machines are technology, not products. Picturephone, for instance, was a technology addressed to no problem. It failed as a product. The profits are made by those who use technology to solve the problems at hand. We're going to businesses today and telling them how to do their business as to the use of our services and products."

Picturephone has been reincarnated as a teleconferencing service to meet the need for business meetings within organizations with offices located throughout the country. It offers an alternative to the problems and costs of the travel required for face-to-face meetings. Beshaw summoned up the changes at AT&T, remembering the failure of the railroads to become transportation companies: "We've gone through being the telephone company to become a communications company."

The future of that communications company was described to a House Subcommittee on Postal Personnel and Modernization in April 1978 by AT&T Network Planning Director Joseph Bader. Referring to the company's hundreds of millions of circuit miles of wire and cable, plus its hundreds of millions of circuit miles of microwave and satellite facilities, with some 20,000 switching centers capable of 10 million billion possible connections, otherwise known as the "public switched network" (PSN), Bader envisioned its becoming a system "permitting the user to communicate, in any form desired, with any other user at any time and at any place."

With further installation of computer-based, stored-program control (SPC) and common channel interoffice signaling (CCIS), the switching control signaling network installed along side voice lines, Bader sees the public switched network becoming a "telecommunications network of communications computers" through which "the customized telecommunications needs of each customer can be met."

Bell Labs' Vice-President George Dacey, in an address to the American Newspaper Publishers Association in 1978, spoke about the development of human speech within computers. For man and machine to better

upon release. The interruptions become pulses that are sensed and processed by the central office equipment. With push-button tone, a set of voice frequencies given to each number activates frequency-discriminating equipment. Instead of an interrupted DC signal as for dialer phones, push-button systems use AC voice frequency signaling, which is suited to the electronic exchange equipment that since the late 1960s is being installed throughout the telephone network.

Following step-by-step switching, in the 1930s, electromechanical crossbar mechanisms were developed and first used. Two distinct operations are employed in crossbar switching: control and switching. The control phase serves to select the circuit path prior to connection. Switching makes the actual connection. A crossbar switch contains a number of vertical and a number of horizontal paths. A vertical path can be connected to a horizontal path constituting a connection. Switching information (the dialed number) is received and stored by the controlling mechanisms. With control operations to ferret out circuit paths, speed increases and utilization of facilities is more efficient.

The functions of control operations began to be further exploited in the 1960s in electronic switching systems (ESSs), which employ computers and stored switching logic programs. Output from the computer triggers switches that make the connections. Switches can be electronic, such as semiconductors, or electromechanical, such as magnetically operated minute metal reeds encased in small glass tubes called ferreeds. ESS can be also operated in conjunction with crossbar switching systems. ESS is, of course, speediest with semiconductor crosspoint switches as opposed to any involving mechanical components.

Number 4 ESS is AT&T's largest switching system and it is being widely installed in the 1970s and early 1980s. It is a time-division, digital switching system for tandem and toll operations. Its capacity is 100,000 trunk lines and its stored-program control (SPC) can switch 550,000 calls per hour. Digital signals can be stored for message or store-and-forward switching as well as line switching at a sample rate of 8,000 bps. Stored digitized signals may be taken from storage in a different order than entered, and their time position in a multiplexed channel can be altered, a process known as time slot interchange (TSI). Control signaling between facilities equipped with stored-program control is done on a separate data linking network referred to as common channel interoffice signaling (CCIS). CCIS interconnects all major toll switchers and is planned for extension to local electronic offices in the 1980s. Paralleling voice circuits, CCIS frees them up for greater volume of traffic.

Computers are also being used to expand local loop capacity. The loop switching system (LSS) employs a small computerized switching unit to locate and test circuit paths controlling connections along local loop wire pairs. This can triple their capacity.

The transmitting of telephone calls includes the use of the familiar wires on poles, underground coaxial and optical fiber cables, submarine cable crossing waterways, microwave radio relay on land and in space (satellites), and shortwave transmission for radiotelephone. AT&T's Long Lines department has installed and maintains about 365 million transmission circuit miles, of which about 70 percent are microwave and 30 percent coaxial cable.

Radiotelephone or mobile phone was first introduced in 1946 by AT&T. In the late 1970s, demand began to outgrow capacity. Single high-power base stations have been serving to connect up mobile phone users with called or calling parties at fixed phones. Only twenty-five channels within the allotted bandwidth have been available and that within an area of about 5,000 square miles since the high-power transmissions would interfere with each other if situated closer. To overcome these limitations, identified in the 1950s when research to improve mobile phone service was begun, AT&T introduced Advanced Mobile Phone Service (AMPS) in the 1970s.

Getting away from the use of a single high-power transmitter serving a given large area, the AMPS approach breaks that area into cells that are hexagonally shaped with radii of about eleven miles. Each cell is served by a low-power transmitter, and each is allocated a set of frequencies different from that of its bordering cells so that interference will not be a problem. However, the same frequencies can be used in cells far enough apart where interference is not a problem.

Each cell serves a caller when in its area. Part of the radiotelephone equipment in the vehicle is a small computer that generates a signal constantly to cell base computers which tracks the transmission to keep it clear and strong. As a caller moves out of one cell and into another, the newly entered cell base computer picks up the signal and transfers the call without interruption to an open frequency in its area. The vehicle's computer and the cell base computers are in touch throughout a call to ensure proper transmission and switching of cells' frequencies as required. The

function in the future, computers must be able to hear and understand humans as well as speak. Dacey concluded that "either people must learn to speak machine language or vice versa." Language arts for computers is under ongoing development at Bell Labs. Synthesized-voice recorded messages are already being used by Bell System companies.

No timetable for the speaking computer has come to light, but by 1990, a total computer-based switching network, the SPC Network, will be 70 percent complete, according to Bader, and will permit "customer programmable software to meet changing needs." The national, giant communications brain built by AT&T will be at the public's beck and call with a simple push of a few buttons and a changing memory or two.

By the mid-1980s, electronics will be at the heart of both push-button telephones and, for businesses, private branch exchanges. Equipment will be intelligent, meaning it will be programmable to suit individual needs. For business systems, data and voice services will be more integrated. Bader sees broad expansion of digital transmission capabilities already available in metropolitan areas.

Custom Calling services will become widely available by the mid-1980s, and by 1990, customers in about 2,000 Electronic Switching System (ESS) central offices will be able to receive them. Bader predicts that by 1982, direct-dial conferencing (Threeway Calling) will be a standard offering.

AT&T's seeming universal quest to unify communications resources was apparent in Bader's remarks on data services. Noting the present trend to set up data communications networks separate from the public voice network, and separate from each other, he suggested that a shared-use approach would eventually evolve out of economies that would become obvious in concentrating "in fewer networks or a single network."

Graphic services, such as television, which the Bell System has been transmitting for broadcasters for over three decades via land microwave and satellite, will see more satellite use and incorporation of digital transmission. Facsimile terminals for voice-channel transmission will work at speed rates of a minute per page, while high-speed digital channels will provide transmission of a page in seconds.

a

FIG. 11-3. AT&T phone systems. (a) A communications terminal for transmission of data or text to another terminal and for transmission and reception of data to computer-based data communications systems. (b) The VuSet terminal capabilities include 64 ASCII alphanumeric and space characters (upper-case alpha only), as well as 33 control characters. It operates synchronously over both the switched and private line networks. (Courtesy of AT&T Co.)

b

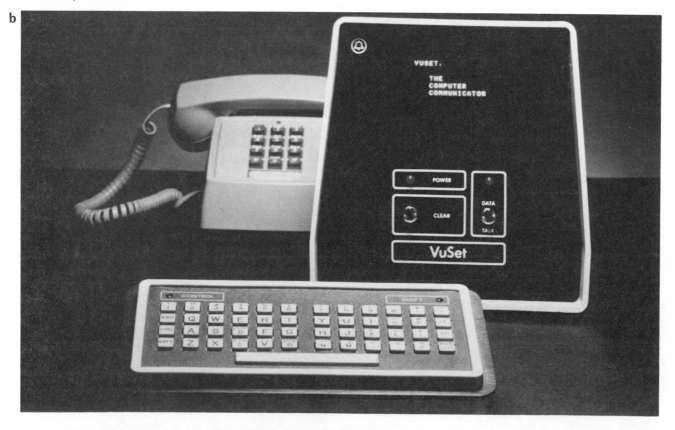

cellular system approach for radiotelephone is anticipated for nationwide development by AT&T in the 1980s and '90s.

The computer in telephony has created new services for subscribers as well as improved some of the older ones. The following are some of the major services and/or technologies developed by AT&T which are, in some cases, changing the nature of the telephone as we have known it.

Private Branch Exchange (PBX) is a telephone system of up to 7,000 phones belonging to a single business or organization. The system may be installed at a single location or serve a set of locations, such as a chain of stores or a business's main office and branches. An attendant at a switching control unit connects all calls. The system is connected to a telephone company central office by trunk line. A PBX system can be automatic (PABX), which means that outgoing calls and calls within the system can be dialed without an attendant. Incoming calls from outside the system are received by an attendant.

Wide Area Telephone Service (WATS) was instituted in 1961 to permit customers to pay a flat, monthly rate for long-distance service if they had a large volume of calls over a wide area. "Inward WATS" refers to 800 number service, which permits incoming only calls on a flat rate basis.

Direct Distance Dialing (DDD) permits the placing of long-distance calls without operator assistance. A feature of upgraded switching technology, DDD also works internationally.

AT&T offers *private line* (PL) services at flat, monthly rates.

Dataphone Digital Service (DDS) is AT&T's data transmission system for handling digitally encoded data from end to end. As an alternative to using modems and the public voice network for data communications, it offers speeds of up to 56,000 bps and is available in over 150 cities.

An *electronic blackboard* incorporates a modem for transmitting handwriting over the phone lines for display on TV monitors at distant locations. The board is pressure-sensitive. Its surface is composed of two electrically conductive layers that make up a horizontal and vertical (X-Y) grid of electrical points. When chalk is pressed against the surface, current flows at each pressed point, producing a series of dots that are transmitted to distant TV monitors for display.

Custom Calling Services are currently available through electronic switching systems. *Call Waiting*

Bader, in his summary remarks to the congressional subcommittee, said: "Undoubtedly, most homes will boast having a telecommunications center with the capacity to send and/or receive voice, data, graphics, visual information. From this center a person might perform his or her job, be educated, shop, vote, be entertained, and perform a host of other functions that today would require that he or she physically leave home. If, as some have suggested, people will not accept such home-bound confinement, then work might be performed at nearby work centers. Limitations of natural resources will make it desirable, to an ever-increasing extent, to replace the transportation of persons to information by the transmission of information to the persons in their homes or local center."

It's clear that AT&T, as a communications company, is looking to a future, in which it will become "the" communications company.

provides an incoming-call signal to a customer already talking on the phone. By hitting the receiver button, one party can be put on hold, while the other is answered. *Call Forwarding* permits the transferring of incoming calls to another number. *Threeway Calling* permits conversation among three separate phones. *Speed Calling* permits shortcut dialing of frequently called numbers. These services are part of what is referred to as the "intelligent network"—the computer-based, stored-program control switching network being installed by AT&T. In addition to the services described above, the intelligent network will eventually permit the storing of special customer instructions in central office computers, for example, to give incoming calls priority handling or to maintain a list of numbers from which reverse charges can be made automatically, services valuable to businesses and other high volume customers. The equipment manufacturers, on the other hand, seek to make the phone itself "intelligent" by incorporating in it features competitive with network offerings.

12

Radio and Sound Recording

Some ten years after Heinrich Hertz's 1887 demonstration of electromagnetic wave transmission and reception, Guglielmo Marconi developed "wireless telegraphy," known today as radio, the generic term denoting the transmission of information by way of electromagnetic propagation. More commonly, radio has come to mean sound transmission as particularly distinguished from television. By the end of the first decade of the twentieth century, with the use of the microphone, derived from Bell's telephone mouthpiece, and improvements to the wireless transmitter/receiver, sound communications through the air was underway.

The microphone, commonly "mike," changes sound pressure into electrical signals. A mike can have a range of sensitivity or pickup that takes in all directions (omnidirectional), in a single direction (cardioid and shotgun), or in two opposite directions (bidirectional). Like a telephone's mouthpiece, microphones have diaphragms—thin membranes which vibrate in reaction to the air pressure of sound hitting them. Three types of mikes are common: dynamic, crystal, and condenser.

In a *dynamic mike*, attached to the diaphragm is a coil of wire that passes between the poles of a magnet. A current is produced in the coil when it moves through the magnetic field of the magnet. Changes in the movement of the coil become changes in current, and thus an electrical copy of the patterns of sound vibrations is made.

In a *crystal* or *piezoelectric mike*, the diaphragm moves a sliver of crystal that is set between two metal plates. The varying vibrations of the crystal cause a varying voltage to be generated from the plates.

A *condenser mike* requires its own power source. A small battery charges a capacitor, the electric-charge-storing component. The amount of stored charges varies depending on the amount of separation between the capacitor's two conducting surfaces. The diaphragm is connected to one of the surfaces, and its vibrations cause that surface to move toward and away from the opposite surface in turn causing stored charge to be released from the capacitor. The changes in the amount of released charge form the electrical counterpart to the sound vibrations moving the diaphragm.

A simple transmitter is composed of signal amplifiers to increase input signal levels, a radio frequency oscillator for generating a carrier wave, a modulator for combining the signal and the carrier, and radio frequency amplifiers for increasing the level of the modulated signal to the antenna.

A signal from a microphone, for instance, is relatively weak and needs to be amplified for the modulator. A modulator requires a given signal level depending on the mode of transmission and the method of modulation (AM, FM, etc.). A common radio frequency oscillator is a crystal type whose operation is based on the same piezoelectric effect as the crystal mike, but in reverse. A sliver of crystal set between two plates will mechanically vibrate when a voltage is fed across the plates. Depending on the cut

FIG. 12-1. Microphones

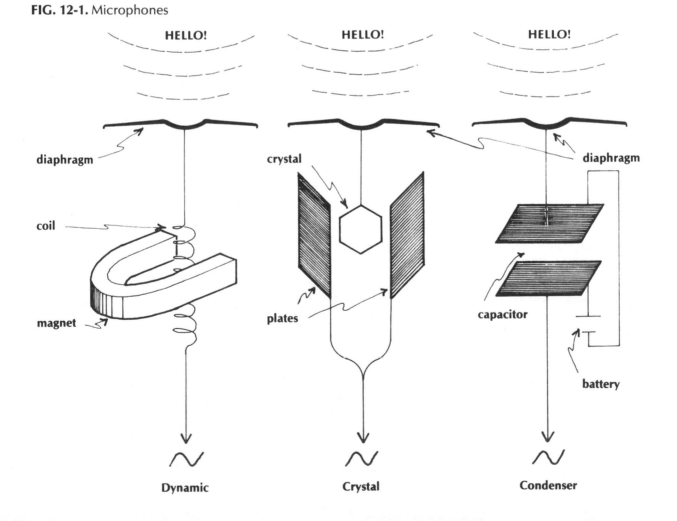

FIG. 12-2. Radio transmitter

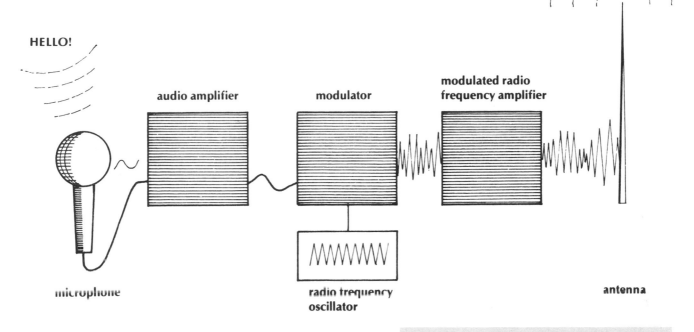

of the crystal and the applied voltage, specific, fixed, or high-frequency oscillations can be generated.

The transmitting process starts with the mike signal fed to a single amplifier and then to the modulator, which is simultaneously fed the carrier from the radio frequency oscillator. The mike signal modulates (AM, FM, etc.) the carrier, and the combined signal is amplified in the radio frequency amplifier on its way to the antenna from which it radiates in space. In stereo transmission, a second carrier or subcarrier is used to transmit the second channel of information. The two signals are multiplexed for transmission and, at the receiver, are separated and fed to different amplifiers and speakers.

A simple or *tuned radio frequency* (TRF) receiver is composed of radio frequency (r.f.) amplifiers for tuning in and increasing the level of the signal received from the antenna, a detector or demodulator for extracting the signal from the carrier frequency, and a signal amplifier for increasing the signal to the required level for output to the loudspeaker(s). A received signal is tuned, amplified, and demodulated. The signal, stripped of its carrier, is amplified for driving the speaker(s).

A superheterodyne receiver, the type most commonly used, is composed of an r.f. amplifier, as in a TRF receiver, for tuning and increasing the level of the signal from the antenna; an oscillator to generate a *beat frequency*, which provides further selectivity

censes are issued by bodies empowered by the public, both nationally and internationally. A license, like one for operating an automobile on public highways, permits spectrum use within the limits of the rules established by the regulating groups.

The spectrum is divided for use according to three parameters: space, place, and volume. Space is the bandwidth required for a particular type of transmission. Place is where that band of frequencies is located in the spectrum. Volume is the amount of power permitted for radiating a transmission which effects its reach. Rules are addressed to operator conduct for communications over the air and to equipment requirements. The spectrum is allocated for use internationally through the United Nations' International Telecommunications Union (ITU), which is composed of nations ratifying the Telecommunications Convention (as of 1981, 154 nations). A secretariat and Frequency Registration Board are located in Geneva, Switzerland, for handling ITU frequency management activities. The ITU is assisted by a number of international bodies which have special interests in particular areas of communications. Among them are the International Radio Consultative Committee (CCIR), and the International Telegraph and Telephone Consultative Com-

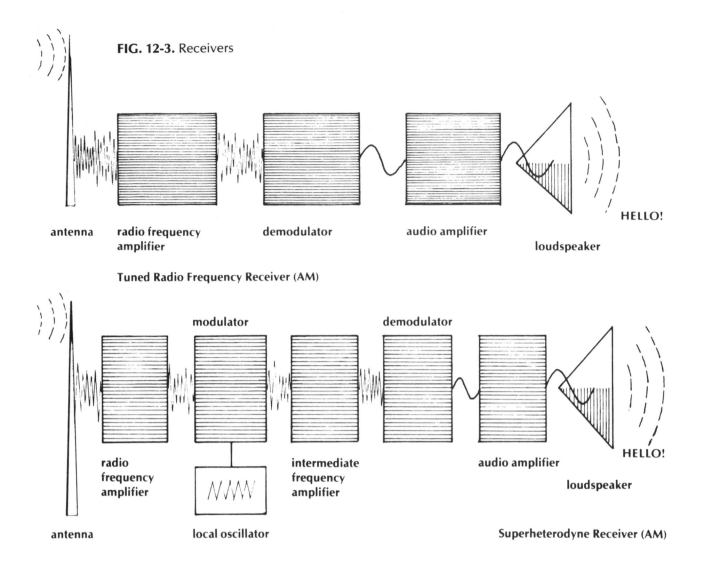

FIG. 12-3. Receivers

antenna   radio frequency   demodulator   audio amplifier   loudspeaker
           amplifier

HELLO!

Tuned Radio Frequency Receiver (AM)

modulator   demodulator

radio   intermediate   audio amplifier   loudspeaker
frequency   frequency
amplifier   amplifier

antenna   local oscillator   **Superheterodyne Receiver (AM)**

HELLO!

mittee (CCITT), both which directly assist the ITU helping to establish technical standards. The ITU coordinates with the International Civil Aviation Organziation (ICAO), the International Maritime Consultative Organization (IMCO), the World Meteorological Organization (WMO), the International Electrotechnical Commission (IEC), and the International Oceanographic Commission (IOC).

Each nation conforms to the International Radio Regulations of the ITU, which divides the earth into three regions. Each region has some differences of allocations. The United States is in Region 2. Blocks of frequencies are allocated to specific uses or types of services, such as amateur services for hobby or personal use as opposed to business or for-

in the tuning process; a mixer for combining the beat frequency with the r.f. signal to make an intermediate frequency (i.f.); and then a detector and a signal amplifier, as in the TRF receiver, for demodulation and amplification of the signal for output.

High-frequency transmissions are more difficult to free of interference from other frequencies than transmissions at lower frequencies. To optimize selectivity or tuning of a high-frequency signal, *heterodyning*, or beating, is performed. Beating two frequencies together produces a third which is equal to the sum or difference of the first two. For example, to lower a high-frequency signal of 1,500 kHz, it is combined with a beat frequency of 1,000 kHz, which results in a difference signal or i.f. of 500 kHz, at which selectivity is more easily accomplished.

Tuning is most commonly accomplished using a variable capacitor for setting the resistance factors in a circuit, which determines the *band pass* or range of frequencies that can pass through it. By balancing the magnetic resistance (inductance) and the electric resistance (capacitance) in a given AC circuit, a frequency can be produced which oscillates in resonance with a transmitted r.f. signal. A tuned or resonant frequency is received while all others are "blocked."

The reception process in a heterodyne (synonymous with superheterodyne) receiver starts with initial tuning and amplification of an r.f. signal from the antenna, followed by the mixing of the beat frequency and the r.f. signal to produce the lower inter-

profit use. Each nation, in turn, regulates the spectrum within its borders, assigning specific frequencies of the designated blocks for its licensees' uses.

In the United States, spectrum management is divided between the president and the Congress. The president, formerly through the Office of Telecommunication Policy with the Interdepartment Radio Advisory Committee and now through the National Telecommunications and Information Administration (NTIA) of the Department of Commerce, controls the frequencies used by the federal government. The NTIA has the technical support of the Institute for Tele-

FIG. 12-4. Speakers

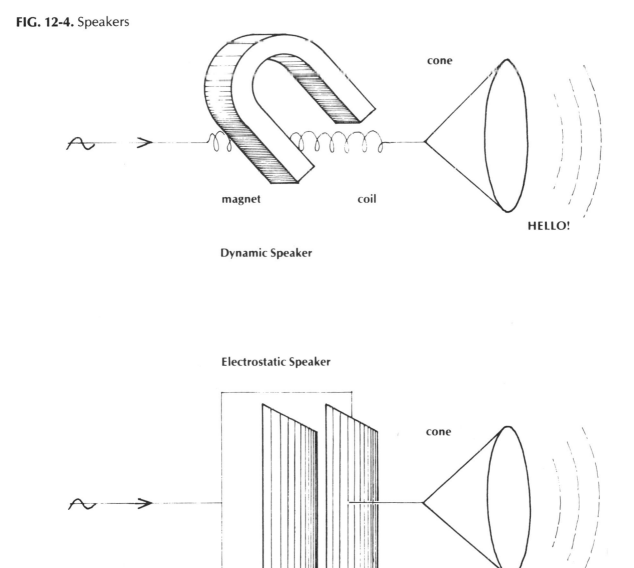

Dynamic Speaker

Electrostatic Speaker

communications Sciences (ITS). The Congress, through the Federal Communications Commission (FCC) created by the 1934 Communications Act (to be revised in the early 1980s), controls the frequencies used by state and local governments and private entities. The FCC is assisted by the Electromagnetic Radiation Management Advisory Council (ERMAC), the Frequency Management Advisory Council (FMAC), the National Television System Committee (NTSC), the Television Allocations Study Organization (TASO), the Radio Technical Committee for Aeronautics (RTCA), the Radio Technical Committee for Marine Services (RTCM), and the Land Mobile Advisory Committee (LMAC).

In addition to the government organizations are several industry associations of note that provide important technical and marketing information. The Electronics Industry Association (EIA) develops industry-wide standards for equipment and marketing data for the industry, as well as acts as a lobby in legislative matters. The Institute of Electrical and Electronic Engineers (IEEE) is concerned with technical standards and developments and has joined together with the EIA to form the Joint Technical Advisory Council (JTAC), which provides unbiased technical evaluations of problems related to the use of the spectrum.

The main services for which the spectrum is used are as follows.

Amateur is one of the oldest services and has served, aside from its personal and hobby uses, emergency communications, the training of operators, and experimental developments of radio. Amateur bands are small, but spread out through the spectrum.

Broadcasting services are for reception by the general public. They can be sound, TV, or other. Primarily, broadcasting is AM and FM radio and VHF and UHF television in prescribed broad bands of the spectrum.

Fixed or *point-to-point* services involve transmission between fixed stations, such as microwave relays, satellites, radiotelephone and telegraph transmitters and receivers, etc. Frequencies assigned for fixed services can be shared by nonconflicting users, such as the 5,000–5,450 kHz band, which includes fixed aeronautical, fixed in Alaska, international fixed public, and police.

Mobile services involve the communica-

mediate frequency. The beat frequency is determined by setting the tuning dial. The i.f. signal is fed to a detector for demodulation and is followed by amplification for output.

Demodulation is the process of rectifying an AM signal. An amplitude-modulated signal is composed of a carrier frequency with changing amplitude levels which represent the information. Rectifying serves to discard the carrier frequency by changing the signal to DC, which preserves the amplitude variations—the information. In FM receivers, the FM signal is converted to AM before demodulation.

The loudspeaker works in reverse of the microphone; it changes electrical signals into air pressure waves—sound. The two most common types of speakers are the dynamic and the electrostatic speaker. In the dynamic speaker, a coil is connected to a cone-shaped paper vibrator. The audio signal is fed to the coil, which passes between the poles of a magnet. When the signal flows in the coil, a magnetic field is produced which interacts with the magnetic field of the magnet, causing the coil to move. The cone moves in turn, causing air pressure waves that replicate the original sound.

In the electrostatic speaker, a capacitor consisting of two metal plates separated by air is fed the signal. The signal causes a variation in the amount of electrostatic charge between the plates, which, in turn, varies the distance between them. The moving plate to which a cone vibrator is fixed produces the sound waves.

SOUND RECORDING

Sound recording goes back to the early nineteenth century and was, at first, mechanically accomplished. In addition to the work of Edison, Emil Berliner, considered the father of the record as we know it, in the 1880s began his work with the ideas Charles Cros had in the 1870s to improve upon a system called the "phonoautograph" developed by Leon Scott de Martinville in 1856, which in turn was related to a system conceived by Thomas Young in 1807.

The mechanical or acoustic recorder consisted of a stylus or needle attached to a diaphragm which vibrated when air pressure hit it, causing the needle to vibrate accordingly. The needle cut minute zigzagging grooves into wax, tin foil, or black paint surfaces fixed to a revolving cylinder driven by a small motor. The grooves represented a kind of "written sound." For playback the stylus was placed in the grooves as the cylinder was rotated. The needle vibrated and caused the diaphragm to produce corresponding air pressure waves, which were amplified by use of a large horn or megaphone.

The introduction of electricity into the playback system changed the stylus from a primary sound generator to a transducer for changing the needle's mechanical vibrations into oscillations of an electrical signal. As an electrical signal, it can be amplified and fed to loudspeakers. The rotating cylinder was displaced by the flat, spinning turntable driven by an electric motor at specific revolutions per minute (rpm). The needle is most commonly diamond tipped. The pickup can be either piezoelectric or magnetic type. The signal from the pickup is fed through a preamplifier, which includes controls for tone and volume, to a power amplifier for increasing the level of the signal for speaker output from fractions of microwatts to tens of watts. For stereo playback, the stylus picks up two separate signals etched in the groove, and the pickup feeds them out to two separate preamplifiers, amplifiers, and speakers.

The primary standards that have been developed in record manufacturing are: (1) the disk format, (2) 45 and 33 1/3 rpm turntable speeds, (3) side-to-side groove etching for mono and side-to-side/up-and-down groove etching for stereo, and (4) an average of 225 grooves per inch. The "pressing" of records is accomplished by making a master disk using a cutting stylus to etch the grooves. The source of sound most commonly used for disk mastering is an audio tape recording. After cutting, the master disk is coated with a combination of metals, a process that renders a mold or negative impression of the disk. The mold is used to impress heated plastic for copies.

In the 1940s, *audio tape recording* was developed out of earlier forms of magnetic recording, which began with the use of steel wire, followed by steel tape and then coated paper tape. Since magnetizing metal is a process of making the spin direction of its atoms' electrons the same, patterns of magnetization can be formed to represent electrical signals—in this case, sound signals. Magnetic tape is composed of a plastic (Mylar) ribbon of widths from one-half inch to two inches, coated on one side with a bonding paste containing many minute particles of metal—iron oxide, for instance.

To magnetize the tape's iron oxide, the electrical signals are fed to a recording head, which is made up

tions between moving vehicles and between a fixed station and moving vehicle and can be on land, at sea, or in the air. The very high and ultrahigh frequency (VHF and UHF) bands are used for business and industry mobile services. For interest, here are the frequencies for mobile distress calls: mobile telegraph distress at 500 kHz; mobile telephone distress at 2,182 kHz; and mobile marine radiotelephone at 156.8 MHz.

Radio astronomy services are for reception of radio waves of cosmic origin.

Radiodetermination services are employed for determining position or obtaining information regarding position by using radio waves, such as with ships at sea (radio navigation).

Space services are for communications with space vehicles, such as satellites for telemetering and telecommanding. The major communications satellites operate in the UHF and superhigh frequency (SHF) bands at 4–6 GHz and 7–8 GHz. Space systems have been allocated almost all spectrum space from 40 to 275 GHz at the far, high end of the spectrum.

Some specific applications of services are illustrated in the following definitions drawn from the FCC Rules and Regulations.

Disaster communications services can be fixed or mobile and provide communications in connection with disasters or in cases where usual communications facilities are inoperative or nonexistent and temporarily required.

Domestic public radiocommunications services can be land mobile and fixed and are open for public correspondence in the United States.

International fixed public radio services are for public correspondences between the United States and any other point.

Personal radio services can be fixed or mobile, are for business or personal use, and can be used for radio remote control, as of model airplanes. CB is a personal radio service.

Earth exploration–satellite services are for transmissions between earth and space stations for gathering earth observation data.

Standard frequency services provide transmission of highly precise, specified frequencies for general reception which are used as technical and scientific standards.

In the fall of 1979, the World Administrative Radio Conference (WARC) of the ITU, held every twenty years to attend to the matters of frequency allocations among the nations, took place in Geneva. The procedure for allocations in the past has been on a first-come, first-served basis. The problem solving was primarily technical, to avoid radio interference and the like. Politics was pretty much absent from ITU conferences until recently, when a new wrinkle appeared in the international communications fabric. In the last twenty years, a great number of newly developing nations have emerged, and they constituted about two-thirds of the delegates at the 1979 WARC.

At a 1977 ITU meeting on satellite broadcasting, concerned about their lack of technological resources and consequent lack of readiness to request frequencies allocations, especially regarding satellites, the new nations challenged the first-come, first-served idea of allocations. They voted in a proposal for a new allocations system whereby they would receive spectrum space for their future use. The allocate-now, use-later idea has pervaded the WARC also. Under consideration at the WARC were some 14,000 proposals from the member delegates representing their nations' requests and raising many issues that clearly delineated the interests of the majority, poorer nations from those of the minority, high-technology nations. The conference was allotted ten weeks, out of which came a report sometime in 1980. The report became the basis for rules and regulations for international spectrum use for the next twenty-year period.

of a coil wrapped around a C-shaped magnet. Signal passing through the coil causes a magnetic field to form between the poles of the magnet. As the tape is drawn past the changing magnetic field between the poles of the recording head, its iron particles are magnetized in bunches, or *domains*, and the changing patterns of the signal are "magnetically frozen" on the tape, virtually forever or until erased—"remagnetized."

If you could see magnetic domains on tape, a recorded sound of 8,000 Hz would be seen as 8,000 domains along a length of tape drawn past the recording head in one second. The intensity of the sound would be seen in the magnetic field strength of the domains. The faster the tape moves, the more of it there is per second for the storage of signal. For instance, a tape moving at 15 inches per second (ips), the professional recording standard, provides more physical space for our 8,000 Hz signal than does a tape moving at $1\frac{7}{8}$ ips, which is the consumer recording standard along with $3\frac{3}{4}$ and $7\frac{1}{2}$ ips. This means better fidelity, especially at the higher frequencies.

Among the various formats for audio recording are reel-to-reel for tape in a range of sizes ($\frac{1}{8}$, $\frac{1}{4}$, $\frac{1}{2}$, $\frac{3}{4}$, 1, and 2 inches), $\frac{1}{8}$-inch cassette or cartridge, and 8-track cartridge for homes and car tape players. The term *track* refers to a single channel of audio information which, on the tape, is the narrow area on which a channel is recorded. Multitrack recording can involve many simultaneously recorded channels (up to thirty-two or more), which are mixed together after the recording session and before the making of a master disk or commercial tape for the market. A stereo recording is made up of two final tracks carrying two different components of the sound for playback through two amplifiers and two speakers. Quadraphonic (or quad) recording has four final tracks, requiring four amplifiers and four speakers for full appreciation of its playback.

Audio tape playback incorporates a recording head which functions in reverse, producing an electrical signal in response to the magnetic signal from the tape. As the tape passes the head, the stored magnetic energy generates a magnetic field between the poles of the head's magnet, which causes electrical current to flow in the coil. The electrical signal is, of course, a copy of the magnetic signal.

The recording of sound on photographic film for the cinema is referred to as *optical recording*. Here, electrical sound signals are converted to light patterns and back again. In a basic system, a mike signal or a

FIG. 12-5. Audio synthesizer

sound signal from a recorder is fed to a coil-and-magnet device, like that of a speaker except that the coil is attached to an iris. The coil vibrates in response to the electrical signal and causes the iris to open and close, allowing more or less of a beam's light to pass onto the edge of a moving strip of film. The developed film thus has a set a varying bands of lights and darks which represent the patterns of the recorded sound. A sound head on the projector changes the light patterns back into electrical signals, which in turn are fed to an amplifier and speaker for playback and synchronization with the picture. The sound head incorporates a light beamed through the film onto a photoconductive cell, changing light into electricity.

Important to sound transmission and recording are the following systems and pieces of equipment.

Digital recording will replace analog recording in the years to come. Since its beginning, the recording of sound has been an analog process: Electrical signals representing sound are continuously changing AC frequency rates, voltages, or currents which comprise complex waveforms subject to noise and distortion inherent in the equipment. In the late 1970s, a number of professional recording studios installed the first digital recording equipment for the production of recording masters. Rather than the complex waveforms of analog signals, digital equipment converts the information of a sound—its frequency, amplitude, waveform (which determines timbre), and wave envelope (which describes the attack and decay of a tone)—to binary computer code at a sampling rate of 50,000 times per second, a frequency more than twice the top end of a sound frequency that we can hear—20,000 Hz. Only numbers are recorded on tape, thereby eliminating the problems that degrade the analog recording. Home digital recording playback requires a digital-to-analog converter to drive conventional amplifiers and speakers. Digital sound technology is predicted to become widely available in the middle to late 1980s.

Sound synthesizers for creating electronic music are becoming a primary tool of contemporary composers and performers in almost all types of music. Traditionally, musical instruments have functioned as sound generators based on any of four basic designs: (1) strings that are stretched between two points and plucked or across which another stretched string(s) is drawn; (2) woodwinds, which require that air be blown against a reed to vibrate a confined air column; (3) brasses, which require that air be forced through a confined air column; and (4) percussion, which entails the striking of a surface by hand or stick. Amplification of the resulting sound is accomplished by use of a resonator. In the 1960s, electrified amplification began to be widely used. An instrument's output was changed into electrical signals for amplification and fed to loudspeakers, which greatly increased the volume, also giving musicians a new set of tone and loudness controls to work during performance. Sound synthesis employs electronic circuits directly to generate and modify electrical signals with audible-range AC frequencies. No "real" sound input is required. The oscillator is the main circuit of a synthesizer. It can provide a sound source and be used to control aspects of another oscillator's generated sound, such as periodic control of amplitude to produce wowing effects, or periodic control of frequency filtration to produce undulations of pitch, etc. A synthesizer is made up of sound producers, which, in addition to oscillators, are noise generators and inputs for external sources. Noise generators produce "pink noise," a signal with all audible frequencies at random amplitudes, with an emphasis on the lower frequencies, and "white noise," the same with the emphasis on the higher frequencies. Filters, amplifiers, mixers, and voltage regulators are the other components of a synthesizer. By varying the voltages fed to the components, oscillation rates, amplification powers, filtering of frequency bands (band passes), attack (start of sound) and decay (end of a sound) durations, and wave shapes can be controlled. Thus, an operator has unlimited possibilities for making renditions of familiar sounds as well as creating sounds that have never been heard before. A synthesizer in combination with a computer constitutes a sound-making system capable of complex and long-duration sequencing of sounds into recorded works, either programs for performance by computerized synthesizer or finished pieces ready for disk or tape distribution.

Carrier current radio has been used for office and home intercom systems and campus-only college radio stations. Simply, it is the use of power transmission lines for radio (sound) communications. By modulating a high-frequency AC carrier wave which is superimposed on power lines, transmissions can be made between points within the network of the electric system. Each electrical outlet on the wall can be tapped by the appropriate receiver and/or transmitter for handling the signal. Carrier current operations are not limited to electric power lines. In principle, a carrier current can be superimposed on any type of electrical transmission lines, such as telephone or telegraph wires.

13

Television and Video Recording

TV TRANSMISSION AND RECEPTION

Philo T. Farnsworth and Vladimir Zworykin separately invented electronic television in the early 1920s. Since the beginning of operations of the first commercial TV station, WNBT of New York, in 1941, television has become the mass medium of choice for entertainment and news throughout the world.

In a television system, light is converted into electrical signals, transmitted or stored on video tape, and fed for display to a TV screen—or cathode ray tube (CRT)—which converts the electrical signals into light emitted from the screen.

To make an electrical signal of a vision field, the location of points in the field, as well as their intensity and color (frequency), must be noted. Raster scanning is the process by which locations of visual points in a scene are represented in the conversion of light to electricity and back again.

The television camera is made up of a light-sensitive circuit, most commonly a vacuum tube containing an electrode gun, deflection coils, and a face or signal plate. Located at the rear end of the cylinder-shaped tube, the electron gun provides a fine, constant stream of electrons hitting the inner side of the signal plate. The electromagnetic deflection coils, which are wrapped around the tube near its center, control the vertical and horizontal movements of the stream of electrons.

The signal plate is made up of several layers. First, the innermost layer, the photoconductive layer, is hit by the stream of electrons from the inside, and by particles of light (photons) from the outside—the scene focused on the tube's face by a lens. As photons hit the photoconductive layer, its electrical resistance is lowered and electrons from the gun can pass through. The more photons, the lower the resistance, the greater the number of electrons pass. The next layer,

FIG. 13-1. The television system

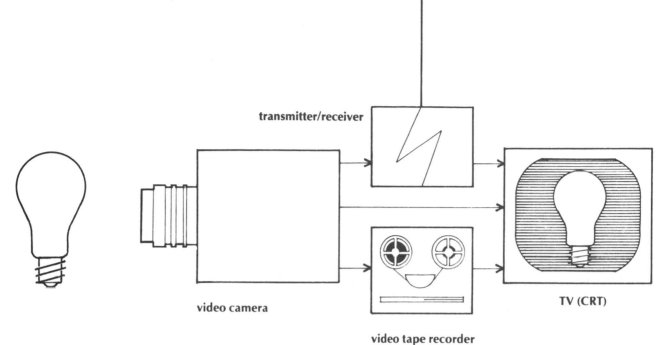

transmitter/receiver

video camera

video tape recorder

TV (CRT)

the conductive layer, is encircled by a target ring, which drains off the electrons that have passed from the stream through the photoconductive layer onto the conductive layer. The electrical signal that is drained off by the target ring is the video signal—an electrical representation of the light in the scene.

Scanning is done by steering the stream of electrons with the deflection coils, which are driven by oscillators set at specific frequencies (rates of time) to provide synchronization of the up and down movements. In the U.S. system, the stream of electrons is first swept horizontally from the right side to the left, taking about fifty microseconds. Then, for about ten microseconds, retrace occurs; the stream is returned to the right side, during which time the signal is blanked. At the same time as the horizontal oscillator drives the electron stream back and forth, the vertical oscillator, at a much slower rate, drives it down and up. The process of horizontal sweeping and retrace occurs 262.5 times before it is vertically driven downward to the bottom of the raster—the imaging area. Then the vertical deflection coil guides the electron stream back to the top, during which time the signal is blanked. The scanning of 262.5 lines occurs sixty times a second and is called a field. The first 262.5 lines make up the odd field—lines 1, 3, 5, etc. After vertical retrace, the even lines—2, 4, 6, etc.—are scanned and make up the even field. The

FIG. 13-2. (a) TV camera; (b) video cassette recorder; (c) TV (Courtesy of RCA)

two fields are interlaced or interwoven to make up a frame of 525 lines, which occurs thirty times a second. A frame contains the total information of a scene.

Scanning systems vary throughout the world. South America and Japan employ the 30-frames-per-second, 525-line system. The number of frames per second usually coincides with a country's electrical system's AC rate, which is either 50 cycles or 60 cycles. Therefore, many European and Asian countries with 50-cycle AC have a 25-frames-per-second TV system rather than 30 frames. Horizontal frequencies can be greater and thus produce more lines, such as 819 in the French system and 625 in England and the U.S.S.R.

A composite video signal contains two types of signals: picture and synchronization (sync) signals. Picture signals are the light information, while the sync signals are the horizontal and vertical instructions for locating each picture signal in its proper place in the raster.

Solid-state cameras became commercially available in 1980. Using charge-coupled devices (CCDs), made on silicon chips, electron-gun scanning tubes are eliminated. The CCD sensor, composed of a grid of about 300 by 500 elements (about 164,000 pixels), converts light into electrical charges from which the video signal is put together. The cameras using CCDs are compatible with standard TV displays.

In television, detail is distinguished primarily by the intensity or black-and-white components of light. Contrast (blackness) and brightness (luminance or whiteness) of a TV signal are controlled on a TV set commonly with tuning knobs. Good TV picture resolution—detail—is a function of how many discrete signal notations are made, for instance, during a horizontal sweep in the scanning process. In the CCD

FIG. 13-3. Charge-coupled device (CCD) camera (Courtesy of RCA)

sensor, for every point on the grid of the silicon chip, a discrete signal is generated. In the process of scanning, when a stream of electrons is moving across a line, a signal is equated to a duration of time. How fast a notation is made determines how resolved the image is. For the black-and-white components of light, 300 discrete signals or "lines of resolution" is an acceptable standard.

For color in TV, three elements are noted: hue, or tint; saturation, or color; and luminance, or intensity. The color TV picture is derived from three primary color lights: red, green, and blue (RGB). By combining these colors together and varying their saturation and luminance, any color light in the whole visible spectrum can be produced. Color cameras are made with one or a combination of tubes, from two to four. As it enters the camera, the light is split into several beams and directed through color filters to tubes. Each tube converts the filtered light fed exclusively to it into an electrical signal representing the color. These outputs are then combined. The final color TV signal is composed of three parallel signals: the Y signal, which is the black-and-white (b/w) information, and the I and Q signals, which are the color and saturation information.

Three color systems are used throughout the world. They are essentially different in their methods of mixing together the components of color and the frequencies selected for modulating the color signal for transmission. In the United States, the National Television Standards Committee (NTSC) color standard is used. The Phase Alteration Line (PAL) system is used throughout most of Europe, except for France, which employs a system called SECAM (*Séquential Couleur à Mémoire*), which controls the color at the point of broadcast, requiring no color controls on the receiver. To improve NTSC color, in the late 1970s, U.S. manufacturers began cooperating with broadcasters to develop better color tuning accuracy by building circuits into receivers to detect an automatic color tuning signal transmitted in the vertical interval by the broadcasters.

The broadcasting of television entails transmission of a signal with a 6-MHz bandwidth to accommodate all the picture and sound information. The b/w portion of the picture is amplitude-modulated (AM), its color components are phase-modulated (PM), and the sound is frequency-modulated (FM). Two bands of the radio spectrum are used for TV broadcasting: VHF for channels 2 to 13 falling between 54 and 216 MHz; and UHF for channels 14 to 84 falling between 470 and 890 MHz.

The TV display is either a receiver for reception and display of broadcast signals, or a monitor for display of video signals fed directly to it from a camera or video tape source. A receiver incorporates the necessary circuits for demodulating a radio frequency carrier to separate out the video signal. From that point on, the receiver and monitor are the same, amplifiers and a CRT, which functions like a camera tube in reverse, changing electricity into light. The CRT contains an electron gun, deflection coils for controlling the electron stream's movements, and face plate (the screen) with an inner coating of phosphors, which give off light when hit by electrons. The video signal containing picture and vertical and horizontal sync information is separated into its components. Each sync signal is fed to its appropriate oscillator to drive the appropriate deflection coil of the CRT. The picture signal is fed to the electron gun and controls the amount of electrons passed from the gun to the screen. The more electrons hitting a given spot of phosphors, the more light emitted.

For display of color, either three electron guns or a single gun producing three electron streams is used. The Y signal containing the b/w information is fed to all the electron streams, while the information of each color is fed to the gun(s), each to control its own electron stream. The inner coating of the screen is coated with three types of phosphors: one to emit red light, one for green, and one for blue light. The RGB phosphors are arranged into a great number of trios, either in a dot or bar pattern. To ensure proper convergence of electron streams onto their appropriate

FIG. 13-4

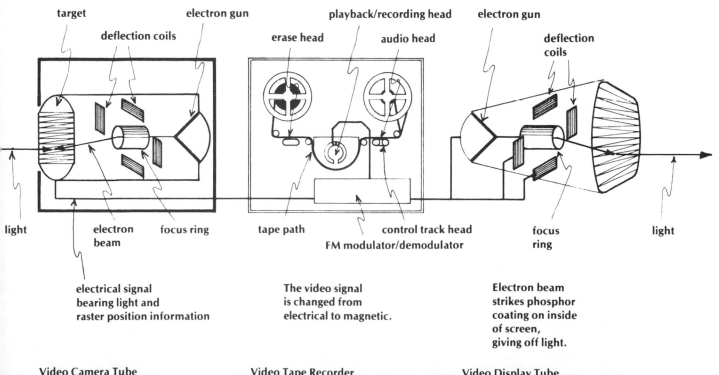

target   electron gun   playback/recording head   electron gun

deflection coils   erase head   audio head   deflection coils

light   electron beam   focus ring   tape path   control track head   focus ring   light

FM modulator/demodulator

electrical signal bearing light and raster position information

The video signal is changed from electrical to magnetic.

Electron beam strikes phosphor coating on inside of screen, giving off light.

Video Camera Tube   Video Tape Recorder   Video Display Tube phosphors, a shadow mask is placed near the screen between it and the gun(s). It is a thin metal sheet with perforations equal in number and pattern to the phosphors, and it functions somewhat like a strainer.

Television reception is similar to that of superheterodyne radio reception, which employs an intermediate frequency (i.f.), a lower-frequency carrier within the receiver. Since demodulation is easier at lower frequencies, an i.f. at a level well below the broadcast carrier is used. In television reception are two i.f.'s; one for sound and one for picture. The separation of the color, b/w, and sync portions of the composite video signal entails the use of additional demodulators after the composite video has been separated from the i.f. carrier.

VIDEO RECORDING

Recording composite video signals on magnetic tape is like sound recording, whereby the electrical signals are converted to magnetic signals and stored as patterns of magnetized groupings (domains) of metal particles. A video signal, however, is not recorded "as is" onto the tape. The b/w portion of the signal is, most commonly, frequency-modulated, while the color portion of the signal (if any) may be directly recorded, as are sound signals. In the video recorder, the recording heads move as well as the tape. The video signal is composed of so much information per second—30 frames, each made up of 525 lines of roughly 300 discrete signal levels per line—that head and tape speed must be driven at relatively high rates to be able to convert signal and have the space to store it.

Standard recording formats are of two types: quadruplex and helical scan. The *quadruplex* (quad) system consists of four heads placed on a wheel revolving at a ninety-degree angle to the tape (2-inch) as it passes at 15 ips. Quad recording has been the technology used by broadcasters, though that will likely change in the 1980s with the recent development of a high-standard, helical system and soon-to-come digital recording systems. In *helical scan* recording, the tape is wrapped around a head drum in which a set of two recording heads spin. The tape is guided around the drum in a helix or spiral path. Whereas quad recording lays down the information vertically on the tape, helical scan lays it down diagonally. Helical recorders have been built for 2-inch tape, but primarily use 1, 3/4, 1/2, and 1/4 inch, which includes the

FIG. 13-5. Video equipment: (a) special effects generator (SEG) for mixing together images of different cameras; (b) half-inch color reel-to-reel editor; (c) video projection system (Courtesy of Panasonic Co.)

a

b

c

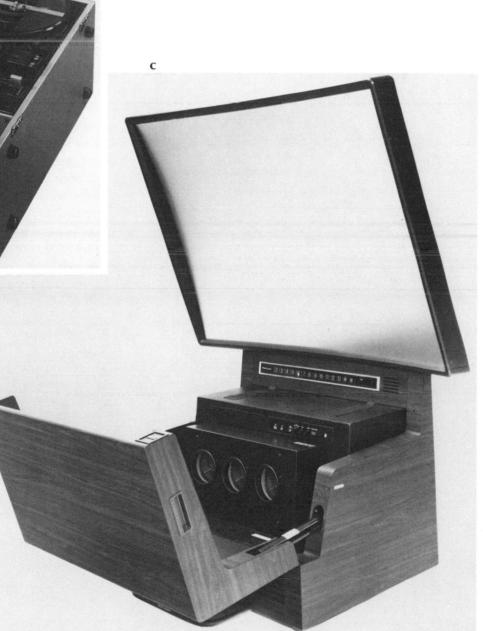

new Type C broadcast helical scan 1-inch format, ³/₄-inch U-matic cassette systems, and the home ¹/₂-inch cassette systems (Betamax and video home system, or VHS). Most nonprofessional helical scan recorders have tape speeds of 7¹/₂ ips.

In standard helical recording, the diagonal lines of signal are separated by blank lines, which serve as guardbands that prevent crosstalk interference between lines during playback. As the home video cassette recorder (VCR) market grew in the late 1970s, there was a demand for greater tape economy. This meant slower tape speeds so that more signal could be stored in less space without a loss of quality. The result is the azimuth recording system, which does away with the guardbands and alternates the storage pattern angle of every other line of signal. One of the two heads will write and read only the signal at one angle, and the other head will write and read only the signal at the other angle. This eliminates crosstalk while gaining space. The use of thinner-backed tape also extends playing time.

A video tape recorder (VTR) is made up (in order of which the tape passes first) of (1) an erase head that wipes away all previous signal for new recording and does nothing in playback, (2) the video heads that write and read signal, and (3) a sound recording and playback head, which also contains a control track head. The control track is the VTR's synchronization signal which is laid down in the record mode and read in playback to coordinate the two main motors, one moving the tape (capstan motor) and the other spinning the video heads (head drum motor) to keep the signal stable.

The two types of recorders are reel-to-reel and cassette. *Reel-to-reel* refers to having the video tape on

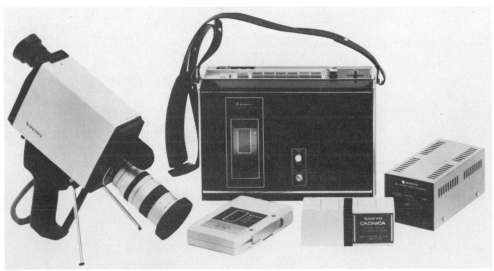

FIG. 13-6. Lightweight portable video cassette recording system, including hand-held camera, recorder, and both batteries and adaptor for AC wall outlet (Courtesy of Sanyo Electric, Inc.)

FIG. 13-7. This video disk player uses a laser to write and read information. (Courtesy of MCA Discovision)

an open reel and requires manual threading of the tape along the tape path to a take-up reel. *Cassettes* are closed, hard plastic containers housing the tape and are inserted into a compartment in the recorder for automatic threading. Cassettes also contain their own take-up reel.

There are two primary formats for video disk recording that have been developed in the 1970s. One employs a laser and encodes signal optically; the other, like sound disk recording, depends on capacitance variations. The systems that began to be marketed on a limited basis in the late 1970s are playback-only devices. Both the laser and capacitance-type disks store thirty minutes or 54,000 frames of information on a side. The laser type often uses only one side of its disk, while the capacitance type can use both.

Some manufacturers are attempting to develop a machine with both playback and record capabilities, either by the use of two lasers, one for recording and the other for playback, or by the use of a magnetic disk recorder, which permits recording a number of tracks of information in the walls of grooves etched into a magnetically sensitive disk. The use of holograms, photographic images made with lasers, has also been developed for a disk player. Video and sound information are stored in 3-D images measuring about a square millimeter and positioned on the disk's surface in a continuous train.

In the capacitance-type system, signal is recorded onto a vinyl disk coated with a layer of metal under a layer of insulating plastic. A stylus of sapphire with a metal-wrapped tip tracks a spiral path over the disk's surface. The disk revolves at a rate of hundreds of rpm, having thousands of grooves per inch. Signal is etched into the grooves by a highly focused electron beam as microscopic slots of varying widths and separations from each other. As the stylus passes over these slots, varying levels of capacitance are detected. The system is actually a mobile capacitor in which varying amounts of stored charge are fixed between two plates separated by an insulator; one plate is the stylus, the other is the disk's metal layer. The output from the stylus is fed to an oscillator whose frequency is varied by the changing signal read from the disk. That varied frequency is the video signal.

In the laser system, signal is recorded in the form of bumpy indentations along a spiral track on the underside of an aluminum disk. For playback, no contact is made between the disk and a stylus-type sensor. The reading device is a laser beam focused onto the spinning track. Rotation is nearly 2,000 rpm. The spaces between the bumps vary in relation to the variations of recorded signal. These spaces are flat and reflect flashes of light back onto a photodetector. The light flashes are of different durations and are converted to the electrical TV signal.

CABLE TELEVISION

Cable TV began as an antenna service for rural viewers who wanted better reception of distant city broadcasting stations. In the 1950s, cable TV systems were first being built. In the 1980s, cable TV is on its way to becoming a national electronic highway to and from the home for all kinds of one-way and two-way communications traffic, including shopping, banking, remote accessing of libraries and information banks, schooling, connecting security services, voting, and reading utility meters, as well as having a choice of programming from potentially hundreds of TV and radio channels.

Cable systems are at present constructed using coaxial cable, which is capable of conducting a multitude of wideband signals simultaneously. In the future, cable systems will install optical fibers, which have even greater signal-carrying capacity. A system consists of reception antennas, a headend housing signal processing equipment, and distribution cables and amplifiers.

The antennas are for reception of standard signals broadcast by TV and FM radio stations. Signals may also be relayed via land microwave network, such as closed-circuit sports events transmitted from a distant arena. In this case, an additional microwave antenna would be set up with the others. There may also be a satellite earth station for reception of satellite-relayed transmissions, such as programs from a "superstation"—an independent commercial TV station developing its own national audience.

The headend houses the system's retransmission equipment for amplifying received signals and modulating them on channels (carrier frequencies), in some cases, different from the original carriers. This is done, for example, when the number of signals delivered to a subscriber exceeds the thirteen that can be tuned by the TV set. In this case, a separate tuner box is supplied by the cable company with enough station slots to accommodate all the signals being received and/or originated at the headend.

In addition to supplying better reception of broadcast programs, locally originated signals can be fed through the headend to the home sets. The term *local origination* refers to programming activities on cable which are produced within the community, either by the cable TV company or by local media organizations. Such programs are either live or taped and fed from a studio, public meeting place, sports field, etc., to the headend, where they are modulated on a specified channel for transmission to subscriber TVs. The cable operator can lease channels, and, if the system's subscribership is over 3,500, channel time is made available at no cost to members of the public (public access). Limited costs can be charged for studio and T.V. equipment use for public access programming. Locally originated programming is never transmitted into the air; reception is only via the cable.

Other types of nonbroadcast signals that cable systems can supply to and from the homes of its subscribers include the connection of alarm systems between homes and police and fire departments; water, gas, and electricity metering for remote readings for billing purposes; and two-way polling systems between homes and a centralized computer for instantaneous tabulation. The cable system might be likened to an electronic switchboard serving to interconnect home, business, government, education, and entertainment terminals for the exchange of information. As of 1980, few two-way cable systems have been built in the United States, and none has included the means for transmitting audio and visual information from the home. To date, viewers have been provided home response terminals for answering questions posed during programs. In limited experiments using terminals based on the push-button telephone, viewers are able to interactively access information and shop using the cable. The technologies exist; economic feasibility needs to follow.

The distribution network is made up of trunk lines, which are the major arteries of the system carrying signals from the headend along the primary roadways in the system's geographical area. Split off from trunk lines are the feeder lines, which extend service down the side streets. Drop lines are split off from feeders into subscriber homes. Amplifiers are placed along the cable network to increase signal strength periodically. For two-way transmission—or what is referred to as "downstream" (from the headend) and "upstream" (to the headend) signaling capabilities—amplifiers must be used in each direction.

TELETEXT AND VIDEOTEXT

Teletext has become the generic term for the broadcasting of alphanumerics and graphics using the vertical interval reference of the transmitted video signal. Formatted into pages of information, teletext permits viewer selection via keypad of sports, news, weather, travel and entertainment schedules, captioning for the hearing impaired, and the like on a home TV set fitted with special decoding circuitry. Data can be superimposed on TV pictures or displayed on a blanked screen. On sets without decoders, the signals are undetectable and cause no interference to regular reception. Thousands of pages of up-to-date information on the broadest range of topics will constitute what some industry members call a genuine "electronic magazine."

Teletext-type systems are being operated on a limited basis in Japan, Germany, France (the ANTIOPE system), and England (the BBC's CEEFAX and the British Independent Broadcasters' ORACLE systems). Also in use is the Viewdata system of the British post office. However, Viewdata uses telephone lines rather than free air for its transmissions. As a program to integrate the telephone, the computer and the television, Viewdata permits a subscriber to telephone for information, which is displayed on the TV. The system also allows electronic mail services among its subscribers.

In the teletext method, the vertical interval reference (VIR), also called the vertical blanking interval, consists of twenty-one lines of scanning in which no picture signal exists. Occurring sixty times every second, the twenty-one lines represent the time it takes to direct the electron gun from the bottom of the raster to the top between fields. Only a few lines (two to six) are used for teletext transmission, permitting the display of twenty-four rows of forty characters across. With the use of multiplexing and data packing techniques, pages of information are output cyclically from computers or magnetic disks at rates of speed to make them constantly available to the viewer.

As of 1981, teletext in the United States was being studied by the Electronics Industry Association's Broadcast Television Systems (BTS) Committee, made up of network and manufacturer representatives and observers from government agencies and industry associations, as well as communications representatives of Canada and Mexico. BTS studies have employed modified French and British systems. The broadcasting industry has been investing in teletext as an expansion of its medium in pursuit of new areas of revenue, most probably from advertising support of the "electronic magazine."

Videotex is the generic term for the type of system operated by the British post office, Viewdata. In the United States and Canada, it is under development as an outgrowth of existing services that provide computerized cataloguing via data transmission (on-line) to libraries. Videotex systems will be designed around a central data bank that may be accessed by home subscribers using a decoder capable of storing a number of pages of information loaded into it from the central bank, thereby allowing the subscriber to use the information at a later time disconnected from the system, or off-line. Like teletext systems, videotex data banks will contain a wide array of information, including entries from an encyclopedia, video games, and community information. Banking services will also be available. Any TV set will be adaptable for information display received via telephone lines at rates between 300 and 500 bps. Support of the system will be from subscriber fees.

3-D TELEVISION

Depth in real space is perceived by the brain processing two separate, almost identical images, one from each eye. The two images, both of the same scene, are from slightly different positions, separated by the distance between the eyes, some two and a half inches. The slight differences in the two images are the brain's clues to depth perception.

The principle of paired images has been used for 3-D displays since the stereoscopic viewers of the nineteenth century. Like today's ViewMaster viewers, two pictures of the same scene are made from slightly different positions. When seen though the viewer, an image for each eye, the images merge into one 3-D scene.

The 3-D movies of the 1950s were shot with two cameras, each capturing the scene from a slightly different position. Two projectors, similarly positioned, were used to show the film. One projector had a green filter, giving an overall green cast to its image, while the other had a red filter, giving a red cast to its image. A viewer had to wear a pair of glasses in which one lens was a red filter and the other a green filter. Each eye saw only the image of the color of its lens, thereby creating for the brain the two distinct images required for depth perception.

The use of Polaroid filters is an improvement on red/green filters, which are good with only black-and-white photography. Polaroid permits total color. A Polaroid lens, in effect, blocks the light traveling in either a vertical or horizontal plane, depending on the lens. When projecting a film, each projector has a Polaroid filter, one allowing the vertical waves to pass, the other allowing the horizontal waves to pass. Polaroid glasses are worn by viewers. One lens is vertically polarized, the other horizontally polarized. Here, again, two images are created for the brain to process and perceive depth.

With "CinemaScope" 3-D movies, glasses became unnecessary, in part because a special screen was constructed of transparent, vertical, prismatic strips. When the pair of films was projected, each projector had a filter of opaque, vertical stripes which blocked projection of thin slivers of the image. In one image, the odd-numbered stripes were blocked. In the other, the even-numbered stripes were blocked. Careful registration of the two images produced a complete and total image composed of alternating slivers of image from each. The prismatic elements of the screen acted to refract the light from each image's set of slivers, providing the viewer with two separate images of the same scene and thus the perception of depth.

Since 1977, 3-D television has been a reality in Japan in the programming of cartoons for children. The Japanese system is based on the Pulfrich pendulum effect. When one eye views a scene through a light gray filter, while the other eye's vision is not filtered, swinging movements in the scene appear to be circling elliptically. In static scenes, however, no depth perception is perceived. The cartoons are specifically designed for viewing with the appropriate glasses. Nothing is done electroncially.

Digital Optical Technology System (DOTS) is another quasi-3-D system in which the computer plays an important role. When a scene is viewed by a camera, the main area of interest is sharply focused, leaving the background and foreground slightly out of focus or blurred. The computer is used to modify the blurred areas. For instance, the background blur is broken into two sides; one side is given a red tint and the other a blue-green tint. The foreground blur is treated oppositely. DOTS requires the wearing of glasses that have one red-tinted lens and one blue-green-tinted lens. Viewing the processed image produces a sense of depth between the background and foreground around a sharply focused center of interest.

The CinemaScope-type 3-D TV system requires modification to TV screens to include prismatic elements and to production and broadcasting equipment. DOTS requires no major changes to the present broadcasting system, but includes the use of the computer and glasses for viewing. As of early 1980, broadcasters and 3-D systems developers have yet to settle upon a standard for 3-D television in the United States. The ultimate in 3-D viewing, in any case, will be in the development of holography, a process by which the patterns of light that define objects and scenes will be transmitted and projected into viewing rooms, producing the kind of three-dimensionality around which we shall even be able to walk.

HOLOGRAPHY

Holography, the making of three-dimensional images, either moving or still, is being developed as a medium for data storage for computers. It has grown greatly since the development of the laser, though its invention (by Dennis Gabor in 1949) preceded that of the laser. Like photography, which uses light-sensitive chemicals to capture reflected light patterns off objects in a focused field of vision, holography also employs a photographic emulsion. The emulsion is a gelatin with tiny crystal of silver bromide which is spread on a transparent plate of glass or plastic material.

In the making of a hologram, a laser beam is split into two beams: an object beam, which is spread by a lens onto the subject; and a reference beam, which is directed onto the photographic plate. The object beam is reflected off the subject onto the photographic plate also. When the two sets of light waves from the two beams meet, they form an interference wavefront called a diffraction grating. It is this grating that

In the early 1920s, KDKA, the first radio broadcasting station, began operating in Pittsburgh. Some thirty years earlier, broadcasting started with the German Hertz's experiments proving the Englishman Maxwell's theory of electromagnetic waves. The Italian Marconi built the first transmitter and receiver and brought radio communications to all the ships at sea using the American Morse's code. In 1904, the Englishman John A. Fleming invented the diode vacuum tube for detecting radio waves. Two years later, the American Lee De Forest developed the

is recorded onto the plate. The plate is exposed for a length of time from one second to twenty minutes depending on the power of the laser, the emulsion sensitivity, and the subject's reflected light. It is then developed to wash away the silver, leaving the bromide crystals in an invisible pattern, noting the diffraction grating of the two beams of light.

To reconstruct the image, the plate must be illuminated by a bright source of light. The image can be viewed in two ways. When illumination of the plate is done from the original angle of the reference beam, the 3-D image appears within the plate in the identical position in which it was originally. This is called the *virtual image*. When the plate is illuminated from the back, a so-called *real image* appears in front of the plate. However, the image is a mirror reflection, back to front, with reverse perspective—the background elements are larger and those in the foreground are smaller. Such an image is referred to as *pseudoscopic*. To rectify the pseudoscopic effects of the image, a

FIG. 13-8. Holographic recording

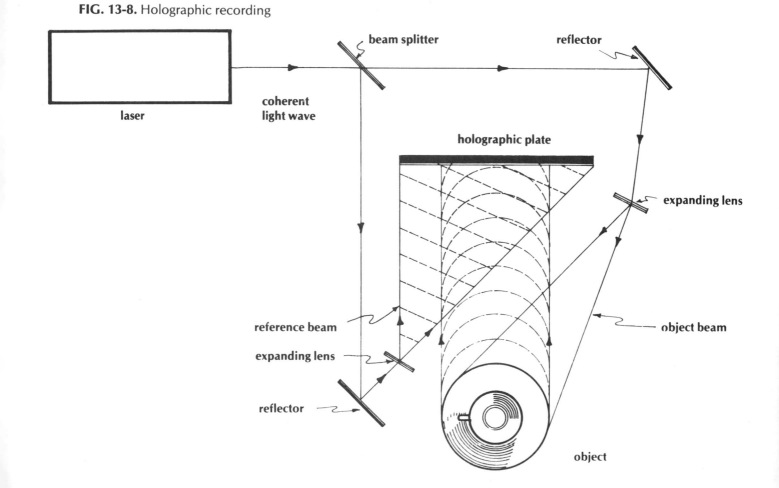

second hologram of it is made. This results in an image projected in front of the plate that is correctly oriented as to front and back and perspective. It is called an *orthoscopic image.*

By using a cylindrical plate or box made up of four plates, a subject can be recorded from all sides, resulting in an image of the entire subject viewable from all sides. Any number of holograms can be made on the same plate by slightly shifting the angle of the reference beam for each image. Holograms are primarily monochrome, but color is possible by the process of making three separate monochrome holograms (a red, a green, and a blue) and superimposing them. Integral holography is the process of making a moving hologram by using many photographic views of the same subject and then transferring them to holograms displayed in a cylindrical format. This is a means of overcoming the limits of direct holography to capture movement. In the process of making a hologram of a real subject, the slightest bit of movement during exposure wipes out the diffraction grating. The use of pulsed lasers, which project an instantaneous beam and thereby produce successive, instantaneous diffraction gratings, are capable of capturing changing light patterns or movement, but they require high power to help make up for the shorter exposure time.

FIG. 13-9. Jim Baker, chief engineer at WABC-TV

triode vacuum tube, which provided the means for blending signals with waves for transmission. De Forest made an attempt at broadcasting in 1910 when he set up a transmitter at the Metropolitan Opera for a performance of *Tosca* with Caruso. Few could listen to it for lack of receivers and very poor fidelity. In the next decade, the American Edwin Armstrong gave us the continuous wave oscillator, so that radio could speak, and what have become basic to all electronic communications we know today, the superheterodyne circuit—a means for amplifying and distinguishing even the weakest of signals detected at the receiver.

The development of broadcast television, the free-air transmission of pictures, took place in 1922 and is credited to the American Philo T. Farnsworth. AT&T was into the act about five years later with the first closed-circuit (by wire) transmission, which hooked up NYC and Washington, D.C. This led to AT&T's development of coaxial cable, the wire required for carrying TV signals. The General Electric Company was right there in 1928 with its own in-plant TV broadcasting. In 1930, G.E., RCA, and Westinghouse pooled their best talents in an effort to make television viable and lucrative. At the 1939 World's Fair in New York, TV got its public debut, but it was another decade before it became the infant of its present self.

Since the late 1940s, TV technology has grown to include multicamera switching, long-distance hookups, video tape recording, color TV, worldwide satellite transmission, portable equipment for electronic news production, instant replay, slow motion, and computerization of switching, signal processing for quality enhancement, editing, electronic image making, and automated program transmission. The impact of technology can be clearly seen in the ever-changing resources of the television maker. Keeping up with the state of the art, if not ahead of it, is the name of the game.

WABC-TV's Chief Engineer Jim Baker, in a fall 1978 interview, stated the bottom line: "Any equipment that saves me money or gives me new flexibility or enhances production, we go for it. Go back a few years and let's talk about color slow-motion equipment. CBS had it first in black-and-white. So we went to Ampex and for so many months of exclusive use, we paid for development of a color system. It attracts viewers.'' ABC, NBC with its parent company RCA, and CBS all maintain engineering staffs that keep close watch on new products, work with vendors to develop needed products, and do their own product development.

Electronic news operations clearly have displaced film in the news gathering area just within the decade of the 1970s. Until 1974, WABC was an all-film news operation. Electronic news has its roots in the 1960s, when the Japanese electronics industry introduced hand-held, low-cost, b/w video tape recording equipment for the nonbroadcast producer. The ''portapak,'' as it was called, was picked up by educators, psychologists, sociologists, artists, and an antiestablishment, alternate-media youth population that took it to the streets with a flamboyance and intimacy unseen in professional TV work.

In the early 1970s, looking for a way to cut costs of news film productions, CBS began to experiment with the substandard technology and eventually developed a more suitable line of equipment with a Japanese camera maker and an American tape recorder manufacturer. However, its choice of recorder, utilizing video tape of 1-inch width, did not allow the over-the-shoulder portability of the

FIG. 13-10. At WABC-TV, two-inch recorders are a production mainstay, earmarked for obsolescence in the face of newer, small-format video systems.

FIG. 13-11. WABC-TV's ''Eyewitness News'' studio during a quiet hour

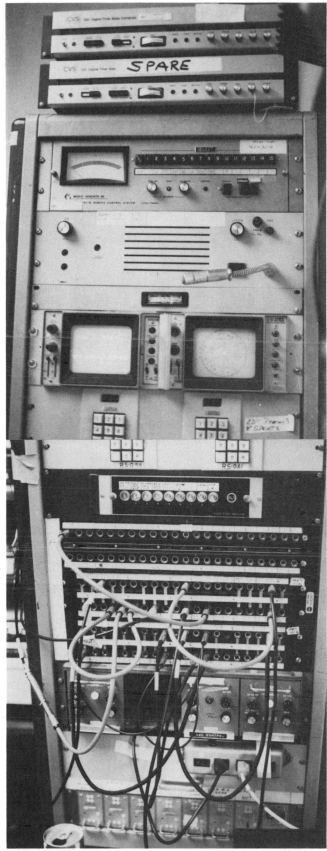

FIG. 13-12. A rack of video-tape editing equipment used in the editing room

portapak with its ½-inch video tape. Soon after, Sony introduced the ¾-inch video cassette recorder, which by the mid-1970s gained wide use for location work in all areas of production, for station, independent, and ad producers alike. The time-base corrector (TBC) came out about the same time, ensuring the success of the ¾-inch format; with a TBC you could transfer up to the industry-standard 2-inch tape machines. The time-base corrector eliminates substandard signal elements inherent in the smaller-format recording. Though the TBC could have, and on occasion has, permitted the use of ½-inch recording for broadcast, mechanical problems have worked against the broad use of ½-inch equipment. Newly developed ½-inch cassette, not reel-to-reel, recorders were introduced in the late 1970s, again, to the consumer market. Some smaller city stations are using such equipment in their news gathering operations.

The need for electronic news portability and maintenance of high signal standards for broadcasting has brought into being several major pieces of equipment that use computer circuitry. In addition to lower cost and improved TBCs, noise reducers that separate the signal from the background noise and increase the signal-to-noise ratio have become necessities in the postproduction processes of editing and airing.

Video tape editing is a process of electronically transferring selected images and sound from an original recording to another tape, the program master. In comparison to film, tape is not physically cut, nor can one see the images by holding a strip of tape up to the light. Those features in film editing make it a direct and tangible process. With tape, on the other hand, a recorder and TV monitor must be used to see an image. In the early 1970s, the Society of Motion Picture and Television Engineers (SMPTE) established a video tape time-code standard that brought together a number of different systems for location coding of images on tape. With a time code, you could review tapes, log precise locations of material, prepare an edit scenario on paper, give it to an operator of a computerized editing system, and sit back and watch it be put together. Referred to as "on-line" in editing parlance, it became widely used in the late 1970s at TV stations and independent TV labs.

FIG. 13-13. The editing system for electronic news gathering (ENG) operations consists of two ³/₄-inch video cassette recorders interconnected through a rack of equipment for processing picture and sound as they are transferred from original material to edited program.

"Off-line" editing, referring to the use of nonautomated editing systems, also began to employ edit controllers that offered limited programming capabilities. Much so-called rough editing is done off-line prior to commitment to on-line processing.

"The thing we're seeing now is our movement from analog to digital," Baker pointed out. The TBC was an early digital processing device. Its job is to make the duration of each time segment of picture information the same. This can be better accomplished handling signals as precise numbers than handling them as changing levels of electricity. "Frame synchronizers are digital devices. They take a signal from a foreign source and delay it until it's in time with a studio camera so you can mix the two, or however many, without problems," Baker explained. "Once it's in digital form, you can do anything with a signal, change its size, locate it anywhere in the picture area, flip it around, anything. We get better-quality signals by handling them digitally; the signal is there and nothing can distort it. It's only a matter of time, after the old technology is paid for, until we'll have digital tape storage."

The 1980s will see the demise of 2-inch video tape. In the late 1970s, SMPTE established a new 1-inch tape format standard that met and exceeded the older 2-inch technology standards. Paul Rossi, an engineer at WOR-TV in New York, indicated in the summer of 1979 that in another couple of years WOR would be all 1-inch, doing away with the smaller ³/₄-inch and older 2-inch machinery. The indication was that there's another generation of analog recording devices to come before digital recording.

Jim Baker explained the financial considerations of technological change as he described how the job of chief engineer has changed over the years: "My job has changed from being a technical chief to a financial and management function. Somebody in the technical side has to provide information in terms of budget and capital planning in the technical area. It started years back that broadcasting was a technical activity. Then programming people took over, followed by sales people. Now it's financial people, and the bottom line is profit. Financial controls are tighter. Most broadcast operations have gone into five- or ten-year plans for the tax benefits like credits and equipment depreciation, all the things that can affect the bottom line. Today, the capital plan is for seven years' depreciation on, for instance, a TBC. But there's no way we'll make seven years. It may certainly work that long, but new technologies will have us putting it on the shelf a lot sooner. The first equipment we bought for our electronic news in 1975 is now only used for backup."

Broadcasting in the United States is considered a local service compared with the national broadcasting services of Canada, England, and most other countries. Though the major networks approximate national coverage, broadcasting is under local station control. For example, ABC only owns New York, Detroit, Los Angeles, Chicago, and San Francisco stations. About another 190 locally controlled stations throughout the United States are affiliates. Efforts by nonnetwork programmers to gain access to national audiences were initiated in the 1970s through cable TV and satellite. Home Box Office (HBO), the nationally available pay TV entertainment cable channel, approximates a national network. Other specialized programming services offering sports, news, movies, and other programs distributed nationally using satellite and cable TV also are becoming national. Some independent VHF and UHF TV stations in New York, in Atlanta, and on the West Coast add national figures to their local ratings by using satellite and cable TV to get into homes around the country far beyond the reach of their local broadcast capability.

"We are restricted by the FCC from doing it that way. We have our national reach through our affiliates," Baker pointed out. "If Home Box Office could get three dollars per month throughout the U.S., it could outbid us on every major event, and that could really change things." On the other hand, the use of satellite for distributing syndicated programs to TV stations was introduced in March 1979, when RCA Americom, the domestic satellite division of the company that fifty years earlier had pioneered broadcasting with its creation of NBC, offered to put satellite receiving dishes at all 725 commercial TV stations in the United States at its own expense. The system was proposed as an alternative to conventional means of sending packaged programs to stations, which included the mails and air freight.

Looking to the future, Baker listed broader use of digital technology in transmission, the use of fiber optics to accommodate the larger bandwidths that digital signals require, and the use of the vertical interval part of the composite TV signal for carrying other information for display on the screen. "Digital transmission directly to the home could substantially improve picture quality, but it would make present home receivers obsolete. We would like to improve our 525-line system and our color standard also. The networks could afford it, but, for the public, in terms of receivers, it would be costly. The vertical interval reference (VIR) could be used for bilingual programming or stereo sound. We've encoded it with weather information, information for the hearing impaired, teletext display, all kinds of things. A decoder at the receiver would allow the viewer to receive all kinds of additional information at the same time we're transmitting a program. The FCC does not allow us to use the vertical interval at this time. We'd be in competition with AT&T. We're a protected monopoly, like the phone company."

During a tour of the electronic news operations, Baker summed up the situation of the syndrome to keep up technologically when he described an old b/w portable camera as his "save your ass" camera. "If it was the only camera you had, it would save your ass. If everybody is there covering an event and you don't have the best color, you're no good. If you are the only one there with black and white, you're the winner."

Technology Times

Telefutures

Given the complexity of the world we've inherited and continue to shape for ourselves, it's natural to telecommunicate. Surely the future will bring us new technologies to broaden and enhance human telecommunications. Full-spectrum, multidimensional telesensing will eventually emerge out of our further comprehension and application of the laws of energy conversion.

Right now (as of 1982), in shiny white-tiled, stainless steel laboratories around the globe, a new generation of Bells and Edisons, Marconis and Farnsworths, are on the move to create the unimagined technologies of tomorrow, today. In a recent report in *Popular Science,* prototype telesmell and teletouch devices were featured in the journal's "Telestory" section.

Working in an old factory in Massachusetts, a group of laid-off perfume chemists calling themselves "Scent Chemi" developed the chemisensor. The device is a 5-inch-square plastic circuit board with 100 ½-inch by ½-inch squares arranged in a 10 × 10 grid. Each square is doped with a compound that has demonstrated what the group calls "chemosympathy" to one of the basic elements. For example, the compound that is chemisympathetic to fluorine gives off an electric charge when fluorine is within 1 centimeter of the compound. The greater the amount of fluorine, the higher the electric charge. Each quadrant of the grid contains a compound that is chemosympathetic to one particular element. The 10 × 10 array permits chemosensing of almost all the basic elements. Since smells are composed of minute particles of matter suspended in the air and detected by nerve sensors in the tissues of the nose, the chemisensor is designed to detect all the basic elements in their proper proportion that make up matter floating in the air around it.

The electrical signals from each chemosympathetically activated quadrant of the sensor are frequency-modulated (FM) and transmitted to a receiver, another chemisensor, which reverses the process. The chemists demonstrated that when an amount of the same compound used to sense a particular element is electrically stimulated, it gives off traces of that element in amounts corresponding to that of the electrical stimulation charge. The bigger the charge, the bigger the release. Signals are transmitted with grid location codes to ensure that each signal from the transmitter is fed to the appropriate quadrant in the receiver. A fan is built into the enclosure, in which the chemisensor fits with the required amplifiers and modulator/demodulators for transmission and reception. When in the sending mode, the fan sucks air toward the sensor; when in the receiving mode, the fan blows air through the grid into the environment to amplify the release of the elements. The day is coming soon when the springtime smells of the Champs Elysées can be breathed in living rooms throughout the world.

Less developed, but promising, is the "handulator," designed for use with the telephone. A first step toward teletouch, the handulator is a remotely operated, soft rubber robotic hand, which the touchee holds and places as instructed by the toucher. The toucher wears a glove knitted of circuits interwoven into a plastic yarn. As the inserted hand moves, circuits are squeezed together or stretched apart, which changes the resistance between them. The output

FIG. 13-14. Chemisensor odor transmitter/receiver

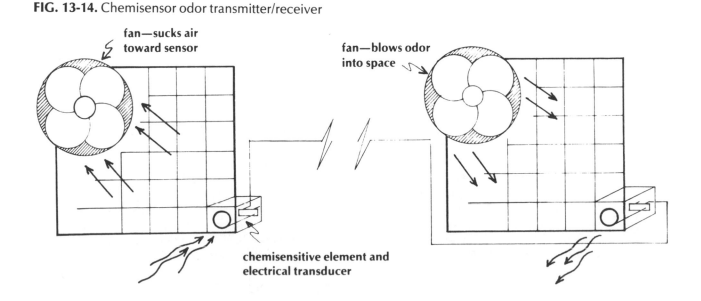

fan—sucks air toward sensor

fan—blows odor into space

chemisensitive element and electrical transducer

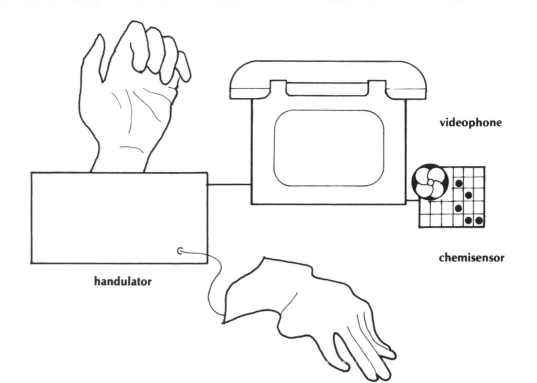

videophone

chemisensor

handulator

signal includes a coding of the location of each of the almost half a million circuits, as well as its resistance. The signal is amplitude-modulated (AM) and multiplexed with the telephone signal. When fed to the handulator receiver (the robotic hand), the toucher's movements are replicated.

Its Viennese inventor, Hans Zupped, envisions the handulator being widely used with videophone to give people sight, sound, and touch contact over great distance. In Zupped's words, "It's a big hand for us shy types, and a little push for mankind." Just another indicator that the drive to telecommunicate is irrepressible.

Glossary:
Telecommunications

Digital communications is the transmission of information—letters and numbers, voice, facsimile, video—by coding it into discrete on/off electronic signals, as differentiated from analog transmission, in which a signal is a measure in time of a continuous flow of electricity.

Data communications is the digital transmission of letters, numbers, words, and text. The term distinguishes data from voice and image transmissions. Data communica-

tions services are provided by communications utilities using worldwide or limited networks of copper wire and/or fiber optic lines and land-based and satellite microwave transmission.

Facsimile (or fax) is the transmission of a page of information, a printed or handwritten page or image. Facsimile transmission rates run between about five minutes and less than a minute per page (as of 1981).

Voice communications is the transmission of sound in the human hearing range. Voice or audio, sound in general, can be transmitted either as analog or digital signals.

Video communications is the transmission of images not limited to the page, as with facsimile. Slow-scan TV is a form of video communications for transmitting still images. Video can be transmitted, like voice, either digitally or by analog signals.

Optical communications is the use of light for transmitting digitally encoded information. Optical fibers and lasers make up a technology that offers the maximum transmitting capacity using devices that occupy little physical space.

Teletext is the use of a portion of a transmitted video signal for simultaneous transmission of other information in text form. A segment of the TV signal does not carry actual picture information; thus, it can carry data that can be displayed on a TV receiver with an appropriate decoder.

Electronic mail or **electronic message system** (EMS) refers to the electronic creation, transmission, and reception of messages. The computer is the "post office" for electronic mail. Terminals connected by telecommunications lines are the "mailboxes" and delivery agents. When a message is sent, the recipient is electronically signaled and can "open the mail" when time allows and electronically answer it.

Electronic funds tranfer (EFT) is to banking what electronic mail is to postal correspondence. Predecessors of total electronic banking came into wide use in the late 1970s; for example, electronic cash registers or point-of-sale terminals, automatic bank tellers, and electronic clearinghouse systems like those employed to electronically deliver a government check to its recipient's bank account.

Teleprocessing is the use of telecommunication networks to connect geographically separated terminals with centralized processing resources. "Teleprocessors" might someday replace telephones and provide voice, image, and data communications over telecommunications lines made of fiber optics.

Telemedicine is the use of telecommunications, particularly television, for transmitting medical data, such as x-rays or live images of a patient, to a distantly located specialist for consultation.

Teleconferencing is the use of telecommunications for conducting an "electronic meeting" among people at distant locations. Considered an alternative to travel and face-to-face meetings, a teleconference is conducted with two-way audio, video, and, as required, data and facsimile transmission.

Telemetry is the transmission of data derived from instruments measuring changing conditions (e.g., of gases, pressure, or temperature) in the environment or in machines. These data are often used for control operations of other machines, as in weapons guidance control, automated utility meter reading, stationhouse-connected fire and burglary alarms.

Cable television is the connection of private homes to a community antenna system primarily for better reception of TV pictures. Cable TV hookups are made with coaxial cable that can accommodate more information than telephone line wire pairs. Cable TV, also called *broadband communications,* which can provide for two-way communications, is considered to be the telecommunications plant of the future for home information needs.

Satellite communications is the use of space-orbited microwave relays or transponders for transmitting information around the globe. Direct home or office reception of satellite-transmitted information is only in limited use (as of 1981) owing to expense, regulatory restrictions, and possible health hazards.

PART III

AUTOMATIC INFORMATION PROCESSING

THE motivation for developing information processing machines, since the beginning of recorded time, has been to limit the drudgery of the long and tedious work involved in calculation. We are natural-born counters wanting to be precise in a world in which precision is a stepchild. With numbers as our language we observe dimensions, quantities, movements, time, etc., creating the frameworks of science. The seventeenth-century German mathematician Gottfried Leibniz put it this way: "It is unworthy of excellent men to lose hours like slaves in the labor of calculation." Not only excellent men, but men of all qualities and women, too, generally seem to display disdain for the "labor of calculation."

The abacus might be considered the oldest known technological aid for calculation. Formed out of seventy beads strung on ten stretched wires with a capacity to signify values in the billions, the abacus is today still used for addition, subtraction, multiplication, and division with surprising swiftness. In a competition held in the mid-1940s between an abacus and an electric calculator, each in the hands of a skilled operator, the abacus proved faster on all accounts.

Mechanized calculation was invented in 1642 by Blaise Pascal, who was then nineteen years old, as an aid to ease his father's accounting tasks. The Pascal calculator was operated by the use of a stylus to turn wheels inscribed with the numbers 0 to 9. The device could be used for addition and subtraction. Later in the century, Leibniz invented his wheel-based calculator for multiplication, division, and calculation of roots.

The next big step in the pursuit to ease the labor of calculation occurred in the early 1800s. The Englishman Charles Babbage designed his "Difference Engine" for the calculation of mathematical tables, which, since the 1600s, had become an important aspect of the work of scientists and mathematicians. Babbage went on to design his "Analytical Engine,"

FIG. III-1. Pascal's calculator (Courtesy of IBM Corp.)

FIG. III-2. Leibniz's calculator (Courtesy of IBM Corp.)

for which he is considered the father of contemporary electronic computers. Though never totally built because production methods required for some of its parts were lacking, the Analytical Engine contained within its design all the elements of a modern information processing system: an input section for entering data; a memory or storage section for holding the data to be processed; an arithmetic unit for processing; and an output section for printing out results. The machine was also to have used punched cards encoded with a planned program of instructions. Punched cards had been developed in the late 1700s and were successfully used by the Frenchman Joseph-Marie Jacquard for the automatic control of weaving looms. The daughter of the English poet Lord Byron, Augusta Byron (Lady Lovelace), a mathematician working with Babbage, might be considered the mother of contemporary computer programming, for it was she who devised the binary mathematics out of

FIG. III-3. IBM replica of Babbage's Difference Engine (Courtesy of IBM Corp.)

which George Boole created his algebra, upon which logic switching in electronic computers is based.

From this point on, American ingenuity dominates the pursuit. Around the end of the nineteenth century, the U.S. Census Bureau was discovering that the data collected every ten years were beginning to take almost that long to tabulate. In response to the problem, Herman Hollerith, a statistician, developed a format for using punched cards into which information could be coded during collection in the field. After completion the cards were sent to the bureau, where they were run through a machine Hollerith had designed for tabulating data. A hole in a card completed an electrical circuit, which advanced a counter. A counter kept an accumulated total of each type of data, such as age and sex, as successive cards were fed into the machine. Hollerith's success led him to form the Tabulating Machine Company, which became the International Business Machine (IBM) Corporation in 1924. In the 1940s, after years of development and use of punched-card technology, electronics, via the vacuum tube, was introduced into automatic data processing, resulting in the exponential expansion of calculation by machine.

No single inventor can be identified as the person most responsible for the development of electronic information processing. In 1937, a Harvard physics graduate student, Howard Aiken, conceived plans for a machine to solve differential equations. IBM aided him, and they completed the Automatic Sequence Controlled Calculator in 1944. The device used electromechanical relays and could do addition and subtraction of twenty-three-digit numbers in three-tenths of a second and multiply such figures in six seconds. Also in the late 1930s, a professor at Iowa State College, John Atanasoff, conceived plans for an electronic digital computer. In 1946, it was completed by J. Presper Eckert, a student at the University of Pennsylvania, and John W. Mauchly, a

FIG. III-4. Hollerith's tabulating machine (Courtesy of IBM Corp.)

FIG. III-5. The first generation of IBM computers: (a) Mark I and (b) the 1401 (Courtesy of IBM Corp.)

physicist at the school. The Electronic Numerical Integrator and Calculator (ENIAC) was built for the U.S. Army for ballistic firing tables. It was composed of vacuum tubes and no mechanical parts. Tube failure rates were high and the device lacked a way of storing instructions, thus requiring time-consuming manipulations of circuits externally for changing programs.

In 1946, at Princeton's Institute for Advanced Studies, von Neumann, Goldstine, and Burks put in writing the first comprehensive description of the organization and operation of a digital computer in which the program of instruction was stored within the machine. Two major breakthroughs are credited to the design of what is called the "von Neumann machine": (1) storing of the program instructions in the computer's memory along with data, the instructions being number codes to trigger the appropriate circuits to perform specific functions; and (2) encoding of data and instructions in binary form made up of only two elements, which would be compatible with computer circuits, which are either "on" or "off." The Electronic Discrete Variable Automatic Computer (EDVAC), the first von Neumann machine, was built in 1950 and was the first electronic digital computer of the first generation of computers as we know them today. Sometime in the mid-1950s, magnetic cores replaced vacuum tubes in the memory sections of computers. But it was not until 1959 and the development of transistors that vacuum tubes in the central processing unit (CPU) were displaced. With the advent of transistors, the second generation of computers became available in the early 1960s. During the 1960s, development of microelectronics took place and the integrated circuit displaced the single transistor, which brought the third generation of computers in the mid-1960s.

The development of the successive generations of digital computer technology has brought increased data capacity, processing complexity, and speed. The turning over of the labor of calculation to the subatomic world of electrons began the current age of information processing, which Pascal and Leibniz would have hailed as the technological coming of the Age of Reason where machines of logic are accessible to humanity in its pursuit of knowledge.

The speed of punched-card tabulation was one addition per second. The earliest of the first-generation computers could perform ten additions per second. EDVAC performed one addition in a few milliseconds. And UNIVAC, a computer built in 1951 for the Census Bureau, did an add operation in a couple of microseconds. Second-generation equipment was considerably reduced in size from the room-filling mammoths of the preceding generation. Speeds dropped well into the microsecond range for all operations of the computer. Third-generation speeds are in terms of nanoseconds (billionths of a second) and picoseconds (trillionths). Starting with the second generation of computers, peripheral equipment, such as data entry and display devices, keyboards, printers, and CRTs, began to be improved and has been carried into the third generation. Another third-generation improvement is referred to as "modularity." Present-generation computers can be increased in capacity and speed by the simple addition of hardware elements or modules to the basic ma-

FIG. III-6. ENIAC, c. 1946. Manual manipulation of circuits was required for the programming of this early computer. (Courtesy of Sperry Univac, div. of Sperry Corp.)

FIG. III-7. UNIVAC I. Walter Cronkite *(far right)* was shown "the way it was" at the dawn of the Information Age. (Courtesy of Sperry Univac, div. of Sperry Corp.)

Technology Times

Computerized Dispatch in the World's Busiest Firefighting City

Before computers, firefighters in Brooklyn were dispatched to a fire by means of an assembly line of steps that involved a phone, an alarm box receiving board, address books, a conveyer belt, an assignment listing index, a chit board, a two-way radio, and some nine dispatch workers.

In the "manual" system, a fire ticket was written up upon receipt of a call by telephone or alarm box signal. The receiving dispatcher would look up the location and jot down the closest intersection and alarm box. The fire ticket would then be carried by conveyer belt to the decision dispatcher, who would check the assignment index for firehouses in the area and note the assignable units from the chit board, which kept track of who was where. The information would be given to

chines. There is no need to discard old and buy new, within certain limits. The most distinctive capability of third-generation computers is that, at their speeds, a single processor can concurrently handle several tasks. In a manner of speaking, "calculation labor" machines have grown beyond single problem needs to become problem-solving gluttons snorting at the bits for more data and programs.

Fourth-generation computers have yet (as of 1982) to appear. Speeds will surely increase. Voice communications between users and processors is under development. *Firmware* or microcode—preprogrammed instructions stored on, for example, disks and fed into the computer's program memory—will be more widely available for all kinds of applications. The evolution of *software*, or programming of computers, has been along a path away from so-called "low-level" machine language (binary code) toward "high-level" program languages using natural language. Fourth-generation systems will surely produce advances in the area of human and machine interfacing with simplified programming methodologies.

However sophisticated they become, automatic information processors are simply machines for han-

FIG. III-8. A complete microcomputer system with disk storage, printer, and modem for data communications (Courtesy of Apple Computer, Inc.)

FIG. III-9. A microcomputer circuit board with digital I/O capabilities (Courtesy of National Semiconductor Corp.)

FIG. III-10. An electronic test editing typewriter—a so-called "intelligent" typewriter—with diskette storage (Courtesy of Adler-Royal Business Machines, Inc.)

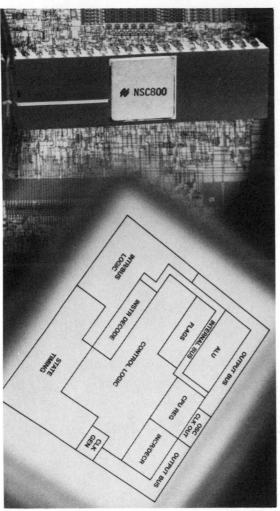

FIG. III-11. Microprocessor chip (Courtesy of National Semiconductor Corp.)

FIG. III-12. A computer without I/O peripherals that uses an integral hard disk storage system (Courtesy of Cromemco, Inc.)

FIG. III-13. A business computer system made up of *(left to right)* a printer, diskette storage, and CRT/keyboard I/O terminal (Courtesy of Royal Business Machines, Inc.)

FIG. III-14. The IBM System 34, a small business computer system (Courtesy of IBM Corp.)

the radio dispatcher, who would announce the call, which would be picked up by the radio operator at the firehouse, who would write it down—and off they would go. All this would take about two minutes. That was before 1978, when the computer came to dispatching in Brooklyn.

Brooklyn's firefighting resources are part of the New York Fire Department. In a city of worldwide distinctions, its borough of Brooklyn has the dubious distinction of being the world's busiest firefighting city. Russell Ramsey, Brooklyn's chief fire alarm dispatcher, with the department since 1956, had some apprehension about computerized

dling the labor of calculation. However fast, capable of concurrent processing, and versatile they become, they are not thinking machines. They cannot intuit or emote or be consciously creative. For performing the logic-based operations that are a significant function of our thinking, computers are proving to be invaluable sidekicks. Without logic or systems of operation, ideas could not be realized; the imagined bridge could not be built, the dreamed flight into space could not be undertaken, the expressed music could not be written and performed. The computer is a tool for shaping, managing, and enhancing our lives and our world. It is to our intellectual capacity as the motor is to our physical capacity.

FIG. III-15. Joe Friedman explaining features of the dispatch system he helped develop

FIG. III-16. A dispatcher at the computerized workstation provided with fingertip access to the information and resources he needs to answer an alarm

dispatch when it was first introduced. In a fall 1978 interview, he said, "I thought automation would cut jobs. Actually because the computer requires data be fed it, we have an additional person on staff."

Ramsey described his earlier familiarity with computers as limited to "paying bills." His "brain was picked" by the computer people for program design in the various phases of development. Ramsey sees "100 percent change" in dispatching since the computer assumed the work that previously "left dispatchers physically and mentally exhausted at the end of a shift."

Billy LaDelle, a liaison dispatcher, described the computer as necessary for handling the volume of alarms, which outgrew manual operations. Some half-million alarms yearly are received, some 200,000 of them false. At a cost of about a half million dollars, the computer dispatch system has cut alarm processing time from two minutes to forty seconds or less.

When a call comes in by phone, the information is fed into the computer, which instantaneously displays the required additional information, such as cross streets and area firehouses. The computer will report an incorrect address, alerting the receiving dispatcher to obtain further information from the caller. "The computer can be used for a phonetic search," explained programmer Joe Friedman of the Fire Department's Computer Services, who is assigned to the Brooklyn dispatch center and who worked on the development of the system. "The computer can supply up to eight alternates of sounds—for example, Kosciusko: Kosgusho, Kosioshko, etc.—which helps in making out a garbled location."

The alarm boxes are fed directly into the computer. With the Emergency Reporting System (ERS), the voice contact alarm boxes, the dispatcher intercedes and must converse with a caller before a full response is executed. If no response is forthcoming, the alarm is considered false; however, a single piece of equipment is dispatched to the site. The Box Alarm Readout System (BARS) gives off an electromechanical signal and is handled by the computer with a full response of four pieces of equipment.

The firehouses now have teleprinters that provide a printout of the information. "In the past," explained LaDelle, "a radio operator at the station had to listen to all calls and write down his own. Today, a printout only appears at the station it's sent to, and it's all there on paper ready to be torn off and taken." Attempts are made to give as much detailed information as possible on the printout, such as, "smoke on the thirteenth floor, street address between such and such streets, phone number of the site of the fire."

The computer has automated the paperwork of periodical reporting. What once took two to three hours of daily work to compile is now accomplished in minutes. Statistical studies are performed monthly from the daily reports. "We can see," said Friedman, "in particular time frames what has been happening, like midnight activity in false alarms."

The computer is programmed to display maps of sites with equipment inventories, unit status, and so on. A decision dispatcher uses two terminals to track activity in the field. As required, voice contact can be made with units at stations, en route, and at the site of a fire. "It's in the long-range plan," Ramsey reported, "to do inventory-type services like TIPS (Tactical Information about Perilous Situations) for industrial and high-rise buildings." In Kansas City, as early as 1977, the computer was providing dispatchers access to compiled information to pass on to firefighting units in the field about dangerous animals at the site, or invalid people and their room of occupancy, noxious chemical storage areas, a victim's doctor and preferred hospital, and so on.

The New York system, to be operational citywide by the early 1980s, is one of many newly installed computerized dispatch systems in the United States. Because of the area's high volume of alarms, the Brooklyn system has been a model for major cities throughout the world.

14
Analog and Digital

Analog and digital are the two methods by which we represent data in machines. The term *analog* refers to maintaining a likeness; for example, a varying electrical signal in a phone line is a likeness of the varying sound pressure waves spoken into the mouthpiece. Analog computers process analog data, such as in production processes where, for example, heat is used (oil and steel refining) and wherever data are in the form of physical values (temperature, voltage, pressure, etc.) and analog-to-digital conversion is time-consuming or uneconomical. The term *digital* refers to the numerical representation of data, a form into which any data can be put or encoded. Digital computers are the computing machines that have evolved since humans began to count and use numbers to represent things, such as baskets of grain, heights of mountains, or lengths of lives. The digital computer is the primary tool of automatic information processing.

15
Data Processing Cycle

Data are processed in a series of steps referred to, in the industry, as the data processing (DP) cycle, a sequence of actions that has accompanied information processing at least since Pascal's father sat down to use his son's calculator to put his accounts in order. The data he (1) *collected* were the figures representing the expenditures and receipts he had incurred over a given period which he wanted to update. The (2) *conversion of data to machine-readable form* was accomplished in his use of the stylus to set the dials on the calculator as he entered successive figures, taking great care to (3) *check* that his entries were correct. The elder Pascal needed to add and subtract numbers representing transactions to let him know what resources were available for new transactions. He set dials that rotated wheels that moved gears that rotated adjacent wheels that moved more gears and dials, (4) *manipulating the data* and (5) *displaying* its sums and differences. He then (6) *stored* his results by writing them into his books for future reference.

Except for collecting and checking or verifying data, the steps of the DP cycle are a reflection of the functions of the major sections of a computing system and are performed automatically. Collection and verification are the human tasks and the areas in which most information processing errors occur. Having the appropriate data for the problem to be solved and ensuring that they are entered correctly are prerequisites for the useful application of automatic information processors.

16
Processing Methods

With automatic information processing systems, you can either "drop off" the job (computer-ready data and program) and "pick it up later" or "do it yourself." *Batch processing* refers to the "drop off, pick up later" method associated with large computer centers. In such cases, a job is loaded into the computer and run through to completion without operator intervention. Batching grew out of the use and procedures related to Hollerith punched cards. All data had to be coded onto the cards before tabulation. A stack of cards was loaded into a tabulating machine, and card by card the information was processed until the stack was depleted. Batch processing is most suitable and widely used for jobs performed on a regular basis, such as monthly billing, and for which the data are readily accessible in machine form, such as customer records maintained on magnetic disk files or punched cards.

The "do it yourself" method entails being *on-line* or *interactive* with the computer by way of a data entry device (e.g., a keyboard) and output device (e.g., video display terminal [VDT]) for step-by-step display of commands and results. In this way, user and machine converse in a high-level computer language to get the job done. An application of an on-line, interactive, or real-time system is word processing, by which a user can edit the text of a newsletter and prepare its pages for output to a printing device.

Time sharing is a notable feature of interactive processing that permits a number of users working at their own input/output stations hooked into a large computer to simultaneously work on their own jobs. The speed of the computer is so great that, between the time an amount of data is processed and more data for the same problem are retrieved from memory for further processing, the computer can work on data from other jobs. Each user is attended to in revolving succession of time at a rate at which, most often, a user experiences no delays in getting the work done.

17

Components of Processors

A computer system is made up of four major sections along the lines Babbage indicated in the 1800s: (1) the *input* section for entering data, making it machine-readable; (2) the *central processing unit* (CPU or mainframe) composed of *memory* for holding data in-process (operand) and instructions for processing, an *arithmetic/logic unit* (ALU), and a *control unit* (CU); (3) the *output* section for display of results; and (4) the storage section or *external storage devices* for holding results and/or other data in machine-readable form for future processing and/or later display.

No matter what size the computer is, it must have input and output sections and a CPU. A computer can do its work without external storage capability; however, its addition provides for processing of more data than that which can be maintained in the CPU's memory. The ALU, the "brain" of the system, performs the calculation or manipulation of data, such as add, divide, shift left or right, on the data that is received from memory. The CU, or "nerve center," directs traffic throughout the system and itself receives from memory the stored instructions to enable it to keep all the components working together.

18

Sizes of Systems

In the beginning, there was ENIAC that begat EDVAC that begat UNIVAC and, thus, the computer begat evolutions of itself. As generation succeeded generation, new families emerged to fulfill the potentials of new technology and to meet the needs of the times. In 1981, five families of electronic information processors are available: large mainframe computers or *maxicomputers;* medium-size or *midicomputers;* small business or *minicomputers;* personal or *microcomputers;* and *microprocessors,* which are tiny computer circuits without input and output sections.

For describing each family of computer here, ten major parameters are considered:

1. Expressed in amount of letters and/or numbers is the size of the central processing unit's memory, which holds processible data together with processing instructions that are sent to the arithmetic/logic unit and control unit, respectively, for execution.

2. The flow of data/instructions from memory to ALU and CU is along a path so many binary digits (bits) wide depending on the size of the computer.

3. In the computer, data are in the form of binary notations made up of so many bits, commonly in groups of 4, 8, 16, 32. A group of bits is called a *word.* The length of the word is the number of bits that can be handled by the CPU per processing step.

4. The time it takes for data/instructions to get from memory to ALU and CU affects the overall processing time of the computer.

5. The execution time is the time it takes the CU and ALU to carry out an instruction on data.

6. The computer is built with its logic circuits capable of being interconnected in different configurations to accomplish different functions, such as add, subtract, or shift left or right. The extent of processing circuit versatility is expressed in the number of instructions that the computer can be programmed to carry out.

7. Programming languages are used to tell the computer what is to be done. Some eight major pro-

Technology Times

A Revolution in the Information Age

Skimming the journals of the information-processing world and attending the computer industry's trade conferences of the late 1970s provided clear indication that a major revolution was under way in the computer industry and thus in the business world, its biggest marketplace. The dominance of the "Big Mother" computers, as a friend at IBM calls them, was being toppled by the decentralizing forces of mini- and microcomputers. The effect was a redistribution of information-processing power from centralized computer facilities to many locally based facilities. A further effect was the opening of access to the information flow.

Essential to this revolution had been the growth of miniaturization in electronics. A room-size machine of the 1940s had been replaced in the 1970s by a device no larger than a fingernail. In using electricity for information handling, the smallest devices give the highest speed and capacity. Computer technology has been on a course of ever smaller, smarter, and lower-cost components, and the end is not yet in sight.

One of the rallying cries of the revolution was "user orientation." Data processing professionals were no longer the exclusive operators of the tools. Managers, office clerks, bookkeepers, analysts, researchers, and

gramming languages are widely used, and a computer is designed to be programmed by one or more of these languages.

8. Computers, capable of a variety of processing methods, such as batch and interactive, must be of certain capacity levels and speeds and must have several channels for input and output devices.

9. Ready-made applications programs for many different jobs, which are common to many users, have been developed over the years. Their number and availability can expand or limit the ease of use of a computer system.

10. Costs (expressed in very round numbers) are the final major consideration.

The large computers are designed to hold in CPU memory the most data/instructions (over 8 million letters and/or numbers, which is equal to about 6,500 book pages), which are sent down the widest path (64 bits for carrying two 32-bit words) at the fastest rate of travel (about 500 nanoseconds) to the ALU and CU for the quickest execution per instruction time (about 50 nanoseconds). The large computers are built with about 150 instructions usable by all eight major programming languages. They batch process, multiprogram (handle many programs simultaneously), and have many channels for input/output devices for interactive processing and time sharing. Thousands of ready-made applications programs are available for use with them and their cost is in the millions.

For hundreds of thousands of dollars midicomputers are available with considerably reduced memory size (one-seventeenth the size of a large computer, or about 375 book pages), a memory-to-ALU/CU path one-quarter that of the maxis (16 bits wide), and a word length of 32 bits, equal to the large com-

Table 18.1. COMPUTER SIZES

Computer	Memory Size	Data Path Width	Word Length	Data Retrieval Time	Execution Time	Number of Instructions	Languages	Costs
Large computers	8 Million letters/ numbers	64 bits	two 32 bits	500 nano-seconds	50 nanoseconds	150	8	$1,000,000s
Midicomputers	0.5 million letters/ numbers	16 bits	32 bits	1000 nano-seconds	300 nanoseconds	140	8	$100,000s
Minicomputers	0.25 million letters/ numbers	16 bits	16 to 32 bits	1000 nano-seconds	300 nanoseconds	80	4	$10,000s
Personal computers	6,500 letters/ numbers	8 bits	8 to 16 bits	micro-seconds	microseconds	80	3	$1,000s
Microprocessors	—	—	4 to 16 bits	micro-seconds	microseconds	—	—	$10s

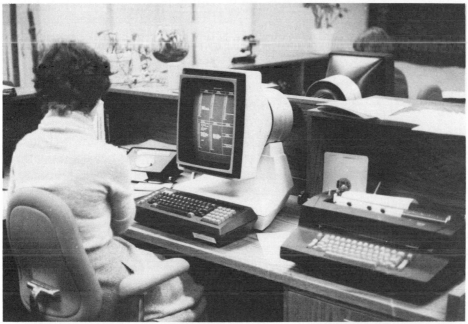

FIG. 18-1. Experimental offices of the future at Citicorp in New York City, 1979

others were sitting down at computer consoles and directly controlling the machines using simple, interactive, English-based languages. The development of programming languages clearly reflected a long-established trend toward user orientation. Many highly technical languages had been refined for the lay user, and that put programming at the fingertips of the nonprofessional many. The most recent developments have been toward a natural English, so users need only speak or type normally and the machines will obey.

The way computers were used to process information had also taken a turn toward optimizing user control. Batch processing, the early method (still in use), required that all data related to a problem be entered en masse. Processing was performed and results produced without intervention by an operator. With the advent of keyboard terminal access to computers, data entry could be made interactively, under the control of the operator according to his or her special requirements. With batch processing the work was done at a distant location. With interactive terminals the processing power was put at the desks of the workers.

The manner in which information was stored for processing had been traditionally file-like. Within an organization, each department's information was maintained separately, each with limited access. To obtain a picture of the total information of the organization, reports from each department were combined. Introduced in the 1970s, data bases offered a new approach for maintaining data: They organized the total information of a company into one comprehensive unit accessible for both specific and general data retrieval. Data bases became a new standard for organizing information.

Miniaturization, user orientation, simple computer languages, interactive entry and output facilities, data bases, and the means for interconnecting distant processing stations comprised what the industry began calling DDP—distributed data processing. A terminal at every desk, a computer for every office, and all offices interconnected had become the aim of computer manufacturers, dealers, and customers.

An IBM manufacturing expert, Mike Kutcher, compared the events of the late 1970s to the invention of the fractional horsepower motor during the early industrial revo-

puter. The travel time of data/instructions from memory to the ALU and CU is twice that of maxis (about 1,000 nanoseconds), and the per-instruction processing time is about 300 nanoseconds, which is six times as long as that of the maxis. The number of instructions in midicomputers is a little less than the large computers at 140, which are also usable by all eight major programming languages. The midis have only a few channels for input and output devices but are otherwise equal to maxis in processing method versatility and in availability and number of ready-made applications programs.

The minicomputers or small business computers have a memory size half that of the midis (fewer than 200 book pages); their data/instruction path is the same as midis (16 bits wide), but their word length could be reduced from 32 bits to 16 bits. Compared with midis, minicomputers are only a trifle slower in memory-to-ALU/CU travel time and execution of instruction, but they can handle only about eighty instructions usable by only four major programming languages. The minis can do multiprogramming with only two programs, and for time sharing they must be specially designed, or *dedicated*. They have only one channel for input/output devices, but can be built with an integrated telecommunications system for real-time processing. Note that telecommunications capabilities for large and medium-size computers are provided by separate systems interconnected with the computers. Ready-made programs for minis number in the hundreds, and minicomputer costs are in the tens of thousands of dollars.

The personal computers or microcomputers are the most limited in processing power and data capacity, having a word length of 8 bits, memory equal to about five book pages, and execution speeds in microseconds. Micros, like minis, handle about eighty instructions usable by only three major programming languages. They do not permit batch processing, multi-programming, or time sharing and have only a single channel for input/output devices. Ready-made applications programs are limited in number, but are under development. Microcomputers cost in the thousands of dollars.

At the heart or, more appropriately, the "head" of the microcomputer is the microprocessor, which is also used in automobiles, ovens, heating systems, and the like for single-task processing applications, such as controlling the on/off cycles of a heating system. Costing in the tens of dollars, microprocessors are most commonly designed with word lengths of 4, 8, and 16 bits and execution speeds in microseconds. The microprocessor is made up of a large-scale-integrated circuit that performs the function of the ALU and CU. In some cases, main memory is not included within the same integrated circuit or chip. The microprocessor in its largest dimensions is also used for minicomputer CPUs. As techniques of miniaturizing circuitry improve, the capacity and speed of microprocessors will increase and their use in electronic information processing machines at all levels will grow.

lution. The machines of the first factories of the early 1800s were driven with a jackshaft—a long shaft powered by a large engine. All manufacturing machines were connected by belts to the jackshaft and under the control of the central power source. With the advent of the small, individual motor came the splintering of the central factory. The impact of the small computer on "Big Mother" is analogous to the small motor on the jackshaft: decentralization, the result.

In the business world, the existence of an alternative to the headquartered, large computer facility began pitting regional site managers against central corporate executives over the question of control of information—the power for decision making. The ultimate changes that will accrue to business structures owing to redistribution of the information processing power are still indeterminable.

Issues like those raised in the 1960s around political decentralization began to emerge in the late 1970s in the business world. The revolution of a past decade had made its way into the technological environment, and on the corporate walls a new revolutionary type of graffiti appeared: "Viva DDP—*Democratize* Data Processing!"

19

Processing Applications

Since the days of Pascal and Leibniz, the "labor of calculation" has greatly expanded. Today's computers can perform numerous tasks, unimagined in the 1600s, for carrying on business and scientific research, operating government, maintaining the home. The capabilities of computers, regardless of size, are as follows.

Data organization. Data entered into a computer can be examined and subsequently recorded into one or more files as indicated by programmed instructions. For example, in processing a telephone order for an item in a store, the data are fed to both shipping and customer billing files. Properly stored and indexed data provide for easy access and quick retrieval, a benefit of data organization.

Data (and word) processing. Data, either numerical or textual, can be processed by the computer for calculation or text manipulation, such as sorting (putting data in order), clustering (grouping things of similar characteristics together), merging (combining of files), searching (finding an item in a file), and listing (linking items together). An important aspect of the processing capability is the potential for user/machine interaction in accessing files, input of new data, test calculations, new data, etc., in a series of inquiries and responses.

Generation of information. The output of results of computer processing can be thought of as "raw data turned into useful information," such as reports, letters, financial statements, customer bills, payroll checks, library search printouts, engineering drawings, and animated graphics on CRTs.

Government, business, and scientific institutions have been the primary users of computers. At first, only large organizations could afford the high costs of computers. As small-systems technology developed, new users and markets have emerged, producing new user classifications: small business, professional, and personal.

Small-business applications most often require minicomputer capacity; however, the personal microcomputer manufacturers have been developing systems to meet small-business needs. Like large businesses, small businesses regularly process accounting and financial information—for example, sales figures, costs, research and development, overhead and administrative expenses, inventories, available cash, investments, accounts payable and receivable, prepaid and accrued expenses, property, buildings, machines, taxes, debt, and so on. Business information is processed weekly, monthly, and so on, for production of needed financial statements, budgets, tax reports, and the like. The computer permits display of reports in any time frame, and present figures can be shown in comparison with a previous period's figures or with budgeted or forecast data.

Financial analyses can be made by comparing various data to determine inventory turnover, gross and net profit margins, return on investment, and other measures of business activity. Forecasting can be done by using projected data, such as anticipated sales figures or tax increases, to produce the usual statements and reports.

Most accounting and financial business needs are fulfilled by data organization, relatively simple processing, and a great amount of information generation—reports. The use of a computer, whatever its size and cost, is justifiable when the volume of business data and the need for reports are so great that manual processing and reporting are too time-consuming and uneconomical.

Other activities of business, large and small, depend on computers in a variety of ways:

Marketing data that are properly stored for easy access can aid business marketing activities, such as market research, customer services, advertising, sales promotion, market and product planning, etc. With an easy-to-access body of information, business decision makers have a tool for identifying trends and other patterns of the marketplace. Quick production of customer and mailing lists is another potential benefit.

Business operations and production information systems aid day-to-day handling of orders, schedules, inventories, work assignments, and monitoring of performance and overall work-load planning. The use of a large computer or many interconnected smaller devices guides a business's in-house activities from ordering to shipping. Business managers can access and interact with data at any stage of the operations/production line to direct and redirect the process to fit management needs.

Technology Times

The "Big Board" Bears Automation

From under an old buttonwood tree on Wall Street in 1792, and a newly built coffeehouse down the block in 1793, has come today's "Big Board," the New York Stock Exchange (NYSE). It serves now, as it did then, as a membership securities marketplace. With a present membership of some 1,400 traders handling tens of millions of shares every trading day, it is the world capital of capital investment.

The establishment of a membership marketplace (one open only to members) grew out of the need to organize the scattered trading of government stocks and bank and insurance company shares that cropped up in the post–Revolutionary War period. Twenty-four men made up the original membership, and they handled all buy and sell orders of securities traded through the Exchange. Anyone else wanting to complete a transaction had to commission the services of a member or his firm. It is the same today.

Membership is not without its requirements. In addition to dues and other monetary outlays, member firms are required to issue financial statements to customers on demand, maintain certain levels of capital, have annual audits and be open to spot checks, file twelve financial reports yearly, expose loans and borrowings, and maintain fidelity insurance.

Issuers of stocks listed on the Exchange have agreed to provide shareowners with the opportunity to vote for company directors and on other matters that have an impact on ownership status.

Trading practices of 1792 and of the late 1970s vary little. A buyer and a seller are put together and a deal is made. Transactions are made public, so market prices are fairly controlled. When you want to buy or sell securities, you contact a broker whose firm is a member of the exchange on which the security is listed. The broker gives you the latest information on prices for the particular stock. Referred to as a "quote," it consists of the highest bid being made and the lowest asking price being offered. For example, a quote of

FIG. 19-1. (a) Before and (b) after electronification on the floor of the New York Stock Exchange (Photo by Edward C. Topple courtesy of NYSE)

a

26 to 26.25 (dollars) means that $26.00 per share is the highest bid being made at that moment by potential buyers, while $26.25 is the lowest asking price being put forth by potential sellers. When you give the broker the go-ahead, the order is passed to the firm's representative at the exchange. The exchange "floor broker" calls out the order to other brokers at the post where the stock is traded. Or the specialist, an exchange member who handles that particular stock and few others, may buy or sell from his own accounts in order to keep the trading active if there are no other offerings. When a transaction

Business engineering and research work employs computers as tools to aid engineers and designers in solving complex calculations, for visualizing designs graphically on CRTs, and in research.

Personnel data maintained in an appropriately secure computerized file are an aid in keeping employee records (job descriptions, benefit and recruitment files, etc.) in a business with a large number of workers.

Office management activities involve the use of computers for primarily word processing of correspondences and memos, preparation of reports, press releases, brochures, instruction manuals, and other everyday literary tasks of business executives and secretaries.

Professional applications using microcomputers are for filing and file maintenance, limited financial record keeping, generation of reports and word processing common in the practices of doctors, lawyers, and other one-person or small-group personal service businesses.

Personal applications, also microcomputer-based, are home financial management and record keeping, remote control of home environment systems, education, and games for entertainment.

The applications thus far mentioned have to do

is made, whether with another floor broker or with a specialist, it is written down on a piece of paper and reported back to the phone clerk who received the incoming order from the outside broker. Once the transaction is completed, within a few minutes it is transmitted over the ticker-tape network countrywide, throughout Canada, and in other foreign cities.

In addition to simple buy and sell orders, there are three other types that add conditions to buy or sell orders: (1) a limit-order dictates that buying must be done only at a specified price or lower and that the order is good for a

b

specified time period or until canceled; (2) a limit-sell order specifies a sales price or above and time constraint; (3) a stop order means to bail out or buy up if a certain price is reached, and here, too, time constraints can be specified.

During the minutes it takes to get a quote, give an order, and have that communicated to the floor, prices can change. Thus, the most critical element in a trade is the man or woman on the floor who negotiates the best prices in face-to-face trading. As NYSE specialist Donald Dinsmore put it in an interview, ''The human element of stock trading will never be eradicated or obsolete, because that is still the essence of a stock trade—bargain, buy, sell, et cetera. We have the job of facilitating the channels between the two parties, not replacing the parties themselves.''

Dinsmore's response was in part to some questions about his use of the then six-month-old computer system called ITS (Intermarket Trading System), which allows NYSE floor traders to transact trades with other exchanges around the country.

In 1975, the U.S. Congress amended the Securities Act and mandated that a national market be developed. Among its purposes were to increase competition among market centers, reduce trading costs, and generate greater interaction of order flow. Like Dinsmore, most professional traders describe the traditional trading procedures as working well. They resist changing something that's already working as well as it is now and has worked for almost two hundred years. You'd think that people who usually reap the benefits of change occurring in other sectors of the economy would welcome it in their own. Or might their conservative response be an insight into an unarticulated wisdom that envisions technology and automation as anti-human or at least uneconomical? After examining the situation, one gets a distinct sense that many fear for their jobs. The fear that technological change will endanger jobs is not limited to blue-collar laborers.

ITS is the way NYSE, the American Stock Exchange (AMEX), and regional exchanges in Boston, Chicago, Philadelphia, and San Francisco took the bull by the horns before the Congress, through the Securities Exchange Commission (SEC), devised a plan of its own. Advocates of ITS note that it is a new market structure built on the acknowledged trends of

FIG. 19-2. An ITS terminal (Photo by Edward C. Topple courtesy of NYSE)

mostly with organizing, processing, and generating information related to commercial and domestic affairs. Worth noting are the scientific applications for which Babbage conceived his computing "engines" and which are often the most awe-inspiring in their results, notably the automatic control of spacecraft circling distant planets, a three-dimensional graphic simulation of the brain, and artificial-intelligence machines learning and composing music.

The application of processing machines, in many instances, serves to do work that people can and do perform themselves. As stated earlier, a computer is justified when it becomes too time-consuming and uneconomical for people to do the work, or when the computer performs tasks that people cannot, as is most obvious in scientific applications. The professional and personal use of systems is not always justifiable. Financial and record-keeping activities in most homes and professional offices are easily accomplished with calculators and file folders costing a small fraction of a microcomputer and, in many ways, as time-efficient. A writer or lawyer might well use word processing capabilities in the preparation of briefs or contracts, but for the doctor or student at home, it's questionable unless word processing is only one use among many to which the system is put on a regular basis. The home or office system can be justified when it also serves as an on-line terminal telecommunicating with a larger computer for in-

FIG. 19-3. John Luddy

the traditional market system. It is evolving and allows input by its participants. Critics of it who subscribe to faster and more comprehensive automation of trading refer to it as merely a communications link.

The Intermarket Trading System, as of 1981, connected up the NYSE, AMEX, Philadelphia, Boston, Midwest, Cincinnati, and Pacific stock exchange floors. When a floor broker or specialist uses the system, working for him is a central computer in New York City run by the Securities Industry Automation Corporation (SIAC). The computer validates, routes, and processes all messages for both storing and reporting. The system maintains and produces a complete audit on all trading and communications between centers. Each center has a series of terminal stations with CRT, keyboard, and hardcopy output. The terminals can also be used prior to floor openings for free-form messages among centers. Part of the system is the Composite Quote System (CQS), which permits display of quotes at the trading post from all centers and flags the best outside offer.

The way it works is that a floor broker or specialist who wants to transact a certain stock goes to the trading post and checks the quote. Suppose he sees that Boston has the best offer. An exchange employee who operates the terminal calls the blank for ordering, which is filled in with the required information including the originating broker's or specialist's identification number and time sent. The Boston trader receives the order on his terminal and must respond within a time frame determined by the originating trader—usually one or two minutes. If no response is forthcoming within the time limit, the system automatically puts the order back in the hands of the originator. If the order is acted upon by the Boston trader's entering his I.D., a ticket is printed out at both stations and is as good as a face-to-face execution. The average trade takes about forty seconds.

"Limit orders are enhanced and better protected by the exposure to a complex of centers," explained John Luddy of the NYSE Marketing Department, a section that was set up in 1978 to deal with selling ITS to the industry, among other things.

"The concern that New York was swallowing up other exchanges prompted the SEC action. This system gives other exchanges a means to latch onto the New York order flow.

ITS allows them to expand their own business through communications on a national level."

Another system that is being watched in the market is the automated trading of the Cincinnati Stock Exchange, which handles less than 1 percent of the volume traded on the NYSE. In that experiment, also overseen by the SEC, the exchange has an "electronic floor." Brokers in their offices are connected via terminals into the exchange, which itself is composed of manned terminals, and all are connected into a computer center based, in fact, in Jersey City. Where are the arias of orders against the chorus of transactions and the accompaniment of bells and blinks and flapping paper sheets, which like hoisted flags signify the great events of trading?

"There's a great feeling of 'why can't we keep things as they are?' " Dinsmore said, "but I'm sure they said that about the telephone, too."

formation retrieval or processing, as for doctors accessing distant medical libraries or families interacting through a national computer games network. For home environment systems control, as for heating, security, air conditioning, and the operation of appliances, the trend is for single-purpose microprocessors to be built into a product dedicated to a particular function, as opposed to the use of a general-purpose computer for centralized control. It is difficult at present to define a configuration for small computer systems, but one thing is sure; Information processing facilities will be found increasingly in the home and office.

Education and entertainment are the small-computer applications that have proved to be most popular and appropriate. The use of personal computers for education in the school and at home provides individualized instruction in a variety of subject areas for which there are ready-made courses widely available. Computer or video games have become a great American "electronic pinball" pastime, providing entertainment at home and in penny arcades, launderettes, and bus terminal waiting rooms.

Computers save time, labor, and costs in the execution of large, repetitive procedures like billing and payroll preparation. They also provide for the accomplishment of jobs that could not be done without computer speeds and large-volume data capacities—such as short-term weather forecasting entailing a multitude of calculations on a voluminous amount of data. And, finally, computers permit simulations of real and/or anticipated conditions by use of mathematical models, as is evidenced in computer-driven flight simulators for pilot training, business forecasting, and scientific experimentation.

20
Punched Cards

The card that Hollerith devised for coding data in the late nineteenth century has survived the turnover of machine generations and is in use today still in great quantities. Punched cards, also called IBM cards, have been the traditional medium of data encoding for machine input and output since Hollerith's day, a tradition to which we pay homage with every reading of the inscription that is boldly placed on every card: "DO NOT STAPLE, SPINDLE, FOLD, OR MUTILATE." Though the punched-card system is beginning to be replaced by other systems of computer data entry, it is well worth noting.

Punched cards are used in batch processing. Each card serves as a record of a single transaction, containing all pertinent data. For example, in a record of a sale of an item on credit, the card contains the name, address, and charge account number of the customer, and the date of sale, stock number, description, price, and tax charges of the item purchased. The cards may be produced for a computer run to make up monthly bills for customers. The cards are laid out in a framework of columns and rows into which holes are punched to encode the data. Holes in various groupings represent letters, numbers, and special characters (e.g., punctuation marks).

Punched-card readers are used to convert card data into machine-readable signals. Conversion is done electrically or optically. Electrical sensing is done by passing each card between an electrically charged roller and a set of brushes. Where there are holes, as the card passes through the mechanism, the brushes make contact with the roller and complete electrical circuits. The passing of each card through the mechanism takes a fixed amount of time (less than a second), which is broken into smaller time segments corresponding to the number of rows on the cards; thus, the location of each hole is identifiable by time. In this way, the reader converts the card code based on spatial position to machine code based on time pulsation. Higher speeds (1,000 cards per minute) are achieved with optical sensing, in which light in place of brushes passes through the holes and is detected by sensors in place of an electrically charged roller.

Holes can be punched into cards with small portable card-punching devices at the data origination point upon acquisition, or by copying data off bills, invoices, etc., after acquisition by use of key-punching equipment. For coding data upon acquisition, there's also the mark-sensing method, for which a special pencil is used instead of a punch. The markings of the pencil can be sensed by a special reader for conversion into machine-readable signals.

The main purpose in considering punched cards is to examine their coding format, which serves as an introduction to data representation in general. Two card layouts are in use: the Hollerith-IBM card with 80 columns and the 96-column card IBM introduced in the late 1960s, often called the System 3 card.

The 80-column card has twelve horizontal rows along which data can be punched. Either one, two, or three rectangular-shaped punches can be put in every column. The card is broken into two areas: digit punching and zone punching. Rows 0–9 are in the digit-punching area, and rows 12, 11, and 0 are in the zone-punching area. The 0 row is used in both areas. Numbers are represented by a single punched hole per column. Alphabetics are represented by two punched holes per column, consisting of a zone punch and a digit punch. The letters A–I are made up of a zone-punched hole from row 12 and one digit-punched hole from rows 1–9; J–R are made up of an 11 zone-punched hole and one digit-punched hole from 1–9; S–Z are made up of a 0 zone-punched hole and one digit-punched hole from 2–9. Most special characters are made up of three punched holes; they include punctuation marks, the asterisk (*), the ampersand (&), the dollar sign ($), the percent symbol (%), and others.

A card can be predesigned for coding a specific type of data. For example, student enrollment cards might be specifically designed to use columns 1–6 for the date (two columns each for the month, day, and year), columns 7–30 for the name, 31–39 for student I.D. number, the next six columns for birthdate, one column for sex, and so on. Such a card would be printed with column headings in the 12 and 11 rows to identify each type of data and would include lines down the columns separating the different data. Each different type of data on a given card is referred to as a field, and all the fields make up the record.

The System 3 IBM card with its 96 columns is one-third the size of the Hollerith-IBM card. It was developed for the minicomputer, and its punches are small round holes that can only be read optically. In principle, it works like the older card, but it stacks its data into three punch areas, each 32 columns wide.

21

Input/Output (I/O)

- The input section is for entering data into a processing system making it machine-readable.
- The output section is for the display of results.

We bridge the gap between human and machine languages by using codes. In the early days of computers, alphanumeric data had to be converted to binary notation and then entered into the computer, often manually by switching circuits directly. Input/ouput (I/O) devices have been developed over the years to provide faster and more efficient automated alphanumeric-to-binary and binary-to-alphanumeric translations. Today, only certain hobby computers use direct circuit switching for data entry.

All data in and out of computers flow through input and output peripherals. *Peripherals* are the extra equipment (keyboards, CRTs, printers, etc.) external to the CPU necessary for processing operations. I/O devices facilitate communications between humans and computers. This translation function is referred to as *interfacing*. To interface one device to another means to connect two devices so that signal flows between them without loss of meaning. I/O devices are, in fact, referred to as "interface peripherals."

Interface peripherals determine the overall speed and efficiency of an automatic information processing system. CPU operation speeds are far greater than those of I/O devices. It takes longer to enter or retrieve from storage an amount of data than it does to process it. As pointed out earlier, good use of this speed discrepancy is made in time-sharing operations. Many newer I/O devices contain microprocessors that enable them to perform processsing tasks independently of the computer. Referred to as "intelligent" terminals, they are capable of handling some of the processing tasks previously performed by the computer, such as checking for validity of data or word length. (A "dumb" terminal is one without such processing capabilities.)

Considering the future for a moment, the ultimate input device could evolve out of work being done today with *magnetoencephalography* (MEG), which is the measuring of magnetic fields generated by brain activity. MEG is related to electroencephalography (EEG), the measuring of electrical activity in the brain, commonly done in medicine to detect brain malfunctioning. Mapping of the brain with MEG has already begun. A map is made to identify areas of the brain according to the neural activities that are carried out in them. In other words, we'll know what

a

FIG. 21-1. (a) Yesteryear's dictating machine has evolved into (b) a computerized system that includes a "word management" switchboard. (Courtesy of Dictaphone Corp.)

b

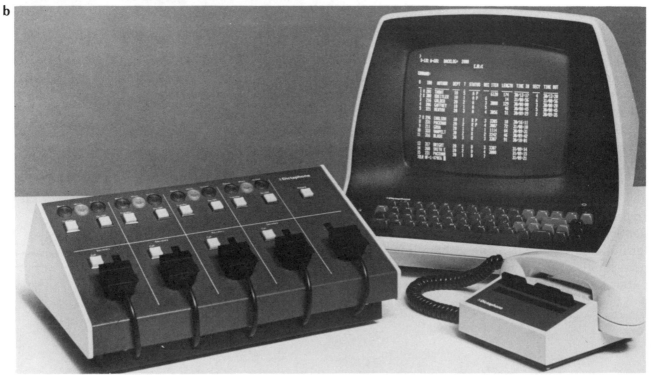

part of the brain is active for each thought process. A computer could be programmed to respond to the magnetic field signals of a given activity and carry out the represented thought process in its own circuits; the end result would be that humans would be able to "think" data and instructions directly into the computer by wearing some type of MEG headgear connecting them to the processing system. Add to that the neurophone, invented in the 1960s, which converts audio signals into signals within the nervous system by using electrical contacts placed on the body. This could provide a medium for the computer to convey information directly to the human mind.

For now (1982), keyboards, CRT screens, and printers are the primary devices interfacing us and our computers.

ANALOG I/O

The use of computers for the control of machines (e.g., automatic piloting of aircraft or cooling and heating of large buildings) involves handling data that are in an analog physical form, such as pressure, temperature, or velocity. To convert physical data into digital form for input into a computer, they must be first converted into an analog electrical signal and then fed through an analog-to-digital (A/D) converter. On the other end, to produce an analog signal output, the processed digital signal is fed through a digital-to-analog (D/A) converter, and then to a device capable of producing the desired physical effect, such as increasing speed, shutting down a furnace, or steering an aircraft.

PERFORATED PAPER TAPE

Akin to punched cards is perforated paper tape. Originally developed for telegraphic uses and still widely used in the communications industry, computer paper tape is primarily limited to smaller-systems applications.

Two coding formats are in use with paper tape: a 5-bit and an 8-bit code. A perforated hole is a binary 1, and no hole is 0. In the 5-bit code, shift symbols are used to distinguish between letters and numbers. Without shift symbols, code groups for all letters and numbers would not be available, since a 5-bit code provides only thirty-two variations of 1s and 0s.

Paper-tape readers, like those for punched cards,

work either electrically or optically to convert code to machine-readable signal. An optical reader can read at a rate of up to 1,000 characters per second. Devices for perforating tape perform at speeds from about 15 to 150 characters per second and are often part of computer output sections. For manual encoding of data onto paper tape, typewriterlike devices are used.

I/O TERMINALS

Terminals are made up of input and output devices built into a single housing. The keyboard is the most common data entry device, while CRTs and teletypewriters are most common for output of data. Display on a CRT is referred to as *softcopy* and is retained only as long as the system is powered. Teletypewriters produce a *hardcopy* of data, or a printed page that can be saved.

KEYBOARDS

A keyboard is made up of an array of switches arranged in columns and rows which are scanned to detect which keys are struck. An integrated circuit (IC), called an encoder, detects key action and transmits the proper binary-coded signal to the com-

FIG. 21-2. Computer terminals with printer/CRT combinations. (Courtesy of Hewlett-Packard Corp.)

FIG. 21-3. A dual minidiskette text editor with communications and a 24-character minidisplay (Courtesy of Exxon Information Systems)

puter and display device. The intelligent keyboard uses an encoder that incorporates a microprocessor that permits reprogramming of key functions. In other words, with an intelligent keyboard, a user may dedicate a key to a particular function required for his or her work, using any 8-bit code for any given key.

The keyboard switching mechanisms most commonly used are two types of magnetic switches, the mechanical switch, reeds, and capacitance.

One of the *magnetic switches* uses a magnet attached to the key plunger that moves toward a circuit (Hall transducer) that produces a voltage when in the presence of a magnetic field. The other magnetic switch also incorporates a magnet attached to the key plunger. The switch is a ferrite core that is magnetically saturated when the plunger magnet is positioned close to it, and unsaturated when the plunger is pulled away from it. The core is periodically sensed. When a key is not depressed, the core remains saturated and no signal is sensed. When a key is depressed, the core is unsaturated and a signal is sensed and fed to the encoder.

The *mechanical switch* uses a metal-to-metal direct contact between the plunger and the switch. They are good for about 10 million switchings. *Reed switches* are also metal contact devices. They are sealed within protective packages, which increases their usage to ten times that of mechanical switches.

Capacitance-based switches depend on the movement of electrically charged plates to produce a variation of signal, which is then amplified and encoded. One plate of a capacitor is connected to the key. When pressed, the key moves in relationship to the other plate of the capacitor, producing a change in the level of charge, and thereby a signal for the encoder.

The keyboard in itself does not produce characters; it only produces the coded signals that represent

TYPEWRITER-STYLE KEYBOARD

FIG. 21-4. (a) A computer terminal for interactive input/output of data and (b) its keyboard (Courtesy of Hazeltine Corp.)

FIG. 21-5. Color graphics terminal (Courtesy of Tektronix, Inc.)

FIG. 21-6. Desk-top data entry terminal (Courtesy of Computer Devices, Inc.)

letters, numbers, and special characters. They can be used to feed data into storage (key-to-storage) such as magnetic tape or disk (key-to-tape and key-to-disk systems). Or the signals can be fed to a character generator for display on a CRT screen or to a printer for hardcopy production.

Printers are of two major types: impact and nonimpact. In *impact printing*, each character or part of a character is formed on paper by impact of a striking mechansim. In *nonimpact printing*, characters are formed by electrical control of ink or the use of certain chemicals that produce visual manifestations on paper.

Serial, dot matrix, drum, and chain printers are the types of impact printers.

The characters of a *serial printer* are fixed to a set of hammers, as in a teletypewriter; fixed to a ball, as in an IBM Selectric typewriter; or set on a wheel, such as the "daisy wheel." Balls and wheels can be removed and typefaces changed. Characters are printed one at a time, so serial printers operate at relatively slow speeds. The range of speeds for all printers is from about 10 characters per second (cps) to 20,000 lines per minute. Serial printers are at the lower end of

FIG. 21-6. Desk-top data entry terminal (Courtesy of Computer Devices, Inc.)

FIG. 21-7. A portable (16-lb.) send/receive computer terminal capable of graphics printing. Its thermal printer has a resolution of 120 points per square inch. (Courtesy of Computer Transceiver Systems, Inc.)

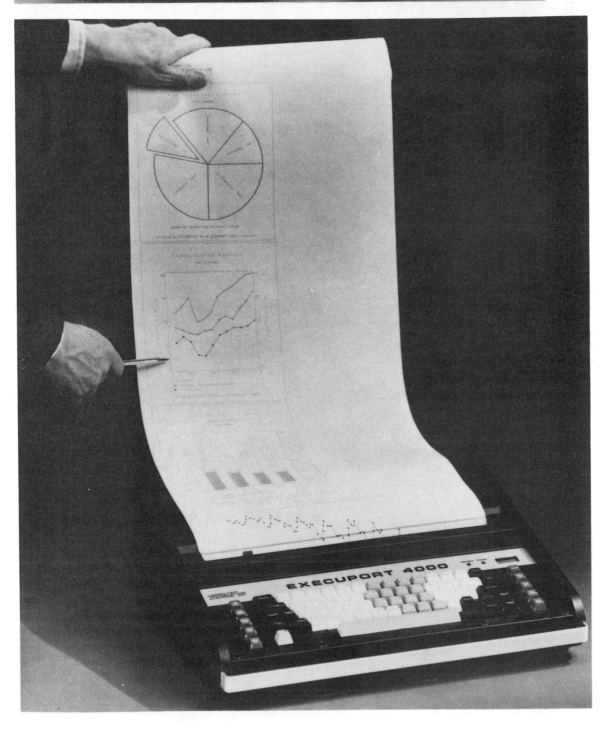

FIG. 21-0. Line printers (Courtesy of Radio Shack, div. of Tandy Corp.)

FIG. 21-9. A text editing system with keyboard for input, diskettes for storage, and CRT for display of work in progress. A separate printer is used for final hardcopy. (Courtesy of Olivetti Corp. of America)

that range, as may be expected. *Dot matrix printers* are serial devices that use a grid of 5 × 7 or 7 × 9 impacting points as character elements to form all letters, numbers, and special characters. Dot matrix printers operate at about 50 to 100 cps.

Drum and *chain printers* are classified as line printers; they print all the characters in a line almost simultaneously. A line commonly contains from 100 to 144 characters. The drum printer is made up of rows of raised type. A row, for example, has the letter *a* in every character position of the line. After all the *a* letters are printed where they are required in a given line, the drum rotates and the *b* letters are printed, and then the *c* letters, and so on. Chain printers use a bicycle-like chain, and each link is a different character. As the chain revolves and characters come into positions on a line, hammers hit against the paper, forcing it into the type so that it captures the impressions. The coordination of hammer strikes and character positioning is done by electronic circuits. Type chains are interchangeable, providing different typefaces. Related to the chain printer is the *print train*, which achieves the highest speeds for impact printers, about 2,000 lines per minute.

Nonimpact printing has been developed to overcome the speed limitations inherent in impact devices, which depend on mechanical contact and movement. Nonimpact printing systems use either special or plain paper subjected to thermal or photographic processes. (For a discussion of printing processes, see chapter 9, "Facsimile Transmission.") Three important nonimpact printing systems are: electrostatic, electrophotographic, and ink jet.

Electrostatic printers contain electrically charged styluses or dot makers grouped in densities of up to 200 per inch. These styluses form the characters as a special paper is drawn past them. An applied toner adheres to those areas that have been "electrically etched" by styluses or dot makers, making the characters visible. Speeds for this type of device run up to 5,000 lines per minute.

Electrophotographic printing employs a light beam (low-powered laser or stream of electrons) to form the characters on a photosensitive surface of a rotating drum. A toner that adheres to the exposed areas of the drum's surface is then transferred to plain paper, rendering the printed page. Such devices can operate at speeds of up to about 20,000 lines per minute. This type of printer permits alteration of character size and use of overlays, such as form blanks.

Ink jet printing is a process of electronically guiding a superfine stream of ink to form characters on paper.

CATHODE RAY TUBES

The CRT (described in chapter 13) is the "blackboard" of a computer terminal station. It provides instantaneous electronic display of alphanumerics and/or graphics such as charts, diagrams, or even perspective drawings, in b/w or color.

For CRT display of alphanumerics, a *character*

generator is used. In a character generator, each character is broken into a dot matrix pattern (5 × 7 or 7 × 9), and that information is stored in a memory device. A character is retrieved from it when the memory is signaled from a keyboard or output from the computer. The character in signal form is fed to circuits that change it to a video signal to direct the CRT's electron stream for display on the screen. Color can be used to enhance alphanumeric displays by use of character generators designed with added color generation circuitry.

For CRT display of graphics, image data are broken into pixels (picture elements) in arrays of 64 × 64, 128 × 96, 256 × 192, etc. Each pixel represents a bit of data. The more pixels, the more resolution and better picture quality to the image. With the use of a device called a light pen, a terminal user can interact directly with the computer to draw, magnify, erase, etc., a selected area of image. The light pen serves as an electronic pointer by sensing a point of light emitted from the screen and feeding a signal back to the computer. The CRT raster or image area is made up of 525 lines drawn thirty times per second by a moving stream of electrons. The computer can detect specific locations on the screen by referencing the light pen signal to the electron stream's movements in time.

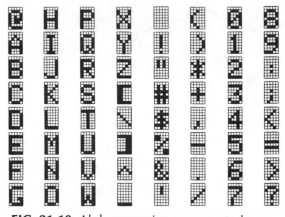

FIG. 21-10. Alphanumerics as generated on a CRT screen

PLOTTERS

For graphic display, an alternative to the CRT is a *plotter*, a device for drawing lines on paper. Plotters are of two major types: electrically driven ink pens and image printing using electrophotographic or electrostatic processes.

Plotters using electronically driven pens can have either flatbeds or drums on which the paper is placed. The pen or a group of pens of different colors is controlled by output data from a computer, storage device, etc., which are converted into signals to move the pen(s) along vertical and horizontal axes, as well as to and from the paper. Alphanumerics as well as graphics can be drawn by these electromechanical plotters.

Electrostatic and electrophotographic processes are the same as discussed above under nonimpact printing. An electrostatic printer is, in fact, referred to as a printer/plotter. The electrophotographic process in plotting may include the use of film upon which the image is exposed, and then the making of a print or hardcopy from that film.

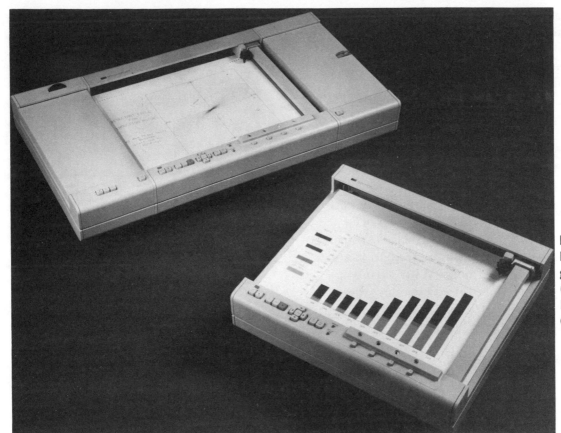

FIG. 21-11.
Plotter/printers for
graphic generation
(Courtesy of
Hewlett-Packard
Corp.)

FIG. 21-12. OCR system (Courtesy of AM Jacquard Systems)

MAGNETIC INK CHARACTER RECOGNITION (MICR)

MICR was developed in the 1960s by the banking industry to replace key-punch entry of data from checks and other banking documents. Familiar to all of us are the oddly formed numbers and special signs at the bottoms of checks. These inscriptions are printed on checks with an ink that contains minute metal particles. When the checks are passed under a reader, an electromagnet magnetizes the metal particles, which then can be sensed magnetically. The character forms were developed for grid format sensing. The sensor converts the characters to binary-coded signals for machine processing of the data.

FIG. 21-13. Bar-code reader terminal (Courtesy of Computer Devices, Inc.)

OPTICAL CHARACTER RECOGNITION (OCR)

OCR is the ability to sense handwritten and printed data by way of light-sensing processes. In an optical reader, light is focused on a page and bounced back to sets of photocells. Where there are no marks, the blank page reflects a significantly greater amount of light than is reflected from the marked areas. OCR has achieved data entry rates twenty-five times faster than key entry. However, it cannot be universally used because all readers cannot decipher all hand-scripts and typefaces. Thus, different optical recognition systems have been developed for special applications, such as tag and tape readers for speedy reading of cash register and adding machine tapes and price tags, required in large retailing operations. Page readers are capable of reading entire 8½ by 14-inch pages with characters in a variety of styles and in what is called "restrained handprint." The standard character forms used for optical recognition are OCR-A, OCR-B, Farrington 7B, and the MICR E13B.

COMPUTER OUTPUT/INPUT MICROGRAPHICS (COM AND CIM)

COM is an up-and-coming alternative to paper computer printouts. It operates at faster rates than printers and cuts down the use of paper. The output from a computer or storage device is recorded on film by photographing data displayed in a CRT or by feeding output signals through an electron gun onto the film in a vacuum, thereby exposing it. CIM is the conversion of microfilm images to electrical signal for data entry. Pages of data can be greatly reduced in size when stored on film in either of two microform film formats: microfilm strips or microfiche, a piece of film about 3 by 5 inches. For viewing microforms, either a manually operated reader or a computer terminal can be used.

SOURCE DATA ACQUISITIONS (SDA)

SDA refers to the direct entry of data into the computer at the point where the data originates. One example is a *point-of-sale* (POS) *system* consisting of a cash register and a data entry terminal combined and connected to the computer. As sales are made and rung up on the cash register, the computer processes the data accordingly. POS systems in retailing include a supermarket system that uses the Universal Product Code (UPC), the striped patterns printed on the wrappers or labels of many products. UPC is a 10-digit code that identifies the product. When the item is passed over an optical reader connected to a computer, the identity is noted and the current price retrieved from a price memory. The amount is displayed at the checkout counter and added to the customer's total.

Voice data entry is accomplished with a voice-recognition terminal that can "understand" a limited

FIG. 21-14. Universal Product Code

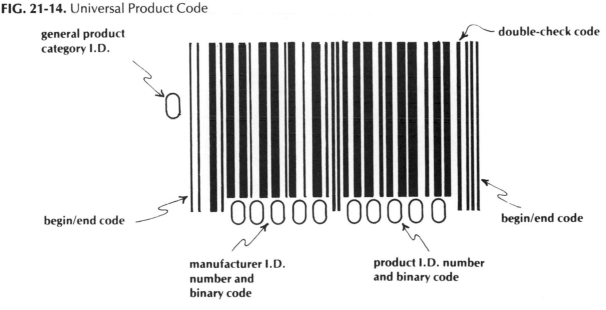

general product category I.D.

double-check code

begin/end code

begin/end code

manufacturer I.D. number and binary code

product I.D. number and binary code

number of words (up to 200) and distinguish voice characteristics of a number of users for which it has been programmed. The user has a microphone connected to the terminal and a small alphanumeric display for verifying his or her input.

Touch-Tone telephones are widely used for both data entry and to make inquiries of the computer about stored data. The twelve-zone keypad serves as an alphanumeric terminal for communicating with a computer. In some cases, the computer output is a voice response, the product of electronic circuits programmed with a limited vocabulary. Such terminals are common in banks and are sometimes used in conjunction with identification or credit cards inserted into readers. The use of cards expedites terminal action and is a security measure in protecting access to individual data files.

With punched cards, a two-symbol system of "holes" and "no holes" is used to represent data. In machines, the holes and no holes become a series of electrical pulses in a continuous string of signal. Such a signal might, for example, be made up of an electric current with two voltage levels, a low voltage to denote no holes and a high voltage for holes. It could be either way. In any case, each discrete voltage or pulse represents an element of data. When that element of data is placed in computer memory, it is stored in a circuit that can be in one of only two possible states. Each signal becomes a "frozen" pulse to be activated when retrieved by the central processing unit. In the CPU, each pulse is fed to processing circuits that put out only one of two possible signals, in this case, a high- or low-voltage pulse. In other words, data in processing machines are always reduced to signal elements of one state or the other of a two-state system.

For translating data to machine-readable language, a code made up of only two symbols is used to represent the two states of signal—binary notation with its 1s and 0s. In what is called positive logic, the 1s represent the high voltage and the 0s the low. In negative logic, the reverse is the case. Either system can be used and is determined by the designer of a machine. Somewhat akin to Morse code, also a two-state system, binary 1s and 0s are grouped together to represent decimal numbers, letters of the alphabet, special characters, and machine control signals such as the shift bar control on a typewriter keyboard. By grouping bits together, we are able to create enough different notations using just 1s and 0s to represent all twenty-six letters, ten decimal numbers, and other special symbols.

The binary number system, like the decimal, uses place value notation. For example, when a decimal number is read, each digit from right to left has a value ten times greater than its neighbor to the right: 1,980 has 0 in the ones column, 8 in the tens column, 9 in the hundreds column, and 1 in the thousands column. With binary numbers, instead of each column

22

Data Representation

Technology Times

Thoughts into Printed Pages at the *New York Times*

Jim Morgan sports a mildly round midsection which substantiates his authoritative personage as he leads curious visitors on tours through the *New York Times* building. He is casually attired like a newspaperman and personable. He speaks with a good combination of humor and informed assuredness, revealing what you might expect from a *Times* company man—an intelligent cynicism tempering a loyalty and pride that in other companies might result in blind obedience and a rote espousal of the company line.

In late 1979, on a noon-hour tour to see the then 15-month-old computerized news system, we were led to a mostly empty newsroom; it was explained that reporters were out on their beats and that sometime around 4 P.M. they would be returning almost en masse to write their stories. The paper goes to press at 9 P.M. and continues printing until 5 A.M., during which time 850,000 copies are produced on weekdays, 1.5

million on Sunday. The *New York Times,* employing 5,000 people, makes its income through advertising (80 percent) and newspaper sales (20 percent). The newsstand price of the paper is less than the amount it costs to produce, we were told: 40¢ for weekday issues, up to $3 for a Sunday issue. Of course, some Sunday issues can bring in as much as $6 million in advertising revenues.

Newspapers are considered to be the first mass medium. They achieved such status in the late 1800s with the advent of steam to power presses, the rotary press, line casting machines (Linotype), and cheaper newsprint. Around the mid-1960s newspaper industry technology began taking another leap forward with computerization, data transmission, and filmsetting machinery. The *New York Times* went completely into printing through electronics on July 3, 1978, after phasing in the new technology over a three-year period that started with automating the advertising department and then sections of the Sunday edition.

"No longer are stories written on typewriters. We use computer terminals upon which you can see the story as you type it on the video display screen. When the story is completed, a press of a button stores it away electronically in the computer, and when the editor wants to consider it, he can bring it onto his terminal for viewing," explained Morgan, who also said there were then 250 terminals, each one costing about $12,000; acquisition of only a small number more was anticipated.

The *Times'*s "news editing system" is a product of the Harris Corporation. Its storage is done on magnetic disk, and stories are erased once they are committed to paper. Some longer-range storage is done, as in the case of stories in progress over a number of days and, probably, for the 350 or so ready-to-go obituaries that are maintained by the *Times.* As Morgan put it, "We have four pages on Carter, seven on Nixon, and these are modified as life goes on. We like to think that when they're ready to go, we're ready to go."

The impact on labor in the production of newspapers has been significant. In the newsroom, no longer is the copy boy or girl shuttling fistfuls of copy from desk to desk. In the composing room, fewer than half of the

being ten times greater, it's only *two* times greater: 1001100 has 0 in the ones column, 0 in the twos column, 1 in the fours column, 1 in the eights column, 0 in the sixteens column, 0 in the thirty-twos column, and 1 in the sixty-fours column.

Conversion from binary to decimal is done by adding up the column values of those columns containing a 1: 1001100 has 1×64, 0×32 and 16, 1×8, 1×4, and 0×2 and 1, which totals 76. Converting a decimal number into binary is done by repeatedly subtracting the largest power of 2 contained in the remainders until you reach zero. For example, in the number 1,980, the largest power of 2 is 2^{10} or 1,024, which means we put a 1 in the far left column of a binary number having ten places (1---------). Subtract 1,024 from 1,980 for a remainder of 956. The largest power of 2 in 956 is 2^9 or 512, which means a 1 is placed in the next column of the binary notation (11--------). Subtract 512 from 956 for a remainder of 444. The largest power of 2 in 444 is 2^8 or 256, which means another 1 in the next column of the binary number (111-------). Subtract 256 from 444 for a remainder of 188. The largest power of 2 in 188 is 2^7 or 128, which means another 1 in the seventh column (1111------). Subtract 128 from 188 for a remainder of 60. The largest power of 2 in 60 is 2^5 or 32, which means in column six (the sixty-four column) we have a 0, but in column five, we can put 1 (111101----). Subtract 32 from 60 for a remainder of 28. The largest power of 2 in 28 is 2^4 or 16, which means another 1 in the next column (1111011---). Subtract 16 from 28 for a remainder of 12. The largest power of 2 in 12 is 2^3 or 8, and thus another 1 in the third column (11110111--). Subtract 8 from 12 for a remainder of 4, which is 2^2, and put another 1 in the second column and, since zero has been reached, nothing in the first column. The complete binary notation for 1,980 is 1111011110.

In the early 1960s, for second-generation machines, computer designers developed what is called *Binary Coded Decimal* (BCD) to simplify numeric and alphabetic binary notations. Each of the decimal digits from 0 to 9 can be represented with a binary number of four bits: 0000 is 0; 0001 is 1; 0010 is 2; 0011 is 3; 0100 is 4; 0101 is 5; 0110 is 6; 0111 is 7; 1000 is 8; and 1001 is 9. In BCD, for example, 1,980 is written 0001 1001 1000 0000. To note letters of the alphabet in BCD, a two-digit zone code is used like that employed in punched-card coding. Each letter has a zone code and 4-bit number code; for example, *d* is 110100.

Table 22-1. **BCD ALPHABET AND NUMBERS**

Letter	Zone	Binary		Number	Zone	Binary
A	11 BA	0001 1		1	00	0001 1
B	11 BA	0010 2		2	00	0010 2
C	11 BA	0011 21		3	00	0011 21
D	11 BA	0100 4		4	00	0100 4
E	11 BA	0101 4 1		5	00	0101 4 1
F	11 BA	0110 42		6	00	0110 42
G	11 BA	0111 421		7	00	0111 421
H	11 BA	1000 8		8	00	1000 8
I	11 BA	1001 8 1		9	00	1001 8 1
J	10 B	0001 1		0	00	1010 8 2
K	10 B	0010 2				
L	10 B	0011 21				
M	10 B	0100 4				
N	10 B	0101 4 1				
O	10 B	0110 42				
P	10 B	0111 421				
Q	10 B	1000 8				
R	10 B	1001 8 1				
S	01 A	0010 2				
T	01 A	0011 21				
U	01 A	0100 4				
V	01 A	0101 4 1				
W	01 A	0110 42				
X	01 A	0111 421				
Y	01 A	1000 8				
Z	01 A	1001 8 1				

It is common among computer professionals to represent the zone and binary digits of BCD code using B and A for zone and 8, 4, 2, and 1 for bits. For instance, the BCD code 11 1111 is referred to as BA 8421.

To further explain: decimal 8 is binary 1000; decimal 4 is binary 0100; decimal 2 is binary 0010; and decimal 1 is binary 0001. Thus, in those places in the 6-digit BCD code where the bit is 1, the decimal equivalent is used. For example, 10 0010 (BCD for the letter *K*) is B 2; another, B 81 is *R* or 10 1001.

1,000 workers formerly employed occupy an area one-fifth its former size. There are no longer 140 Linotype machines producing several column lines of type a minute. Now photocomposing technology integrated into the new editing system generates 1,000 column lines per minute at the flick of an editor's terminal button once he has specified type, sizes, and so forth. The composition room has become a place where strips of ready copy are pasted onto page layout sheets, preparing them for plate production. No longer does an anxious editor run in with new copy and summon the artful skill of a composer to fit it in. And further impact will be felt when and if the *Times* introduces what the computer industry calls pagination—electronic page composing by which whole pages are put together at a terminal and then committed to paper or directly to printing plates.

Movable type had its first impact on the Western world when Johann Gutenberg put it to use in Europe in the fifteenth century to produce a Bible. He used a hand-operated letterpress. A flat bed of type was inked, and a piece of paper pressed against it produced a printed page. Later came auto platen presses, which were larger and, of course, faster, but still letterpress or relief printing devices. Type itself developed from wood-carved to lead-alloy-casted, or what is called "hot type." Linotype machines with their typewriter controls permitted an operator to enter the copy desired to produce the lines of ready type needed for printing. The machine produced, from master characters, newly cast lead type, which after use could be melted down and recycled. Linotype machines could be operated with punched paper tape inputs in lieu of the manned typewriter. Punched tapes could be produced from a distance using telephone lines and electrical impulses (teletypesetting).

A further development of the flatbed presses was the cylinder press. Cylinder presses lent themselves to the use of larger plates and paper rolls. Once mechanized, rolls of paper could be fed through numbers of cylinders. This became the web fed rotary presses used primarily in newspaper production and still in use today. The *Times* has two printing plants; one in New Jersey and one in New York City at which seven presses produce sixteen pages each and which for a

Sunday issue can consume 40,000 gallons of ink. The New York presses are letterpress.

In New Jersey, the presses are offset. Offset printing has become widely used in the latter twentieth century, displacing most letterpress operations. Like lithography, offset printing is based on the mutual repulsion of water and grease. Plates are generally made of thin, flexible metal that can be wrapped around cylinders. A plate is treated so that the nonprinting areas absorb water and the printing areas do not. Thus, when ink is applied, the wet nonprinting areas will reject it, while the dry areas will retain it. The image is not printed directly on paper, but is transferred to a rubber cylinder and then to paper or any other surface.

Platemaking techniques are primarily photographic. Light is passed through a partially opaque, partially transparent film onto a photochemically treated surface. The areas hit by the light and those not hit by it are affected differently when further bathed in chemicals. Either offset or letterpress plates can be made photographically. Lasers are used at the *Times* in the transmission of print-ready pages to the platemaking area and in the platemaking process. In fact, the New Jersey plant receives the laser-scanned pages via microwave transmission from the New York headquarters. To cut distribution costs, the *Wall Street Journal* daily prints in several regions of the United States by transmitting via satellite plate-ready copy to those regional plants.

Filmsetting of copy, often called "cold type," is at the core of the news editing system. It is accomplished at the terminals, and it, too, is a photographic process. Photographic paper is placed on a drum in front of which is a mask with alphanumerics. Light is beamed through the mask onto the paper. The paper is developed and clean copy produced. Reporters can obtain a hardcopy of the stories they type on the CRT screens this way. However, it's the editors who do the actual "typesetting" determining the final shape of the copy.

Tied into the news editing system are forty correspondents overseas, another forty throughout the United States, with a Washington, D.C., bureau of about fifty, plus the New York staff. Overseas reports are received either by telephone (at a cost of $4 million yearly) or Telex. Stories are recorded

Table 22-2. EBCDIC AND HEXIDECIMAL ALPHABET AND NUMBERS

Letter/Number	Bit Group	Hex
a	1000 0001	81
b	1000 0010	82
c	1000 0011	83
d	1000 0100	84
e	1000 0101	85
f	1000 0110	86
g	1000 0111	87
h	1000 1000	88
i	1000 1001	89
j	1001 0001	91
k	1001 0010	92
l	1001 0011	93
m	1001 0100	94
n	1001 0101	95
o	1001 0110	96
p	1001 0111	97
q	1001 1000	98
r	1001 1001	99
s	1010 0010	A2
t	1010 0011	A3
u	1010 0100	A4
v	1010 0101	A5
w	1010 0110	A6
x	1010 0111	A7
y	1010 1000	A8
z	1010 1001	A9
A	1100 0001	C1
B	1100 0010	C2
C	1100 0011	C3
D	1100 0100	C4
E	1100 0101	C5
F	1100 0110	C6
G	1100 0111	C7
H	1100 1000	C8
I	1100 1001	C9
J	1101 0001	D1
K	1101 0010	D2
L	1101 0011	D3
M	1101 0100	D4
N	1101 0101	D5
O	1101 0110	D6
P	1101 0111	D7
Q	1101 1000	D8
R	1101 1001	D9

Table 22-2. EBCDIC AND HEXIDECIMAL
ALPHABET AND NUMBERS

S	1110 0010	E2
T	1110 0011	E3
U	1110 0100	E4
V	1110 0101	E5
W	1110 0110	E6
X	1110 0111	E7
Y	1110 1000	E8
Z	1110 1001	E9

0	1111 0000	F0
1	1111 0001	F1
2	1111 0010	F2
3	1111 0011	F3
4	1111 0100	F4
5	1111 0101	F5
6	1111 0110	F6
7	1111 0111	F7
8	1111 1000	F8
9	1111 1001	F9

For third-generation machines, an 8-bit code was developed to provide greater flexibility than the 6-bit BCD code. *Extended Binary Coded Decimal Interchange Code* (EBCDIC, pronounced eb-sa-dik) is used for most larger computers. EBCDIC employs a 4-bit zone code that indicates whether a notation is numeric or alphabetic. The alphabetic zone code has three signs to indicate which third of the alphabet a letter is in. For example, the word *books* in EBCDIC is written: (b) 1100 0010 (o) 1101 0110 (o) 1101 0110 (k) 1101 0010 (s) 1110 0010. The first 4-bit group is the sign indicating the section of the alphabet; the second 4-bit group is the particular letter. For storage, zone codes may be dropped and data packed to save space. For actual processing, zone codes are dropped or the EBCDIC notation is converted to a straight 14-bit binary code. For entry to and exit from the computer, however, the complete EBCDIC code with zone and digit notations must be used.

Two other binary-related coding systems are widely used in processing machines: hexadecimal and

and transcribed into the computer. Remote, direct hookups to the computer are in limited use in the Westchester, Long Island, and United Nations bureaus. Given portable, lightweight terminals, reporters could type their stories in from the field or the comfort of their own homes.

In answer to a question about the possibility that this system will lead to a "newsroom without walls," one *New York Times* data center manager, Frank Jannucci, said, "Sure, but that's really an editorial decision."

"Newspaper people," as Jim Morgan put it, "didn't like the computer at first. As much as they think of themselves as liberal and open to things, when it came to these terminals, they nutted up for a few weeks. Now they like it."

Theoretically, now a paper reporting a specific event, such as a transcript of a news conference by the president, could be on the streets twenty minutes after the close of that event. However, the printed page in an era of electronics can be considered anachronistic. The need for collection and editorial revision of information is growing, and new formats for receiving that information are being developed and tested. Portable, hand-held "newsfax" machines might not be a bad alternative to newspapers. Electronic storage disks slipped into such devices for display of printed information could make them acceptable to commuters, students, and others. Teletext, the capability of sending/receiving alphanumeric data via TV transmission, offers the *New York Times* another way into the minds of its readers, through home and office TV displays and/or hardcopy printers. The newsroom with its editors and reporters will always be with us. As for the news "paper," that's another question.

octal. *Hexadecimal* is a base 16 system that uses the digits 0–9 and A, B, C, D, E, and F for its sixteen different notations. The sixteen symbols are easily translated into a 4-bit binary notation. In addition to the 4-bit binary numbers for 0–9, as shown above, A is 1010; B is 1011; C is 1100; D is 1101; E is 1110; and F is 1111. Hexadecimal is commonly used for packing information in storage. The EBCDIC notation for *books* in hexadecimal becomes: (b) C2 (o) D6 (o) D6 (k) D2 (s) E2—a considerable saving of space.

Octal is a base 8 system using the digits 0–7. Like hexadecimal, it is used to change large binary numbers into a more easily understood format. Binary-coded octal is commonly used in smaller computer systems. Only three binary digits are needed to encode each octal digit. For example, the octal notation "250" (which is "168" in decimal) is 010 101 000 in binary-coded octal.

Since each data element is either a 1 or 0, it is important that each is in its correct place within a byte. For this purpose, a *parity bit* is added to each byte as a reference for checking that the data are unaltered as they move through a system. Power surges and other intermittent electrical activity can cause bits to change their states. This most commonly occurs to only one bit in a string of millions, and practically never occurs to two closely located or consecutive bits. Since only a bit per byte is likely ever to be altered, checking can be done by using a single parity bit as an indicator of the number of 1s or on-states that exist in the byte. When an error is detected by the machine, an error message is given, and after multiple attempts at corrected transmission, the machine stops and waits for further instructions. The number of parity bits in some machines is as many as five, and can be used to identify the incorrect bit and correct it. EBCDIC uses a ninth bit for parity.

- The central processing unit (CPU) consists of memory for holding data and instructions for processing.
- External storage devices hold results and/or unprocessed data in machine-readable form for future processing and/or later display.

23

Memory and External Storage

It is important to keep in mind the distinction between memory and external or auxiliary storage. Within the CPU of the computer system, data and instruction are maintained in memory—a limited storage area and part of the CPU. Memory devices are semiconductors, magnetic cores, magnetic bubbles, and charge-coupled devices (CCDs). Memory capacities vary from about 70 million bits in large computers to half a million bits in microcomputers. Memory capacity is commonly expressed in bytes, or 8-bit groups; for instance, the memory for a minicomputer is 262K (the symbol K actually equals 2^{10} or 1,024) bytes.

External storage of data is done in devices that are separate from the mainframe (CPU). Externally stored data is shuttled to main memory in the CPU as needed for processing. Output from the CPU can be fed to external storage devices in addition or in lieu of CRT or hardcopy or printed paper display. In this sense, external storage is considered another and important area of I/O operations. Storage media are magnetic tape and magnetic or optical disk.

Data in storage are either in random access or serial format. Random access refers to storing or retrieving data by use of an address for the location in which the data is stored. A random access memory device is arranged in a grid of boxlike locations, each having a vertical and horizontal coordinate—an addressable location. Thereby, bits of data can be stored or retrieved in any sequence and all are handled equally as fast. Random access memories (RAMs), also called read/write memories, are used to store and retrieve data in a random-access fashion. They are used for

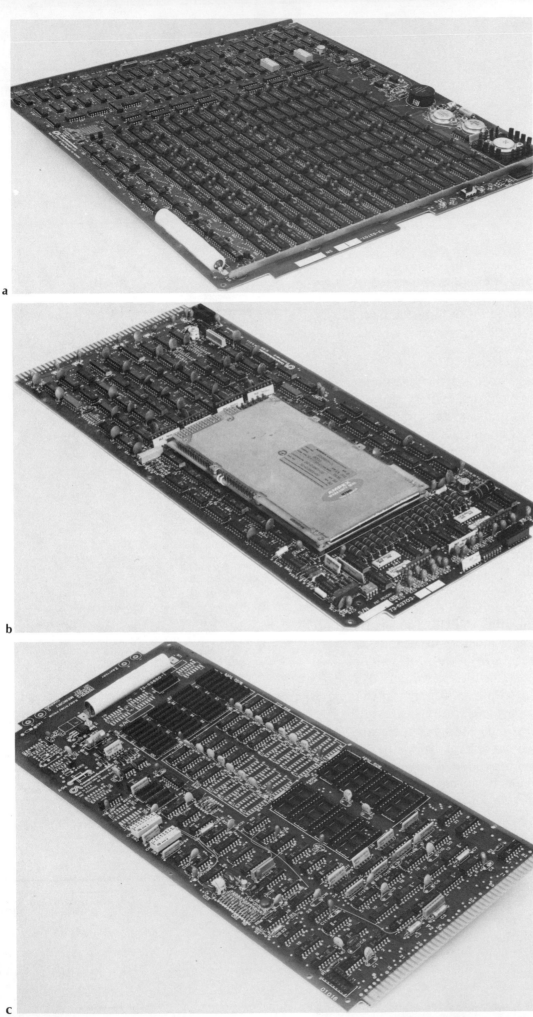

FIG. 23-1. (a) Full-card RAM;
(b) half-card core memory;
(c) RAM/ROM/PROM memory
board; (d) A/D converter
(Courtesy of Computer
Automation, Inc., NAKED MINI
Div.)

a

b

c

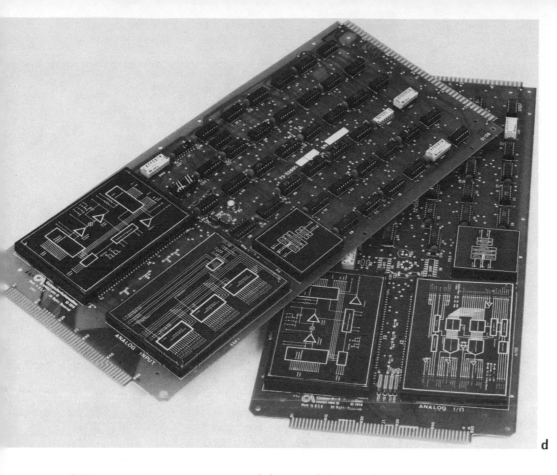

d

CPU memories to store entered data and the results of processing as required. Read-only memories (ROMs) are used also in memories, but for random-access retrieval only. They come from the manufacturer with specific data stored in them. ROMs are used to hold data or instructions that are used repeatedly in a system—for example, the instructions for converting operator commands into machine language. Programmable ROMs (PROMs) and erasable PROMs (EPROMs) are available to users for their own special programming purposes, such as to store special data used in a custom-designed game. RAMs, ROMs, PROMs, and EPROMs are all semiconductor devices. Magnetic cores are another type of memory device used in older, large computers. Cores are also arranged in grid arrays for random-access storage and retrieval of data. (See Chapter 3.)

Another random-access or nonsequential medium in wide use for external storage is the *magnetic disk*—a metal platter with an iron oxide coating. The recording head, like that in a magnetic tape recorder, is an electromagnet used to magnetize groups of tiny metal particles in the coating, making the patterns that represent data. Signals are recorded in binary-coded formats, in two-state magnetic signals. A recording surface is made up of tracks located in sectors. Every track and sector is addressable, giving disk

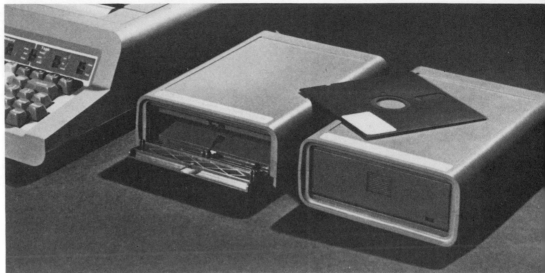

FIG. 23-2. Mini–floppy disk and disk drive for data storage (Courtesy of Computer Devices, Inc.)

storage its random-access feature. Disks can be stacked and both surfaces of each disk used for storage. In such cases, a multihead, comblike assembly is used. In response to signals received from a computer, disk-drive mechanisms, controlling head(s) and disk movement, can locate a specific track in a specific sector and store or retrieve data in tens of milliseconds. Three million bits per square inch is the storage density of disks.

Floppy disks, or *diskettes*, are an outgrowth of magnetic disk storage. They are made with a soft plastic material in lieu of metal and are enclosed in a hard plastic case. Two sizes of floppy disks are in wide use: standard floppy and minifloppy. The standard floppy has about eighty tracks, and the minifloppy has about half that. Access time for the minifloppy is about a half-second; for the floppy, a quarter-second. The disk size with case for the minifloppy is about 5 by 5 inches; for the floppy, 8 by 8 inches. Sectoring of a surface is done either "hard" or "soft." *Hard sectoring* refers to the marking of sector boundaries with holes punched into the disk. *Soft sectoring* requires that sector boundaries be identified with recorded data. Hard sectoring provides all its space for data storage, whereas with soft sectoring, storage space is used for sector identification.

Optical disk storage is under development as a computer storage medium. (For a discussion of related optical disk recording, video disk, see chapter 9.)

The merry-go-round and brass ring make a good analogy for explaining the concept of storing and retrieving data in serial format. Consider each carousel horse as a storage location. The pole from which the brass ring is held out is the point from which data are entered and retrieved from storage locations. Let's say the brass ring is a bit of data taken by the rider on the red horse. To retrieve it, we must wait till the red horse comes around and passes the point again. And so it is with data in serial or sequential storage media, such as magnetic bubbles, CCDs, and magnetic tape. (For a discussion of bubbles and CCDs, see chapter 3.) Serial devices are less costly and more economical for mass storage of data such as banking records. Large computer facilities use both random-access and serial devices.

In large systems, main memory and external storage can be linked so that they effectively are one

FIG. 23-3. Serial access peripheral memory media

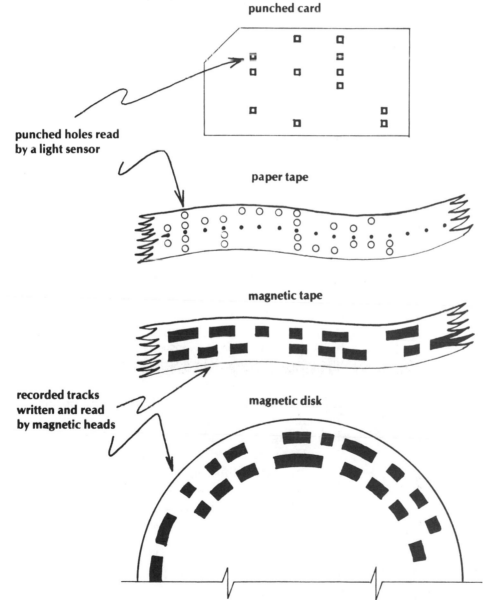

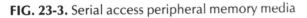

large-capacity memory. *Virtual storage* or *virtual memory* is the term used to describe such a capability. The link is accomplished through special programming designed into the system. So-called "pages" of data are automatically shuttled between main memory and external storage devices as they are needed.

The same type of magnetic tape used for sound and video recording is used for data storage. And the principles of magnetic disk reading and writing are the same for tape—magnetizing and sensing domains of tiny metal particles in a coating, in this case, on a ribbon of flexible plastic (Mylar). Computer tape is $\frac{1}{2}$-inch and is commonly spun onto 2,400- or 600-foot reels. Tape transport mechanisms operate at rates that range from about 20 to 300 ips. Transport mechanisms incorporate two vacuum columns through which the tape is looped to reduce the shock of quick movements involved in the high-speed changes of direction necessary for tape searching operations.

On the average, over 100 million characters can be stored per 2,400-foot reel. Character storage density runs from about 200 to 500 characters per inch in low-density mode, and from 800 to about 6,000 cpi in high-density mode. A magnetic tape system's *transfer rate*—the time it takes for data to be transferred to main memory—is determined by multiplying the tape speed in inches per second times the density in characters per inch. For example, at 6,000 characters per inch on a tape moving at 300 inches per second, the transfer rate is 1.8 million characters per second.

When data are encoded on tape, they are formed into *records*, groups of related characters, such as an individual customer's account information. Records can be grouped together into blocks to bring I/O speeds in line with computer speeds. Records or blocks are separated by gaps of about a half-inch of blank tape. The gaps are an aid in locating the start and end of data groups.

Cassette devices, the same $\frac{1}{4}$-inch systems popular for sound recording, are widely used for economical data storage, especially for microcomputer operations. Data are stored as sounds of two particular frequencies, depending on the standard. The Kansas City standard, for example, uses eight cycles of a 2,400-Hz tone for 1 bits, and four cycles of a 1,200-Hz tone for 0 bits. Each character is separated by two 0 bits. The speed of cassette recorders is $1\frac{7}{8}$ inches per second. Character density is about 16 cpi, thus giving a data transfer rate of 30 characters per second—a relatively slow device.

FIG. 23-4. Cartridge Drive, the size of a standard floppy disk drive, can record 75 megabytes of user data. (Courtesy of 3M)

Considering the function of storage of data in the CPU, two other devices are noteworthy: registers and buffers. *Registers* hold pieces of data on a temporary basis; for example, during the addition of two numbers, a register accumulates the arithmetic results as they are produced. Memory addresses, instruction codes, and data en route to and from main memory are held in registers as they circulate through the system. *Buffers* are also temporary storage devices. Their application is geared to accumulating data from one device functioning at a particular speed for release to another device functioning at another speed. In computer graphics systems, a frame buffer is used to store all the data required to make up a total frame of picture. From the buffer, the data are fed to the image generation circuitry for display on the screen. The data cannot be fed directly from the computer to the screen.

24

Data Manipulation

- The control processing unit (or mainframe) is composed of memory for holding data and instructions for processing, an arithmetic/logic unit—the brain—and a control unit—the nerve center of the system.

The computer is a machine primarily made up of numerous two-state electrical switches and connection lines for interconnecting those switches in various ways at various times to perform a variety of processing tasks. Groups of switches are used to store and process data. Other groups temporarily store and decode memory addresses and instructions. Data and instructions flow between groups of switches under the control of other groups of switches. Switches are to an electronic computer what gears are to a mechanical machine. Both the intermeshing of gears and the sequencing of switches result in the smooth working of their respective machinery.

Memory circuits are made up of two-state switches grouped to hold a number of bits of binary-coded data or instructions. Each group of switches is identified in memory by an address. The memory section contains an address decoder, a group of switches that feeds out the contents of a specified set of memory switches when it is sent an address. Registers—small, temporary memory units in the ALU and CU—are groups of switches used for short-term storage of data, addresses, and instructions that are being acted upon at the moment.

The "nerve center," the CU, controls the flow of messages (data, addresses, instructions) between itself, memory, the ALU, input, and output. It is made up of what can be thought as the "master switches" of the system.

The "brain," the ALU, consists of sets of switches that perform all the processing of data carried out in the computer. Switching algebra, or Boolean logic, governs the way switches are used to carry out arithmetic and logic operations. The basic operations that switches or switching circuits are used to carry out are AND, OR, and NOT. (These operations are discussed in chapter 3.) A switching circuit used in a processing operation has two or more inputs and one output that is a direct result of the inputs. A circuit is an electronic gate that is operated by a set of electrical conditions. Actually, in computers, in most cases, a high- and a low-voltage state is used.

The AND operation, performed by the AND circuit, produces a high voltage (commonly representing a binary 1) at its output when the inputs are all high voltage (1s). If any input is low voltage (a binary 0), the output is low voltage (0). An electronic gate, in a manner of speaking, always opens. The combination of inputs determines which of two possible signals goes through, either a high voltage (1) or a low voltage (0). In terms of logical operations, an example of the AND operation can be seen in the processing task of determining voter eligibility on the basis of citizenship, age, and domicile. If a person is a citizen AND of voting age AND lives within the specified voting district, then that person may vote. If any of the criteria are not met, then that person may not vote.

The OR operation, performed by the OR circuit, produces a high-voltage (1) output from its inputs if any input is high voltage. If all inputs are low voltage, the output is low voltage. An example of the logical operation of OR can be seen in the processing task, again, of determining an aspect of voter eligibility. Assume that a voting place serves several but not all of the districts in a town. To vote at that polling place, a person's domicile must be in district 1, 3, OR 5 of whatever number of districts make up the town. If the domicile is not in district 1, 3, OR 5, the person may not vote at that polling place.

The NOT operation, performed by the NOT circuit, produces an output that is opposite a single input. A high-voltage input produces a low-voltage output and vice versa. In terms of logical operations, NOT is used with AND and OR to make up NAND (NOT AND) and NOR (NOT OR). Keep in mind that, in computers, we are manipulating binary-coded data or voltage levels representing 1s and 0s which, in turn, represent letters, numbers, and special characters. In binary addition, for example, a 1 and a 1 added together make 10; that is, 1 and 1 equals 0, carry the 1 to the next digit place—10. If an AND circuit were used, the result would be 1 and 1 equals 1, which is incorrect. For binary addition, a NAND circuit performs the job.

In a computer, these basic logic circuits are used for

control, memory, arithmetic, and logic operations of binary-coded data, memory addresses, and instructions. Grouped and connected together, simple circuits make up complex circuitry, such as adders, memory cell arrays, and decoders. In the arithmetic/logic unit, for example, a complex of logic circuits can be programmed for connection in a variety of configurations to perform a number of operations, such as addition, subtraction, multiplication, division, rounding numbers, left and right number shifting, and comparing. It's interesting to note that all arithmetic operations in a computer are forms of addition of binary numbers. Binary subtraction is addition in reverse, or complement addition. Division is repeated subtraction, and multiplication is repeated addition. Systems are built consisting only of circuits that can add binary numbers.

PROCESSING SIGNALS

There are three types of signals in a computer during its operation: data signals, memory addresses, and control signals.

FIG. 24-1. The CPU system

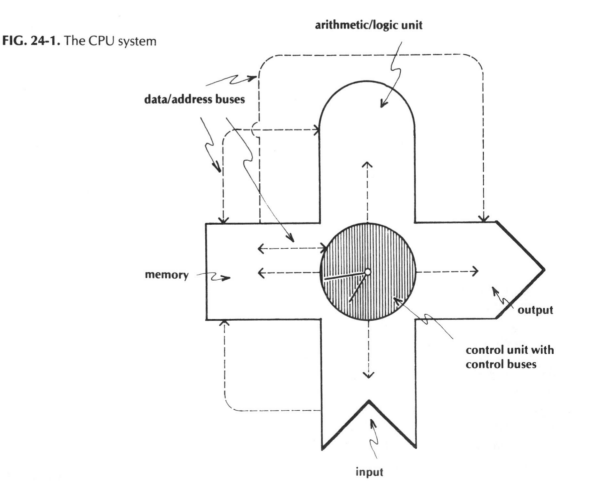

Data signals are the coded information, such as numbers and letters, that have been entered into the computer for processing.

Memory address signals are the memory location codes indicating where data and instructions are stored. Once data and instructions are stored in memory, they are referenced by their addresses.

Control signals are the instructions after they have been retrieved from memory and decoded. They serve to connect up the necessary circuits for accomplishing each processing step.

BUSES

The components of the CPU are tied together by three main connection lines called buses: the control bus, the data/address bus, and the power supply bus. The control and data/address buses are the thoroughfares along which data, memory addresses, and control signals flow between memory, the CU, the ALU, and input and output devices.

The *control bus* carries the control signals from the control unit to other sections of the system.

The *data/address bus* is a two-way path along which data and memory addresses travel between

FIG. 24-2. John Dalton at the DIDS terminal

graphic materials in minutes. However, on domestic affairs he's no better off than the rest of us, often getting information from the TV." In Harden's first months in Washington, he was equally impressed by both the many and varied reservoirs of information that were available, and the lack of swift and easy access to them. Thus, as Zimmerman reported in July 1978 to a Harvard group concerned with computer uses of information, they set out to find a way to develop the means of "delivering better and more timely information for policy and decision making."

The Census Bureau, for example, regularly puts out information that, if delivered within an appropriate time frame and format, could have a positive impact on the formation of domestic policy and decision making. The impediment, however, has been the printed page and the time it has taken to prepare, distribute, and analyze it. Harden and Zimmerman needed something that would cut that time from its days, weeks, and months to seconds, minutes, and hours. Visiting the NASA Goddard Space Flight Center, they came in contact with the Atmospheric and Oceanic Information Processing System (AOIPS), which employed computer-generated color video graphics to enhance satellite imagery for meteorological study. "It occurred to us that AOIPS technology could be used to construct and deliver thematic maps, and we asked NASA and the Census to try it out."

From that has come the Domestic Information Display System (DIDS). A key person in the development of DIDS was John Dalton, heading the Computer Applications Section of AOIPS at Goddard. In a fall 1979 interview, Dalton explained that AOIPS had been working with a computer graphics system since 1974. "It was a turnkey system, for which we developed additional software for specific image manipulations and enhancements, which we wanted for identifying ground features in our satellite images." It only took four months from the time of Harden's request for the experiment to a demonstration of a prototype for decision makers in Congress and the White House. The image analysis computer-driven terminals, a minicomputer with a half-million sixteen-word bits of core memory, three nine-track 800/1,600 bits per inch tape

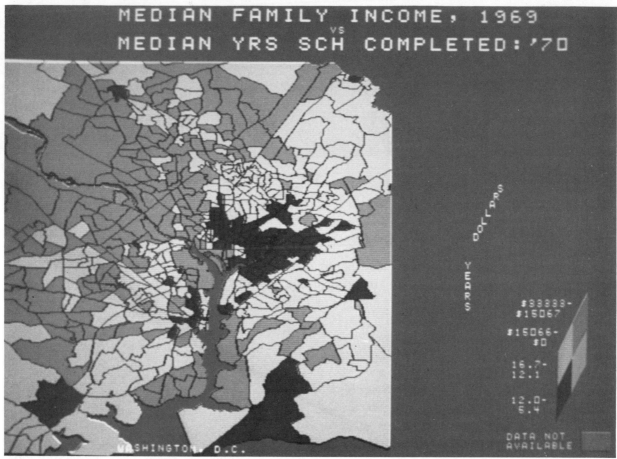

FIG. 24-3. DIDS graphics (Courtesy of NASA)

memory, control unit, and ALU and from input to memory and memory to output.

The *power supply bus* carries electricity to power all circuits of all sections of the system.

When a computer is turned on, all switches, or gates, contain a charge, either a high-voltage or a low-voltage signal. All these two-state switches, in binary-coded 1 or 0 states, are normally disconnected from the control and data/address buses. We might say that signals "bite at their bits" waiting like race-horses for their gates to open. Only one signal at a time can occupy a control and data/address bus. When a gate is opened and connected to a bus, its signal is electrically drawn to another open gate connected to the bus at that same instant. The gate drawing signal to it is switched to the state of that signal. Thus, a signal can be communicated from one part of the system to another. Keep in mind that signals do not abandon one gate to go to another. A signal is extended along the bus to another circuit and is not lost to the gate from which it originates. For instance, when data are retrieved from memory, they are "copied" onto other circuits while still existing in memory until those memory locations are used for some other data.

drives, three 176-megabyte disk drivers for data and software storage, plus several alpha-numeric terminals for software development, kept both "meteorological analysis and DIDS" going until early 1980, when DIDS obtained its own hardware.

On a video screen, DIDS generates maps of the United States composed of colored areas representing statistical information. "Our basic commandment is that all data is publicly available," said Dalton of the information fed into the system; "no confidential data. It's all aggregated to a geographical level like counties. We first used ten categories of information from Census." A map is produced in four seconds. The statistics can be, for example, percentages of those employed in manufacturing in 1970, the estimated per capita income in 1974, or the median school years completed in 1970. There are several geographic levels of display; all the United States, a single state, and a Standard Metropolitan Statistical Area. Data may be aggregated to statewide, county, or congressional district levels. A system user can interact with displays, change colors to enhance clarity, modify statistical limits, zoom in on areas of special interest, combine two variables such as school years completed and per capita income, and call up histograms, which chart changes over periods of years.

By late 1979, more than fifteen federal agencies were participating in the development of DIDS with statistics on population, birth and death rates, education, crime rates, government employment, income, housing, banking, manufacturing, agriculture, federal funds and grants distribution, fuel consumption, public works projects, employment and unemployment, air and water quality, coal production by method, veteran population by period of service, race, and ethnic origin of metropolitan populations, their incomes and occupations, and so on.

In 1974, at an annual meeting of the American Society for Information Science (ASIS), Jimmy Carter, then governor of Georgia, declared his commitment to information as a resource to benefit people.

At the onset of his presidency, the assignment of Harden to the tasks of upgrading information-handling capabilities in the EOP and of exposing staff to information technology and its uses was the first and a significant step in establishing a permanent information support base for all administrations to come. Harden's office of Administration and Information Management was created with two divisions: the Information Systems Division to develop and operate a computer and communications system, and the Information Management and Services Division for actual information processing. Harden's staff worked to obtain appropriate hardware. It also worked with the Information Bank of the *New York Times* and other information repositories in reformatting their data resources to meet the needs of the EOP users, and it led the development of the DIDS project. In an ASIS Bulletin of December 1978, Harden wrote that, "our objective is . . . to provide the technical tools that the [EOP] advisor needs to make better use of information in making decisions."

Going beyond EOP uses, information scientists see, in the DIDS-type display technology, the potential for the average citizen with a home computer to produce simply un-

SERIAL AND PARALLEL SIGNALS

As noted in chapter 18, "Sizes of Systems," the paths along which signal flows are of a variety of bit widths: 4 bits wide, referred to as a *nibble*; 8 bits wide, the *byte*; 16 bits, the *half word*; 32 bits, the *word*; and 64 bits, the *double word*. In computers, circuits can be arranged to handle signal in either a serial or parallel operation.

In *parallel circuitry*, all eight bits of a byte, for example, are operated on simultaneously. The circuitry consists of eight separate circuits arranged side by side for handling a signal consisting of eight side-by-side bits. For each gate, a bus exists.

In *serial circuitry*, a byte is handled by a single gate, one bit after the other. Only a single bus is required. Serial operations are slower and cheaper than parallel operations.

MORE ON CONTROL SIGNALS

The essence of today's "stored-program" computer is that it deals with data and instructions in the same way—as binary-coded electrical signals. Both are stored in memory. When instructions are decoded in the control unit of the computer, they become circuit-connection signals that identify which gates are connected to the bus at a given instant. For example, the instruction "LOAD" means "Send data of a specified memory location to a temporary storage area (register) in the ALU." When entered into the computer, the instruction is written "LOAD 1111." When it is retrieved from memory for execution and decoded, the computer will open the gates of memory location 1111 and those of the register in the ALU causing the register to copy the data in memory. Control signals are, in a manner of speaking, the gatekeepers, opening gates as they are required to perform particular processing steps.

In addition to connecting up circuits between which data flow, control signals connect up arithmetic and logic circuits in the many different configurations required for the many different processing tasks of which the computer is capable. In most computers, that is about a hundred or more distinct processing tasks. A computer does not have separate circuits for each processing task it can perform. The ALU, in which the processing circuitry exists, is made up of a limited number of circuits that can be interconnected in different ways to accomplish each required task. The control signals decoded from an instruction like "ADD" connect up the circuits in a different way than control signals from an instruction like "DIVIDE."

CLOCK

The ALU was referred to earlier as the brain of the system and the CU as its nerve center. Using a physiological analogy once more, the computer also has a "heart": an oscillator or *clock*, part of the control unit, which keeps the beat for all system operations. Clock pulses are fed throughout the computer to all components along the clock's own system of lines. Clock pulse rates can vary in different computers. The faster the rate, the faster the operation of the computer.

MACHINE CYCLE

The computer, like most machines, operates according to a preset sequence of steps, or what is called a *machine cycle*. The machine cycle of a washing machine, for example, consists of these steps: fill with water, wash, drain soapy water, fill again, rinse, drain, spin dry, and stop. Each step takes place in sequence as triggered by a signal from a timer, which also controls the duration of each operation.

The machine cycle of a computer consists of two basic steps: the *instruction* phase or *I-cycle* and the *execution* phase or the *E-cycle*. During the I-cycle, an instruction is fetched from a specified memory location and brought to the control unit, where it is decoded. In the E-cycle, the instruction is carried out. This fetch/execute sequence is repeated for every instruction in a program of instructions. Millions, verging on a billion, of computer machine cycles occur every second in a large computer.

COMPUTER OPERATIONS

To examine the specific steps carried out in a computer, consider the following processing problem. A company is developing an early retirement program and wants to know how many employees would be eligible. It has been determined that two criteria for retirement must be met: the person must be age fifty or over and must have worked at least twenty years for the company. To perform such a job, a search of

derstood maps of vast amounts of statistical data, usually comprehensible to only trained analysts sifting through reams of computer printouts. In *Fast Facts,* a monthly publication from Goddard's Office of Public Affairs, Harvard's Allan Schmidt, executive director of the Laboratory of Computer Graphics and Spatial Analysis, uses the phrase "everyman's maps" in describing the possible role of cartographic displays in aiding local planning and decision making. He projects the case of a community planning a new school and, for a town meeting, the rapid compilation of maps showing the best building sites in terms of economics, growth, and environment. "With sets of understandable facts at hand, citizens could see more easily the adverse effects of their intuitive biases, make compromises, and reach informed decisions that best reflect their own interest."

It is also hoped that that kind of effect will alleviate the struggles that often prevent cooperation between the executive and legislative branches. As Zimmerman put it, "If we are to have a viable constitutional government, differences of opinion must be based on substance and not smoke between the branches. But when each goes off and gets some numbers, and starts comparing apples and oranges, we cannot tell the substance from the immaterial differences. We need to share common sources of information and not rule out the constructive competition that comes at the analytical level. Right now, with statistics, we have several different organizations saying different things. We may not share analytical conclusions, but raw data we can share."

Within federal and state government, DIDS has gained wide acceptance. Numerous users are taking advantage of it. Two Environmental Protection Agency scientists employed DIDS in a study linking diseases and air and water pollution in areas throughout the United States. DIDS maps showing the areas of correlation helped to identify regions needing the most attention. The Drug Enforcement Agency explored DIDS capabilities for mapping the "hot spots" of drug abuse by location and drug to better allocate resources to meet the problem. The Georgia State Department of Offender Rehabilitation produced illustrations for a book on crime in the state showing the correlations of the county judicial circuits' level of felony arrests and convictions per 100,000 population, severity of sentence, and comparisons of offenders given probation and imprisonment.

DIDS is viewed by some as the initiation of a public information network. Proposals for such a resource were presented in the 1960s and 1970s without broad acceptance. The National Data Bank, the sixties version, and FEDNET of the seventies contained technical requirements for centralizing data collection to achieve a computerized exchange. That threatened security, confidentiality, and privacy and was politically unacceptable. In the late 1970s, with the advent of small computer distributed data processing, data bases, and telecommunication hookups, centralized collection is not required. Information can be left at its source and communicated to users when needed. Zimmerman saw DIDS being integrated into a network in which independent data resource centers are connected to a host system that interconnects them for exchanges. The network would permit data exchange, electronic mail, and software exchange. It would be interconnected with other computer networks, extending it outside the DIDS complex.

In 1979, DIDS began operating from the Department of Commerce, which maintained a terminal at its main offices in Washington, D.C. Commerce's Office of Federal Statistical Policy and Standards had been in on DIDS since its inception, as has its overseer, the Office of the Chief Economist. DIDS brought new life to the federal statistical system, and Zimmerman, in a November 1979 paper on DIDS, wrote of the possible formation of a Central Statistical Organization in which to institutionalize DIDS and the public information network.

Meanwhile, in 1980, decentralization came to DIDS. Owing to market developments, microcomputers and new graphic display terminals were acquired at lesser costs than those of the first installation. The use of the small computers with on-site disk storage of data has lessened the need for costly transmission between the Goddard site and a remote terminal.

"The terminal will become as ubiquitous as the telephone," said Zimmerman. "The publishing industry as we know it today is

all employee records must be made to identify those who meet the requirements. Depending on how data are organized in each record, the job could be simple or complex. If data have been entered in any old way, the search to locate the significant pieces of data could be time-consuming. If, on the other hand, data are organized in a consistent format throughout all records, providing easy access to things like first year of employment and date of birth, the job would be expedited. Taking it a step further, the records could contain a retirement eligibility indicator. Assuming the records are up to date, the job becomes one of simply finding those records on which the eligibility indicator is displayed. It is important to know how data are organized before they get to a computer.

For this example, the records are well organized into a consistent format clearly displaying the date of birth and first year of employment. Effectively, the job is to figure out the age and years employed of each employee, and to compare those data with the criteria for retirement eligibility. The pieces of data to be entered into the computer memory for processing are the birth date and first year of employment of each record; age 50 and 20 years work time as the two criteria; and the present date. The processing steps to be taken are as follows: (1) Determine the age of an employee by subtracting the birth date from the present date; (2) compare the result to 50, the age criterion, to determine if the age is lesser or greater; (3) if age eligibility is not met, indicate at the output; if met, go on to determine the number of years employed by subtracting the first year of employment from the present date; (4) compare the result to 20, the worktime criterion, to determine if the years employed are lesser or greater; (5) indicate the result at output. If we wanted a list of the eligible employees, we would also have to enter into memory the names of each and, as a part of step 5, send those names to output that met both eligibility criteria.

A set of instructions (program) revealing the processing steps to be taken is written in a programming language that the computer is "wired" to understand. A programming instruction or command, as pointed out earlier, is a code for a set of signals that causes the computer to connect up specific gates. Instructions and data are entered into the computer memory in specified locations. Once entered, data and instructions are referred to by their memory addresses. For example, the age criterion, 50, is at location 1111.

Consider the execution of the instruction "LOAD 1111" in terms of a computer machine cycle. When the computer is started, it is set to its first position, just as the washing machine must be set at the first position of its cycle. The first instruction is then fetched from memory, where it has been stored. This is done as follows: A signal is fed from the *program counter*— a register in the CU that contains the memory address of the instruction or data being acted upon at the moment. The memory address contained in the program counter is sent to the *address decoder*, which is part of the memory. The decoder is an array of circuits that serves to locate the particular memory cells identified by the address connecting them to the bus so that their contents can be sent to the *instruction decoder* in the CU. Once decoded by the instruction decoder, the instructions become a set of control signals for connecting specific circuits to the bus. In the I-cycle, or instruction phase, "LOAD 1111," which is stored at the address indicated on the program counter, is retrieved and decoded.

The instruction phase is followed by the execute phase, or E-cycle, which carries out the instruction as follows: The program counter displays the address 1111, the location of the data to be acted upon. The memory's address decoder locates and connects the appropriate memory cells to the bus, and the control signals, decoded from the instruction "LOAD," open the gates of the register in the ALU, causing the contents of 1111 to be sent there.

The following terms describe some important aspects of computer operations.

Operand is the term used to denote the thing (data, address, etc.) that is to be operated upon at a given moment.

Synchronous operation is the operation of a computer, as described above, in which all steps proceed in accordance with a clock pulse. In *asynchronous operations*, circuit operations are not related to timing signals from a clock. A sequencing of steps is accomplished by a signal at the end of each step, indicating completion.

Firmware denotes software stored and accessed from a read-only memory (ROM), which is part of the CPU.

Microinstructions are the most basic steps taken by a computer.

Microcode or *microprogramming* is the combining of microinstructions to make up macroinstructions, as in the retirement eligibility problem discussed earlier: The macroinstruction "COMPARE 1111" could be used to represent the several microinstructions involved in comparing an employee's age with the cri-

doomed. It can't continue to put information in a physical form and create an energy-consumptive transportation problem. Electronic media don't do that. In the case of terminals, the end user can decide what and when he wants a physical form. CRT with hardcopy printer; that's clearly the direction of the future, though it may take forty years."

In early 1981, under the Reagan administration's guidance, DIDS found support and a new overseer in the person of Dr. Richard Beale, the director of the Office for Planning Evaluation in the Office of Management and Budget (OMB). DIDS, along with its keeper at the Department of Commerce, Dr. Joe Duncan, moved into the White House as one of Beale's moves to set up the Information System for Policy Planning (ISPP). ISPP services the informational needs of the OMB and operates the National Indicator System (NIS) that provides the president with briefings on domestic affairs. For instance, when Reagan wants to obtain 1980 census data related to the geographic distribution of the elderly, DIDS is brought into action.

Whereas the Carter view of an information system was based on centralizing functions in a Central Statistical Organization, the Reagan view leaves the functions in the departments where they have traditionally been and centralizes policy. As Joe Duncan put it, "Harden, as Carter's director of the Office of Administration and Information Management, thought 'delivery of services,' Beale, Harden's counterpart in the Reagan administration, thinks 'policy making.'"

In any case, DIDS survives and seems to be a "little information pill" of universal benefit.

terion age stored at memory location 1111. Since this operation is repeated for every record that is processed, the several required microinstructions could be programmed into a ROM to be executed every time the macroinstruction "COMPARE 1111" comes up. comes up.

Operation code or *op code* is the part of the instruction representing the specific operations to be carried out.

The numerous switches that make up a computer can be connected in a variety of configurations. Each configuration allows a different operation to be performed. All computers have a specific number of operations (switching configurations). They make up the computer's "instruction set." In large computers, some 150 different operations can be performed by the computer. In small computers, an instruction set can have some 80 operations.

Programming a computer involves selecting a series of operations for performance by the computer, causing it to accomplish a useful task. Programs, or sets of instructions, are written and then entered into the computer memory from which each instruction, in its prescribed sequence, is retrieved by the CPU's control unit for execution.

The basic switching configurations that represent operations of the computer are coded in *machine language*—binary code. Programming in machine language is possible, but obviously highly complex and time-consuming. Thus, special programming languages have been developed to simplify people-to-machine communications.

LANGUAGES

A level above machine language is *assembly*, a so-called *low-level language*. In assembly language, machine codes are represented by mnemonics—short, easy-to-remember names of machine operations such as ADD and LOAD. Memory locations can also be referenced by symbolic names in lieu of machine codes. An *assembler* program is used to translate between the symbolic name and the string of 1s and 0s representing the operation. Assemblers translate on a one-to-one basis; one assembly language statement equals one machine language operation. Assembly languages are machine-dependent, meaning they are written specially for the circuits of specific machines. There are also "cross-assembler" programs, which

25

Programming

Glossary: Automatic Information Processing

Data processing (DP) is the handling of data—numbers, letters, words, statements—in a sequence of operations designed to obtain a specific result. Computer programs provide the sequence of operations controlling the processor. The processing system is made up of data entry (input) and output devices, a processor—computer, minicomputer, or microprocessor—and storage devices. Other parts of a system can include a high-speed printer, a video display terminal (VDT), a copier, and telecommunications devices.

Word processing (WP) evolved from automatic text editing, a system that added electronics and storage capacity to the typewriter, making it possible to (1) display text on a TV screen, (2) electronically correct and alter copy, and (3) obtain high-speed automatic playout—production of the typed page—at the touch of a key. The WP system takes electronic typewriting a step further by adding telecommunications capabilities, thereby hooking up the WP workstation to computers, dictating machines, electronic files, printers, etc., in nearby and distant locations.

Distributed data processing (DDP) refers to decentralized processing facilities using minicomputers in contrast to a large, monolithic processing system.

Multiprocessing refers to the use of more than one computer doing the same job. The additional computers serve as backup systems. The 1981 maiden voyage of the space shuttle *Columbia* was controlled by a five-computer, multiprocessing system.

Multiprogramming refers to the handling of two or more jobs by a single computer. Data entry rates are considerably slower than processing rates: Entry can take seconds or milliseconds, while processing is achieved in microseconds. To use machine time most efficiently, interleaving of many different jobs is common.

Time sharing is the use of a large processing facility by many simultaneous users at different geographic locations, each interacting directly with the computer.

translate symbolic or assembly language written for one computer into the machine code of another, different computer.

The *high-level languages* resemble conversational language. A single statement in a high-level language can instruct a computer to perform several operations. High-level languages, of which there are over one hundred, are machine-independent. They can be used with any computer having the necessary program for translation between levels of language. Such translation programs are called *compilers*. The compiler translates a high-level statement into a series of machine language operations.

Of the hundred or so high-level-programming languages, about a dozen are in common use.

BASIC *(Beginners All-purpose Symbolic Instruction Code)* is a high-level language that was developed at Dartmouth College for time-sharing use of campus computer resources by students. BASIC is an interactive language designed for I/O teletype console. It is widely used in microcomputer systems.

FORTRAN *(Formula Translation)* was developed for scientific and technical problem solving in which mathematics is used. It is a widely known language, though it lacks the facilities to handle characters. FORTRAN IV is used for large systems, while FORTRAN 80 has been developed for small computers.

COBOL *(Common Business Oriented Language)* is designed for business data processing. It was developed by the Conference on Data Systems Languages (CODASYL), a cooperative effort of users and manufacturers. COBOL 80 has been developed for microcomputer systems having the same character processing facilities as COBOL.

PL/1 *(Programming Language/One)* is an outgrowth of efforts to improve FORTRAN. In effect, it combines the facilities of FORTRAN and COBOL and can be used for all purposes. PL/M has been developed for micro systems.

APL *(A Programming Language)* is designed for interactive processing. It is a very high-level language with mathematical operators and was developed by IBM. APL/Z-80 has been developed for a microcomputer system.

ALGOL *(Algorithmic Language)* is popular in Europe. It was created by an international committee and is most suited to mathematical problems.

PASCAL is a language in popular use in the field of computer science.

APT *(Automatically Programmed Tools)* is used

for control of machine tools. It is the language of automation.

GPSS *(General Purpose Simulation System)* is a high-level language used for design and manufacturing problems in which a mathematical model can be developed and tested by simulating conditions related to it.

RPG *(Report Program Generation)* is used for structuring the production of business reports.

Generally, high-level languages are considered either procedure-oriented or problem-oriented. *Problem-oriented* languages are designed for particular applications, for example, RPG, the language for preparing business reports. *Procedure-oriented* languages have a wide range of applications.

SOFTWARE

A computer can do nothing without programs to direct it. In computer parlance, *software* means the programs that make the *hardware*, or computer machinery, perform the operations of which it is capable. "Applications software" refers to programs that are written by users to accomplish specific jobs, such as tabulating census data or doing a payroll.

In the discussion on languages above, translation programs were mentioned: assembler programs, which translate mnemonics to machine code, and compiler programs, which translate high-level language statements to machine code. Such programs function to make the system work. They are part of the *systems software* required to make a total computer system work. A good example of a systems software package is the IBM Disk Operating System (DOS). DOS consists of three groups of programs that are maintained in disk storage and called into action as required during processing.

The *control software* consists of programs to control the orderly flow of both applications and systems programs. It is made up of a start-up program to prepare the computer for operation, and a supervisory and job control program to handle program sequencing. The supervisor programs are kept in memory for tracking and controlling all system operations. The supervisor is itself under the control of the computer operator sitting at the console.

Systems service software consists of a "linkage editor," which is a program that aids translation of computer languages into machine code, and a "li-

Personal computing is the use of relatively low-cost, small computing devices by individuals in the home or the workplace.

Photocomposition/typesetting, pagination, and **automated imposition** are all terms describing the application of electronic processing to the preparation of print. Photocomposition/typesetting is the setting and specification of type and its production by some kind of photographic process. Pagination is the electronic manipulation of blocks of text and graphics in setting up a whole page. Automated imposition is the process by which lasers are used to make plates for printing presses.

Computer graphics is the processing and generating of visual information by computers. Interactive computer graphics refers to the process in which an operator directs and redirects the actions of the computer in constructing an image.

Computer output micrographics (COM) and **computer input micrographics** (CIM) refer to the use of microfilm for storing and retrieving information. Output devices transfer processor data to microforms, and input devices transfer stored data from microforms to processors.

Source data automation (SDA) is the automatic creation and preparation of input data for computers at the place of data origination. Such automation is designed to replace manual preparation procedures, such as keypunching of cards and keyboard entry at terminals.

Data base management system (DBMS) is a framework for storing data designed to optimize access for a number of related uses—for example, the total information of a company's operations compiled into a data base made up of fiscal, inventory, production, and personnel data from which reports of all types can be drawn.

Management information system (MIS), also referred to as *integrated data processing* or *information systems management,* is a business system for organizing past, present, and projected information of all aspects of an organization's activities to enhance timely and effective decision making by managers on all levels of operation.

Encryption is the coding of data to protect its privacy when transmitted over vulnerable communications lines.

Computer-assisted instruction (CAI) is the

use of interactive processing systems in education.

Computer-aided design (CAD) is the use of computers in architectural, engineering, and product design.

Computer-assisted manufacturing (CAM) is the use of computer devices in the manufacturing process.

Robotics is the development of robots—information processing systems that can perform physical tasks such as welding and assembling parts of a product or vacuuming floors.

Artifical intelligence is the development of programs to enable computers to learn and reason, to play chess, prove theorems, etc.

Simulation is the use of processing to construct models of mathematical relationships or real situations, such as an airplane cockpit, and is used for training and problem-solving studies.

The following technologies are also noteworthy.

Optical character recognition (OCR) is the ability of machines to read print by use of light-sensing devices designed to recognize certain typefaces.

Magnetic ink character recognition (MICR) is the ability of machines to read type that is printed on a page in magnetic ink.

Voice activation or **voice recognition** and **voice synthesis** refer to the ability of a machine to understand and speak language. In its infancy, its future promise was well portrayed in the conversing computer of the film *2001*.

Nonimpact printing is accomplished without the use of mechanical devices, such as keys in typewriters and other impact printers. Instead, printing is electronic, as with ink jet, a guided stream of ink propelled onto the paper. The maximum speed of impact printers is 15 characters per second. Electronic printing devices print at rates near 20,000 lines per minute.

brarian," which maintains a list of all programs making up the DOS.

The *processing software* consists of language translation programs, utility programs required by the systems service software, and, finally, the user-written applications programs.

An operating system controls input and output, language translations, and the actual processing of data, which can include arithmetic and logic operations, branching, and the transfer of data and instructions from place to place in the system.

PROBLEM SOLVING

Program writing is the process of selecting and structuring a sequence of computer operations for solving a problem. Programming involves four major steps: (1) clearly defining the problem, (2) determining the algorithm, or method of solution, (3) creating a flow chart, (4) and writing the program. For purposes of explanation, consider the problem posed in the preceding chapter about employee retirement eligibility.

1. *Problem definition:* Given each employee's year of birth and first work year, and eligibility criteria (fifty years or more of age and twenty years or more of work), determine the retirement eligibility of each employee. In defining the problem, the pertinent, available data are identified and the desired result is stated.

2. *Algorithm:* Eligibility status is the result of determining age by subtracting year of birth from the present year and comparing it to see if it is equal to or greater than 50, and if it is, to then determine the work time by subtracting the first work year from the present year and comparing it to see if it is equal to or greater than 20. The algorithm defines the number of steps to take and the processes to follow for the solution of the problem.

3. *Flow charting:* A "map" of the algorithm is made with a set of graphic symbols and short phrases. It depicts each step in its proper sequence. Flow-chart symbols are fairly well standardized, though not 100 percent so.

In Figure 25-1, flow chart A represents the solution for processing one employee's record. It proceeds from START to END and provides no way for continuous processing of records, as does flow chart B.

4. *Program writing:* Programs are written in a high-level language to represent the flow chart. For each flow-chart block, a separate instruction is coded.

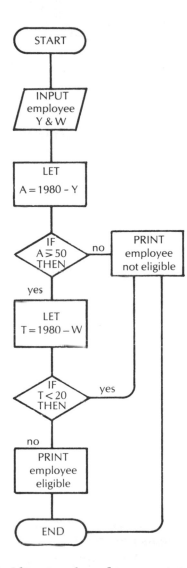

Each coded line is referred to as a *statement*. Each is numbered and appears on a separate line. Numbering determines the sequential order and identifies each instruction. A statement is made up of a number, name, and characters or data values, for example: 80 LET A = 1980 − Y.

Here's the program for determining retirement eligibility written in BASIC. It has been written for interactive processing. In other words, a computer operator at a console would have to call up the program, have the records nearby for entering the data when prompted by the computer. The computer "prompts" are designed into the program.

```
01    REMARK Retirement Eligibility Program

10    PRINT "ENTER NAME—IF NONE ENTER
      NO"

20    INPUT N$
```

```
30     IF N$ = "NO" THEN 160

40     PRINT "ENTER BIRTH YEAR"

50     INPUT Y

60     PRINT "ENTER FIRST WORK YEAR"

70     INPUT W

80     LET A = 1980 – Y

90     IF A $\leqq$ 50 THEN 120

100    PRINT N$; "NOT ELIGIBLE"

110    GOTO 10

120    LET T = 1980 – W

130    IF T < 20 THEN 100

140    PRINT N$; "ELIGIBLE"

150    GOTO 10

160    END
```

REMARKs are for explanation only. They are printed out and appear as the program runs.

PRINT statements are used for display of output. Everything between the quotes is displayed.

Numbering is often done in increments of 5 or 10 to allow room for addition of statements at a later time, if required.

INPUT statements instruct the computer to store the entered data in memory. N$ signifies that a string of characters is the data.

LET statements indicate calculation processes.

IF . . . THEN statements are conditional and used for branching.

GOTO is for looping. "GOTO 10" means, in effect, "Start at the top of the program and run through it again." Note also that IF . . . THEN statements loop to another part of the program.

The above program could be written for batch processing of the same problem. No operator would be required to enter the data in response to prompts. Employee records would have to be stored, for example, on magnetic disk. Each record would be indexed within a file of records, and the files themselves may exist in a data base or complex of stored data, such as the total information of a company's activities. Each significant bit of data would also be indexed and easily referenced for retrieval. The program would instruct the computer to retrieve from storage the input data by identifying its location. In BASIC, file READ statements are used for this purpose.

BIBLIOGRAPHY

Part I: Some Basics

Asimov, Isaac. *Understanding Physics*. New York: New American Library, 1966.

Kondo, H. (ed.). *The New Book of Popular Science*. 6 vols. Danbury, Conn.: Grolier Educational Corp., 1979.

McGraw-Hill Encyclopedia of Science and Technology, Vols. 1-14. New York: McGraw-Hill, 1977.

Scientific American, September 1977.

Shore, Bruce H. *The New Electronics*. New York: McGraw-Hill, 1970.

Part II: Telecommunications

Albert, Arthur L. *Electrical Communications*. New York: John Wiley & Sons, 1950.

Bensinger, Charles. *The Video Guide*. Santa Barbara, Calif.: Video Information Publications, 1979.

Crowley, Thomas H., et al. *Modern Communications*. New York: Columbia University Press, 1962.

Kondo, H. (ed.). *The New Book of Popular Science*. 6 vols. Danbury, Conn.: Grolier Educational Corp., 1979.

McGraw-Hill Encyclopedia of Science and Technology. New York: McGraw-Hill, 1977. Vols. 1-14.

Marsh, Ken. *Independent Video*. New York: Simon & Schuster, 1974.

Martin, James. *Future Development in Communications*. Englewood Cliffs, N.J.: Prentice-Hall, 1977.

"The NASA Role in Major Areas of Human Concern: Communications." Paper, University of Denver, 1973.

Robinson, Glen (ed.). *Communications for Tomorrow*. New York: Aspen Institute for Humanistic Studies/Praeger, 1978.

Squires, T. L. *Telecommunications Pocketbook*. Woburn, Mass.: Butterworth, 1970.

Villchur, Edgar. *The Reproduction of Sound*. Cambridge, Mass.: AR, Inc., 1962.

The Way Things Work. Vols. 1, 2. New York: Simon & Schuster 1967, 1971.

Part III: Automatic Information Processing

Becker, Joseph. *The First Book on Information Science*. Washington, D.C.: USERDA, 1973.

Carver, D. K. *Introduction to Business Data Processing*. New York: John Wiley & Sons, 1979.

Diebold Group. *Automatic Data Processing Handbook*. New York: McGraw-Hill, 1977.

Fink, Stuart, and Barbara Burian. *Business Data Processing*. Des Moines, Iowa: Meredith Corp., 1974.

Kemeny, John. *Man and the Computer*. New York: Scribner's, 1972.

Kondo, H. (ed.). *The New Book of Popular Science*. Danbury, Conn.: Grolier Educational Corp., 1979. Vols. 1-6.

Lewis, T. G. *The Mind Appliance: Home Computer Applications*. Rochelle Park, N.J.: Hayden Book Co., 1978.

McGlynn, Daniel. *Personal Computing*. New York: John Wiley & Sons, 1979.

McGraw-Hill Encyclopedia of Science and Technology, Vols. 1-14. New York: McGraw-Hill, 1977.

Making It Count. Seattle: Boeing Computer Services, 1974.

Martin, James T., and Adrian R. Norman. *The Computerized Society*. Englewood Cliffs, N.J.: Prentice-Hall, 1970.

The Way Things Work. Vols. 1, 2. New York: Simon & Schuster, 1967, 1971.

INDEX

A

Abacus, earliest technological calculation aid, 154
Abbreviations and acronyms (list), 13-14
ABC, *see* WABC-TV
Absorption (of electromagnetic waves), 70
AC, *see* Alternating current
AC frequency oscillation, 39-40
Acoustic coupling (fax machine to telephone lines), 99
Acoustic recorder, 122-23
A/D *see* Analog-to-digital
Addresses (number of memory storage points), 56
Advanced Mobile Phone Service (AMPS), 113
Agencies for regulating spectrum use, 119-120, 121-122
Aiken, Howard, 157
Algebra, Boolean, *see* Boolean logic
ALGOL (algorithmic language), for mathematical problem-solving, 224
Algorithm, 224
Alphanumerics, devices for displaying, 192, 193
Alternating current (AC), 34-35, 37
  capacitors, 42
  inductors, 43
  oscillators, 39-40
  rectifier for changing to DC, 43
ALU, *see* Arithmetic/logic unit
Amateur services, 122
American Industrial Hygiene Association Journal, 93
American National Standards Institute, 102
American Society for Information Science (ASIS), 218
American Standard Code of Information Interchange (ASCII), 102
American Stock Exchange (AMEX), 178, 179
American Telephone and Telegraph, *see* AT&T
Amperage, 31
  Ohm's law and, 33

Ampère, André, 21
Ampex, 145-46
Amplification, amplifiers, 39, 40-41
Amplitude, of electromagnetic waves, 67
Amplitude modulation (AM), 74, 75
Analog, TV, movement toward digital, 148-49
Analog computer, defined, 166
  see also Computers
Analog-to-digital (A/D) conversion, 48-49
  converters, 185, 207
  distortion and, 50
  TV, 148-49
Analog Input/output, 185
Analog signals, 38, 39
Analytical and Difference engines, Babbage's, 154-55
AND/OR circuit, 51
Antennas, uses of, 70-72
APL (A Programming Language), very high-level language for interactive processing, 224
Apple computer, 161
Appliances, household
  amperage levels, 31
  voltage, 32-33
APT (Automatically Programmed Tools), high-level language of automation, 224-25
Arithmetic/logic unit (ALU), "brain" of computer, 168, 169-73, 212-13, 219
Armstrong, Edwin, 145
Artificial intelligence, defined, 226
ASCII code (telegraphy), 102, 104
Assembly (low-level computer language), 223-24
Asynchronous transmission, 74, 76
Atanasoff, John, 157
Atmospheric and Oceanic Information Processing System (AOIPS), 215
AT&T, 77, 149
  in broadcast television development, 145
  computer-based services, 18
  optical communications systems developed by, 92

restructure and new horizons, 110-16
WATS, 115
see also Telephone
Attenuation, techniques for minimizing, 50
Audio tape recording, 123-24
  synthesizer, 125
Automatic data processing (ADP),
  see Automatic information processing; Computers
Automatic Information Processing
  early history and development, 154-58
  uses of, 19
  see all entries under Computers
Automatic sequence controlled calculator, 157

B

Babbage, Charles, "father of electronic computers," 154-55, 168, 179
Babbage's Difference Engine, IBM replica of, 156
Bader, Joseph (AT&T Network Planning Director), 112, 115
Bain, Alexander, 95
Baker, Jim (WABC-TV chief engineer), on current and future technologies, 145-146, 148-49
Bandwidth, 73, 74
  usable or effective, 77
Bandwidth conservation, in facsimile (fax) transmission, 96
Banking, MICR in, 195
Bar code reader terminal, 196
BASIC (Beginners All-purpose Symbolic Instruction Code), 224
  sample program in, 227-29
Batch processing (data processing method), 167, 172
  punched cards in, 181
Batteries, 34-35
  example of capacitor, 42
Baudot code (telegraphy), 102, 103
Beale, Dr. Richard, 221